DIRECTED BY DESIRE

BOOKS BY JUNE JORDAN

Directed by Desire: The Collected Poems of June Jordan, edited by
    Jan Heller Levi and Sara Miles (2005)
Some of Us Did Not Die: New and Selected Essays (2002)
Soldier: A Poet's Childhood (2000)
Affirmative Acts: Political Essays (1998)
Kissing God Goodbye: Poems 1991–1997 (1997)
June Jordan's Poetry for the People: A Revolutionary Blueprint (1995)
I Was Looking at the Ceiling and Then I Saw the Sky (1995)
Haruko/Love Poems (1994)
Technical Difficulties: African-American Notes on the State of the Union (1992)
Naming Our Destiny: New and Selected Poems (1989)
Moving Towards Home: Political Essays (1989)
Lyrical Campaigns: Selected Poems (1989)
On Call: Political Essays (1985)
Living Room: New Poems (1985)
Civil Wars: Observations from the Front Lines of America (1981, 1996)
Kimako's Story (1981)
Passion: New Poems 1977–1980 (1980)
Things that I Do in the Dark: Selected Poems (1977)
New Life: New Room (1975)
New Days: Poems of Exile and Return (1974)
Dry Victories (1972)
Fannie Lou Hamer (1971)
His Own Where (1971)
The Voice of the Children, co-editor (1970)
Soulscript: A Collection of African American Poetry, editor (1970, 2004)
Who Look at Me (1969)
Some Changes (1967, 1971)

Directed by Desire

THE COLLECTED POEMS OF

June Jordan

EDITED BY
JAN HELLER LEVI
AND SARA MILES

 Copper Canyon Press

Cover photo by Gwen Phillips, 1975, courtesy *American Poetry Review* Records,
Rare Book & Manuscript Library, University of Pennsylvania

Copper Canyon Press is in residence at Fort Worden State Park in
Port Townsend, Washington, under the auspices of Centrum Foundation.
Centrum is a gathering place for artists and creative thinkers from around
the world, students of all ages and backgrounds, and audiences seeking
extraordinary cultural enrichment.

LIBRARY OF CONGRESS CATALOGING-IN-PUBLICATION DATA

Jordan, June, 1936–
Directed by desire: the collected poems of June Jordan.
    p.   cm.
ISBN 1-55659-228-0 (alk. paper)
1. Title.
PS3560.073A17 2005
811'54–dc22   2005011701

9 8 7 6 5 4 3 2

FIRST PRINTING

COPPER CANYON PRESS
Post Office Box 271
Port Townsend, Washington 98368
www.coppercanyonpress.org

Contents

NEW DAYS:
POEMS OF EXILE AND RETURN (1974)

Conditions for Leaving

Poems of Exile

Poems of Return

from THINGS THAT I DO IN THE DARK (1977)

For My Own

Directed by Desire

Against the Stillwaters

Towards a Personal Semantics

PASSION (1980)

LIVING ROOM (1985)

from NAMING OUR DESTINY (1989)

North Star

from HARUKO/LOVE POEMS (1994)

KISSING GOD GOODBYE (1997)

LAST POEMS (1997–2001)

Foreword

June Jordan's poetry embraces a half-century in which she dwelt as poet, intellectual, and activist: also as teacher, observer, and recorder. In a sense unusual among twentieth-century poets of the United States, she believed in and lived the urgency of the word – along with action – to resist abuses of power and violations of dignity in – and beyond – her country.

This book appears in a time when reflections of human solidarity, trust, compassion, and respect are in danger of disappearing from our public landscape, when what glares out from public discourse is division – not the great racial and class divides that have afflicted us since colonization but oppositions marked as "cultural": modernity versus regression, fundamentalist faith versus secular reason, "red" versus "blue." Without denying our cruel separations, Jordan went for human commonality, the opportunities for beholding and *being seen* by one another. One of her early poems, "Who Look at Me," was originally written for a book of images of black Americans by white and black visual artists.

> see me brown girl throat
> that throbs from servitude
>
> see me hearing fragile
> leap
> and lead a black boy
> reckless to succeed
> to wrap my pride
> around tomorrow and to go
> there
> without fearing
>
> see me darkly covered ribs
> around my heart across my skull
> thin skin protects the part
> that dulls from longing

Jordan took the world as her field and theme and passion. She studied it, argued with it, went forth to meet it in every way she knew. Along with poems, she wrote children's fiction, speeches, political journalism, musical plays, an opera libretto, and a memoir. But poetry stood at the core of her sensibility. Her teaching began in the 1960s with the founding of a poetry program for black and Puerto Rican youth in Brooklyn called The Voice of the Children; in her late years she created Poetry for the People, a course in the writing and teaching of poetry for students at the University of California–Berkeley. She saw poetry as integrated with everything else she did – journalism, theater work, activism, friendship. Poetry, for her, was no pavilion in a garden, nor simply testimony to her inner life.

She believed, and nourished the belief, that genuine, up-from-the-bottom revolution must include art, laughter, sensual pleasure, and the widest possible human referentiality. She wrote from her experience in a woman's body and a dark skin, though never solely "as" or "for." Sharply critical of nationalism, separatism, chauvinism of all kinds, as tendencies toward narrowness and isolation, she was too aware of democracy's failures to embrace false integrations. Her poetic sensibility was kindred to Blake's scrutiny of innocence and experience; to Whitman's vision of sexual and social breadth; to Gwendolyn Brooks's and Romare Bearden's portrayals of ordinary black people's lives; to James Baldwin's expression of the bitter contradictions within the republic.

Keeping vibrations of hope on the pulse through dispiriting times was part of the task she set herself. She wanted her readers, listeners, students to feel their own latent power – of the word, the deed, of their own beauty and intrinsic value; she wanted each of us to understand how isolation can leave us defenseless and paralyzed. She knew, and wrote about, the power of violence, of hate, but her real theme, which infused her style, was the need, the impulse, for relation. Her writing was above all dialogic:

> reaching for you
> whoever you are
> and
> are you ready?

....

I am a stranger
learning to worship the strangers
around me

whoever you are
whoever I may become.

(from "These Poems")

She was a most personal of political poets. Her poems could be cajoling and vituperative, making love and war simultaneously, as, in this collection, soft-spoken sensual lyrics cohabit with performance pieces. Yet there's a June Jordan persona throughout, *directed by desire,* moving between longings for a physical person and for a wider human solidarity, vocalizing a range from seductive to hortatory, accusing illegitimate authority along with the recalcitrancy of unavailable lovers.

She devised her poems with passion, finesse, and a compressed, individual style. She once defined poems as "voiceprints of language." Hers arc back and forth between manifestos and love lyrics, jazz poetry and sonnets, reportage ("when the witness takes a stand") and murmured lust, "spoken-word" and meditative solos, with mood-shifts and image-juxtapositions to match.

MARCH SONG

Snow knuckles melted to pearls
of black water
Face like a landslide of stars
in the dark

Icicles plunging to waken the grave
Tree berries purple and bitten
by birds

Curves of horizon squeeze
on the sky
Telephone wires glide
down the moon

Outlines of space later
pieces of land
with names like Beirut
where the game is to tear
up the whole Hemisphere
into pieces of children
and patches of sand

Asleep on a pillow the two
of us whisper we know
about apples and hot bread
and honey

Hunting for safety
and eager for peace
We follow the leaders who chew up
the land
with names like Beirut
where the game is to tear
up the whole Hemisphere
into pieces of children
and patches of sand

I'm standing in place
I'm holding your hand
and pieces of children
on patches of sand

Here she breaks what is actually a dactylic metrical line so that the beat is undermined and countered by the line-breaks: a subtle disorienting of form and expectation.

Her flexible, swift mind was tuned to what John Edgar Wideman has called "the continuum of language": intimate lyricism, frontal rhetoric, elegance, fury, meditative solos, dazzling vernacular riffs. These are poems full of specificity—people and places, facts, grocery lists, imaginary scenarios of social change, anecdotes, *talk*—that June Jordan voice, compelling, blandishing, outraged and outrageous, tender and relentless with the trust that her words matter, that someone is listening and ready for them.

She knew many poetries, ancient and modern. Her sonnets, for example, are both silken and surprising:

Supposing we could just go on and on as two
voracious in the days apart as well as when
we side by side (the many ways we do
that) well! I would consider then
perfection possible, or else worthwhile
to think about. Which is to say
I guess the costs of long term tend to pile
up, block and complicate, erase away
the accidental, temporary, near
thing/pulsebeat promises one makes
because the chance, the easy new, is there
in front of you. But still, perfection takes
some sacrifice of falling stars for rare.
And there are stars, but none of you, to spare.

But in her preface to the collection *Passion,* she matched
herself consciously with the tradition of "New World poetry,"
non-European, deriving in North America from Whitman, and
including "Pablo Neruda, Agostinho Neto, Gabriela Mistral,
Langston Hughes, Margaret Walker, and Edward Brathwaite."

> In the poetry of The New World, you meet with a reverence for the
> material world that begins with a reverence for human life, an
> intellectual trust in sensuality as a means of knowledge and of unity,
> an easily deciphered system of reference, aspiration to a believable,
> collective voice and, consequently, emphatic preference for broadly
> accessible language and /or "spoken" use of language, a structure
> of forward energies that interconnects apparently discrete or even
> conflictual elements, saturation by quotidian data, and a deliberate
> balancing of perception with vision: a balancing of sensory report
> with moral exhortation.

(from *Passion: New Poems 1977–1980,* xxiv)

To read through *Directed by Desire* is to see June Jordan, rest-
less in movement, writing always for the voice: sometimes for the
intimate interior room, sometimes more for declamation. Some
of her long declamatory poems, specific to certain moments or
written for public occasions, don't survive on the page absent the
vibrancy of her live breath and bodily presence. Others do, and
will, such as "I Must Become a Menace to My Enemies":

And if I
if I ever let love go
because the hatred and the whisperings
become a phantom dictate I o-
bey in lieu of impulse and realities
(the blossoming flamingos of my
wild mimosa trees)
then let love freeze me
out.

Some of her brief message-poems for friends can seem tenuous and transitory. Others are firmly chiseled epigrams:

POEM NUMBER TWO ON BELL'S THEOREM,
OR THE NEW PHYSICALITY OF LONG DISTANCE LOVE

There is no chance that we will fall apart
There is no chance
There are no parts.

In the last years of her life, when she was often in great pain from metastasized cancer, surgery and chemotherapy, her wit and fury enabled her to go on writing love poems and polemics, some in delicately caressing language, some grimly or hilariously resistant to diminishment. Turn for example to "Racial Profile #2" or the exuberantly scathing rap "Owed to Eminem":

I'm the Slim Lady the real Slim Lady
the real Slim Lady just a little ole lady
uh-huh
uh-huh
I'm the Slim Lady the real Slim Lady
all them other age ladies
just tryin to page me
but I'm Slim Lady the real Slim Lady
and I will
stand up...

I assume that you fume while the
        dollar bills bloom
and you magnify scum while the
        critics stay mum

and you anguish and languish runnin
　　straight to the bank...

　　And she continued, as in "Poem of Commitment," to mingle the
"conflictual elements" of outraged witness and lyrical beauty:

Because cowards attack
by committee
and others kill with bullets
while some numb by numbers
bleeding the body and the language
of a child

....

Who would behold the colorings of a cloud
and legislate its shadows
legislate its shine?

Or confront a cataract of rain
and seek to interdict its speed
and suffocate its sound?

Or disappear the trees
behind a nomenclature
no one knows by heart?

Or count the syllables that invoke
the mother of my tongue?

Or say the game goes the way
of the wind

And the wind blows the way
of the ones who make
and break
the rules?

....

because
because

because as far as I can tell
less than a thousand children playing
in the garden of a thousand flowers
means the broken neck
of birds

I commit my body and my language...

And throughout her ardent, abbreviated life, she did.

– Adrienne Rich

Editors' Note

This book collects June Jordan's published verse, presented here in sequence, beginning with her first book. We also include here the previously unpublished manuscript of the book of poems that she was working on at the time of her death.

We remain deeply grateful to June Jordan for decades of editorial collaboration, love, talk, and friendship, and for the invitation to work together on this volume. We appreciate the advice, support, and inspiration of June's son, friends, colleagues, and students, and the faith and hard work of all at Copper Canyon Press.

– Jan Heller Levi and Sara Miles
Executors, June Jordan Literary Estate

DIRECTED BY DESIRE

These Poems

These poems
they are things that I do
in the dark
reaching for you
whoever you are
and
are you ready?

These words
they are stones in the water
running away

These skeletal lines
they are desperate arms for my longing and love.

I am a stranger
learning to worship the strangers
around me

whoever you are
whoever I may become.

≈ 1969

Who Look at Me

For Christopher my son

Who Look at Me

Who would paint a people
black or white?

∽

For my own I have held
where nothing showed me how
where finally I left alone
to trace another destination

∽

A white stare splits the air
by blindness on the subway
in department stores
The Elevator
                (that unswerving ride
where man ignores the brother
by his side)

A white stare splits obliterates
the nerve-wrung wrist from work
the breaking ankle or
the turning glory
of a spine

∽

Is that how we look to you
a partial nothing clearly real?

who see a solid clarity
of feature
size and shape of some
one head
an unmistaken nose

the fact of afternoon
as darkening
his candle eyes

Older men with swollen neck

(when they finally sit down
who will stand up
for them?)

I cannot remember nor imagine pretty
people treat me
like a doublejointed stick

WHO LOOK AT ME
WHO SEE

the tempering sweetness
of a little girl who wears
her first pair of earrings
and a red dress

the grace of a boy removing
a white mask he makes beautiful

Iron grille across the glass
and frames of motion closed or
charred or closed

The axe lies on the ground
She listening to his coming sound

him
just touching his feet
powerful and wary

anonymous and normal
parents and their offspring
posed in formal

∽

I am

impossible to explain
remote from old and new interpretations
and yet
not exactly

∽

look at the stranger as

he lies more gray than black
on that colorquilt
that
(everyone will say)
seems bright beside him

look
black sailors on the light
green sea the sky keeps blue
the wind blows high
and hard at night
for anyhow anywhere new

∽

Who see starvation at the table
lines of men no work to do
my mother ironing a shirt?

Who see a frozen skin the midnight
of the winter and the hallway cold
to kill you like the dirt?

where kids buy soda pop
in shoeshine parlors
barber shops so they can hear
some laughing

Who look at me?

Who see the children
on their street the torn down door the wall
complete an early losing
                              games of ball
the search to find
a fatherhood a mothering of mind
a multimillion multicolored mirror
of an honest humankind?

                    ∞

look close
and see me black man mouth
for breathing (North and South)
A MAN

I am black alive and looking back at you.

                    ∞

see me brown girl throat
that throbs from servitude

see me hearing fragile
leap
and lead a black boy
reckless to succeed
to wrap my pride
around tomorrow and to go
there
without fearing

see me darkly covered ribs
around my heart across my skull
thin skin protects the part
that dulls from longing

∽

Who see the block we face
the thousand miles of solid alabaster space
inscribed keep off keep out don't touch
and Wait Some More for Half as Much?

∽

To begin is no more agony
than opening your hand

∽

sometimes you have to dance
like spelling
the word joyless

∽

Describe me broken mast
adrift but strong
regardless what may
come along

∽

What do you suppose he hears
every evening?

∽

I am stranded in a hungerland
of great prosperity

∽

shelter happens seldomly and
like an accident
it stops

⁓

No doubt
the jail is white where I am born
but black will bail me out

⁓

We have lived as careful
as a church and prayer
in public

⁓

we reveal

a complicated past
of tinderbox and ruin
where we carried water
for the crops

we come from otherwhere

victim to a rabid cruel cargo crime

to separate and rip apart
the trusting members of one heart

my family

I looked for you
I looked for you

⁓

(slavery:) the insolence

⁓

came to frontiers
of paralyze highways
freedom strictly underground

came here to hatred hope labor love
and lynchlength rope

came a family to a family

❧

I found my father
silently despite the grieving
fury of his life

Afternoons he wore his hat
and held a walking stick

I found my mother
her geography
becomes our home

❧

so little safety
almost nowhere like the place
that childhood plans
in a pounding happy space
between deliberate brown and clapping
hands
that preached a reaping to the wildly
        sleeping earth
brown hands that worked for rain a fire inside
        and food to eat
from birth brown hands
        to hold

❧

New energies of darkness we
disturbed a continent
like seeds

and life grows slowly
so we grew

We became a burly womb
an evening harvest kept by prayers
a hallelujah little room

We grew despite the crazy killing scorn
that broke the brightness to be born

In part we grew
by looking back at you

that white terrain
impossible for black America to thrive
that hostile soil to mazelike toil
backbreaking people into pain

we grew by work by waiting
to be seen
black face black body and black mind
beyond obliterating
homicide of daily insult daily death
the pistol slur the throbbing redneck war
with breath

In part we grew
with heroes who could halt a slaveship
lead the crew
like Cinqué (son
of a Mendi African Chief) he
led in 1839
the *Amistad* Revolt
from slavehood forced
a victory he
killed the captain killed the cook
took charge
a mutiny for manhood
people
called him killer but
some

the Abolitionists
looked back at robbery
of person
murdering of spirit
slavery requires
and one
John Quincy Adams (seventy-three)
defended Cinqué who
by highest court decree
in 1841 stood free
and freely he returned
to Africa
victorious

In part we grew
grandmother husband son
together when the laborblinding day was done

In part we grew
as we were meant to grow
ourselves
with kings and queens no white man knew

we grew by sitting on a stolen chair
by windows and a dream
by setting up a separate sail
to carry life
to start the song

to stop the scream

∽

These times begin the ending of all lies
the fantasies of seasons start and stop
the circle leads to no surprise
for death does not bewilder
only life can kill can mystify can start
and stop like flowers ripening a funeral

like (people) holding hands across the knife
that cuts the casket to an extraordinary size

⁓

Tell the whiplash helmets GO!
and take away
that cream and orange Chevrolet
stripped to inside steel and parked
forever on one wheel

Set the wild dogs chewing up
that pitiful capitulation
plastic flower plastic draperies
to dust the dirt

Break the clothesline
Topple down the clotheslinepole

O My Lives Among The Wounded Buildings
should be dressed in trees and grass

⁓

we will no longer wait for want for watch
for what we will

⁓

We make a music marries room to room.

⁓

listen to that new girl
tears her party dress to sweep
the sidewalk as the elderly slow
preacher nears the mailbox in a black suit
emptyhanded

⁓

Although the world
forgets me

I will say yes
AND NO

❧

NO
to a carnival run by freaks
who take a life
and tie it terrible
behind my back

No One Exists As Number Two
If you deny it you should try
being someone number two

❧

I want to hear something other than a single
ringing on the concrete

❧

I grieve the sorrow roar the sorrow sob
of many more left hand or right
black children and white
men the mountaintop the mob
I grieve the sorrow roar the sorrow sob
the fractured staring at the night

Sometimes America the shamescape
knock-rock territory losing shape
the Southern earth like blood
rolls valleys cold gigantic
weeping willow flood
that lunatic that lovely land
that graveyard growing
trees remark where men
another black man
died he died again
he died

I trust you will remember how we tried to love
above the pocket deadly need to please
and how so many of us died there
on our knees.

Who see the roof and corners of my pride
to be (as you are) free?

WHO LOOK AT ME?

∾ 1971

Some Changes

Dedicated to new peoplelife
with gratitude to R. Buckminster Fuller

For My Mother

for my mother
I would write a list
of promises so solid
loafing fish and onions
okra palm tree coconut
and Khus-Khus paradise
would
hard among the mongoose
enemies delight
a neo-noon-night trick
prosperity

for my father
I would decorate a doorway
weaving women into the daytime
of his travel also
season the snow to rice and peas
to peppery pearls on a flowering
platter drunkards stilt
at breakfast bacchanalia
swaying swift or stubborn
coral rocks
regenerate

for my only love
I would stop the silence

one of these days

won't come too soon
when the blank
familias blank
will fold away
a highly inflammable

balloon eclipsed by seminal
and nubile

loving

In the Times of My Heart

In the times of my heart
the children tell the clock
a hallelujah
           listen people
           listen

The New Pietà:
For the Mothers and Children of Detroit

They wait like darkness not becoming stars
long and early in a wrong one room
he moves no more

Weeping thins the mouth a poor escape from fire
lights to claim to torch the body
burial by war

She and her knees lock slowly closed (a burning door)
not to continue as they bled before
he moves no more

The Wedding

Tyrone married her this afternoon
not smiling as he took the aisle
and her slightly rough hand.

Dizzella listened to the minister
staring at his wrist and twice
forgetting her name:
Do you promise to obey?
Will you honor humility and love
as poor as you are?
Tyrone stood small but next
to her person
trembling. Tyrone stood
straight and bony
black alone with one key
in his pocket.
By marrying today
they made themselves a man
and woman
answered friends or unknown
curious about the Cadillacs
displayed in front of Beaulah Baptist.
Beaulah Baptist
life in general
indifferent
barely known
nor caring to consider
the earlywed Tyrone
and his Dizzella
brave enough
but only two.

The Reception

Doretha wore the short blue lace last night
and William watched her drinking so she fight
with him in flying collar slim-jim orange
tie and alligator belt below the navel pants uptight

"I flirt. You hear me? Yes I flirt.
Been on my pretty knees all week
to clean the rich white downtown dirt
the greedy garbage money reek.

I flirt. Damned right. You look at me."
But William watched her carefully
his mustache shaky she could see
him jealous, "which is how he always be

at parties." Clementine and Wilhelmina
looked at trouble in the light blue lace
and held to George while Roosevelt Senior
circled by the yella high and bitterly light blue face

he liked because she worked
the crowded room like clay like molding men
from dust to muscle jerked
and arms and shoulders moving when

she moved. The Lord Almighty Seagrams bless
Doretha in her short blue dress
and Roosevelt waiting for his chance:
a true gut-funky blues to make her really dance.

Nowadays the Heroes

Nowadays the heroes go out looking
for the cradle in the cold
explore
a cemetery for beginnings
(irony can kill
                the children panic at
the research in the glowing graveyard
what
what about

what about humanity in heat
the arms
the sleep alive?)
             Look.
Look for the life
Look for the reflections of the living
real problem:
money is the sun that makes us shine.

Not a Suicide Poem

no one should feel peculiar living
as they do

next door the neighbors rent their windows

formerly a singing
shatters toneless shards
to line an inmost holdup

drivel salt the stinking coin
iconoclasmic mire
reedy
dull like alcoholic
holy apostolic hireling
herd
inchoate incompatible
and taxing
toll the holy
tell the hireling
             alcoholic
             apostolic
                  tales

terrific reeking epidermal
damage

marrow rot
sebaceous glisten smell
quotidian kaleidoscopic
tricked indecent darling hell

no one should feel peculiar living well

This Man

This old whistle
could not blow
except
to whiskey wheeze
with bandage on his head
temple to temple
black
and dry hands
in his pockets keeping
warm
two trembling fists
clammed
against a stranger
('s) blueandwhite sedan
he
would never drive
could not repair
but damaged
just by standing there.

Fibrous Ruin

Fibrous ruin of the skin not near
not anywhere not torn nor stained
now disappears like leaf and flood

A loose appealing
to the vanishing of many scars lost
by long healing of long loss slipped
quietly across a bruise new broken
from new pain inside
the feeling of let go

Abandoned Baby

Young ash craven
   never near to gold and
   further still from blood

Birth aborted
   risen in that grave of
   other needs dangling

Angles pins and knobs
   discard their use
   to form your tomb

Uncle Bullboy

His brother   after dinner
once a year would play the piano
short and tough in white shirt
plaid suspenders   green tie and
checked trousers.
Two teeth were gold.   His eyes
were pink with alcohol.   His fingers
thumped for Auld Lang Syne.
He played St. Louis Woman
Boogie, Blues, the light
pedestrian.

But one night after dinner
after chitterlings and pigs' feet
after bourbon rum and rye
after turnip greens and mustard greens
and sweet potato pie
Bullboy looking everywhere
realized his brother was not there.

Who would emphasize the luxury
of ice cream by the gallon who would
repeat effusively the glamour not the gall
of five degrees outstanding on the wall?
Which head would nod and then recall
the crimes   the apples stolen from the stalls
the soft coal stolen by the pile?
Who would admire
the eighteenth pair of forty
dollar shoes?
Who could extol their mother with good
brandy as his muse?

His brother   dead from drinking
Bullboy drank to clear his thinking
saw the roach inside the riddle.
Soon the bubbles from his glass
were the only bits of charm
which overcame his folded arms.

Maybe the Birds

Maybe the birds are worried
by the wind

they scream like people
in the hallway

wandering among the walls

In Memoriam:
Martin Luther King, Jr.

I

honey people murder mercy U.S.A.
the milkland turn to monsters teach
to kill to violate pull down destroy
the weakly freedom growing fruit
from being born

America

tomorrow yesterday rip rape
exacerbate despoil disfigure
crazy running threat the
deadly thrall
appall belief dispel
the wildlife burn the breast
the onward tongue
the outward hand
deform the normal rainy
riot sunshine shelter wreck
of darkness derogate
delimit blank
explode deprive
assassinate and batten up
like bullets fatten up
the raving greed
reactivate a springtime
terrorizing

by death by men by more
than you or I can

STOP

2

They sleep who know a regulated place
or pulse or tide or changing sky
according to some universal
stage direction obvious
like shorewashed shells

we share an afternoon of mourning
in between no next predictable
except for wild reversal hearse rehearsal
bleach the blacklong lunging
ritual of fright insanity and more
deplorable abortion
more and
more

If You Saw a Negro Lady

If you saw a Negro lady
sitting on a Tuesday
near the whirl-sludge doors of
Horn & Hardart on the main drag
of downtown Brooklyn

solitary and conspicuous as plain
and neat as walls impossible to
fresco and you watched her self-
conscious features shape about
a Horn & Hardart teaspoon
with a pucker from a cartoon

she would not understand
with spine as straight and solid
as her years of bending over floors
allowed

skin cleared of interest by a ruthless
soap   nails square and yellowclean
from metal files

sitting in a forty-year-old flush
of solitude and prickling
from the new white cotton blouse
concealing nothing she had ever noticed
even when she bathed and never
hummed a bathtub tune nor knew one

If you saw her square
above the dirty
mopped-on antiseptic floors
before the rag-wiped table tops

little finger   broad and stiff
in heavy emulation of a cockney

mannerism
would you turn her treat
into surprise
observing

happy birthday

For Somebody to Start Singing

Song in Memory of Newark, New Jersey

He's a man on the roof
on the run with a gun
he's a man

Boys and little girls
they were bad and they were good
now they're dead

He's a man on the roof
on the run with a gun
he's a man

Had no name and looked
the same but today
the soldiers tremble
at his aim

He's a man on the roof
on the run with a gun
he's a man

The country kept baiting
a people kept waiting
they all stood in line
then they left

He's a man on the roof
on the run with a gun
he's a man

If I have to kill myself
gone burn this box burn
all the locks
that keep me out

He's a man on the roof
on the run with a gun
he's a man

And Who Are You?

1

Leave my eyes
alone
why should I make
believe this place entirely

is white
and I am nothing

pasted to a fantasy
(big black phallus
wide white teeth)
of particles you
blast to pieces asking me
to swallow them as
monster bits

That bit is me.

and even if I wave my arms no
rules will stop the traffic
stop the hatred running near
with ropes and mongrels
on the mind blind cloth
and bloodhounds
at the cradle

2

Don't tell me windmills
like the color of maroon
which was OK
when I first saw a zebra

that's the color of her coat
and in the hallway where she
waits for money once a week
she pulls a spool
of silk along the needles

for a doily

don't tell me windmills
turn no more just
like the horse
that used to lead
the trolleys   you can't
help but smell four legs the
board above for two and hear him
bargaining to tune bananamato
peachpotato   awk   awk
parsley

nothing goes too fast

old fish and unwashed hair why
don't he cut the screwing get
him something nice   sits
on the step a
nylon stocking cap to
cover up his head the cat
fastidious outside
the room
of his secondhand bed

3

Old fish and unwashed hair
you may surmise by reading
the windows
bandaged with the Daily
News from World War

Two which anyway was not the first
that

nothing goes too fast

but slowly like the windmill
like the good milord
and Uncle Remus for a hero

O merrily the children
suffered verily the elevator
Boys with buttons
from the Army and the cleaning
Girls of fifty-five
                    "the children"
suffered as they came to
hear the wild and holy
black book out of the mouths
of the mob and underneath
a hanging tree

    4
Take the acolyte
obsequious and horsey
under lace
              on Monday
off the altar

on the stoop

and no more candles
in the vestibule a no
watt testicle just dangles

take the acolyte his
yellhello for girls his
little sister slow with shoes from '66

a blue harmonica inside her mouth o
sweetly play that Jesu Joy of
Man's Desiring and Desiring and desiring
she
should comb her hair at least or he
could screw forgiveness
for a change move
over but
don't tell me
drums and muscle

on the stoop

sit-in on the stoop
museum
tombstone of the horse maroon
dark dais insane sanctum
if you make it you play ball
    talk loud
    speak low
    drink cheap
    tell lies
    LOOK AT THE PEOPLE

HE LOOKS LIKE A MAN
HE LOOKS LIKE ONE

All the World Moved

All the world moved next to me strange
I grew on my knees
in hats and taffeta trusting
the holy water to run
like grief from a brownstone
cradling.

Blessing a fear of the anywhere
face too pale to be family
my eyes wore ribbons
for Christ on the subway
as weekly as holiness
in Harlem.

God knew no East no West no South
no Skin nothing I learned like
traditions of sin but later
life began and strangely
I survived His innocence
without my own.

Juice of a Lemon on the Trail of Little Yellow

Little Yellow looked at the banana tree and
he looked at the moon and he heard a banana tree baboon
beneath the moon and he sat on the grass
and fell asleep there

Little Yellow nine years old underneath the moon beside
a big banana tree smiled a mango smile as he
listened to a lullaby palm and a naked woman broke
coconuts for him and fed him meat from her mango mammaries

Little Yellow curled himself in a large banana leaf
and he deeply sailed asleep toward the mango moon
Little Yellow traveled to a place where coolies worked
to build a bathtub for the rough and tribal Caribbean

There on that lush cerulean plateau and trapped he
was kept by his boss   brother who positively took
out his teeth and left the mango mouth of Little Yellow
empty

I Live in Subtraction

I live in subtraction.
I hide from rain.
I hold the sun with sleep.
I sleep without the stars.
I can even close my eyes.

I live in subtraction.
I forget your name.
I forbid my heart its mind.
I forgive my mind its dream.
I can end a dream with death.

What Declaration

What declaration can I make to clear
this room of strangers leaving
quickly as an enemy might come?
You look at me not knowing
I must guess what question I can ask
to open every mouth (and mine)
to free the throat (and yours) from fear.
We keep unknown to us
and I apart from me will search
my own deliberation my own you
and you and you, my own.

My Sadness Sits Around Me

My sadness sits around me
        not on haunches not in any
        placement near a move
and the tired roll-on
of a boredom without grief

If there were war
I would watch the hunting
I would chase the dogs
and blow the horn
because blood is commonplace

As I walk in peace
     unencountered unmolested
     unimpinging unbelieving unrevealing
     undesired under every O
My sadness sits around me

Not Looking

Not looking now and then I find you here
not knowing where you are.
Talk to me. Tell me the things I see
fill the table between us or surround
the precipice nobody dares to forget.
Talking takes time takes everything
sooner than I can forget the precipice
and speak to your being there
where I hear you move no nearer
than you were standing on my hands
covered my eyes dreaming about music.

When I or Else

when I or else when you
and I or we
deliberate I lose I
cannot choose if you if
we then near or where
unless I stand as loser
of that losing possibility

that something that I have
or always want more than much
more at
least to have as less and
yes directed by desire

Whereas

Whereas
Judas hung himself
I despise bravura

Whereas
Socrates ignored his wife
I buckle at the brim

Whereas
Judas hung himself
I find no rope as strong

Or

OR
like Atlanta parking lots insatiable
and still
collected kindly by the night

love lies

wrong riding hard
in crazy gear
the hills fly by corruptible
and polar up

and up
the bottom traveling
too proud

Let Me Live with Marriage

Let me live with marriage
as unruly as alive
or else alone and longing
not too long alone.
Love if unduly held by guilt
is guilty with fear
wronging that fixed impulse
to seek and ever more
to bind with love. Oh yes!
I am black within
as is this skin
without one pore
to bleed a pale defense: Will you attack
as cruel
as you claim me cruel? With word with silence
I have flung myself from you. And now
absurd
I sing of stillborn lyrics almost sung.

If this be baffling then the error's proved
To love so long and leave my love unmoved.

Toward a Personal Semantics

if I do take somebody's word on
it means I don't know and you have to
believe if you just don't know

how do I dare to stand as
still as I am still standing

arrows create me
but I am no wish

after all the plunging
myself is no sanctuary
birds feed and fly inside me shattering
the sullen spell of any
accidental

eyeless storm to twist and sting
the tree of my remaining
like the wind

Then It Was

Then it was
our eyes locked slowly
on the pebble wash
of humus leaves and
peeled the plummet belly
of a thundercloud

You bent your neck
beneath a branch my
arms enclosed
and slipped your shadow
over me

Soon we had bathed
the sun fell at our feet
and broke into the sliding
ferment of our warmth

we were an early evening

San Juan

Accidental far into the longer light
or smoking
clouds that lip whole hillsides
spoken nearly foliated full
a free green raveling alive
as blue as pale
as rectilinear

the red the eyebrow
covering a privacy a space
particular ensnarement
flowering roulette

place opening knees night water

color the engine air
on Sunday
silhouette the sound

and silently

some miles away the mountain
the moon
the same

For Christopher

Tonight
    the machinery of shadow
        moves into the light

He is lying there
    not a true invalid
        not dying

Now his face looks blue
        but all of that small body
                will more than do
                        as life.

The lady radiologist
                regardless how and where
                        she turns the knob

will never know
                the plenty of pain
                        growing

parts to arm
        a man inside the boy

practically asleep

Leaves Blow Backward

leaves blow backward with the wind
behind them beautiful
and almost run through atmosphere
of flying birds
or butterflies turn light
more freely than my mouth
learns to kiss by speaking
among aliens.

Nobody Riding the Roads Today

Nobody riding the roads today
But I hear the living rush
far away from my heart

Nobody meeting on the streets
But I rage from the crowded
overtones of emptiness

Nobody sleeping in my bed
But I breathe like windows
broken by emergencies

Nobody laughing anymore
But I see the world split
and twisted up like open stone

Nobody riding the roads today
But I hear the living rush
far away from my heart

Firing Burst His Head

Firing burst his head
excruciation blasted silly
clay declining
blind development
exploding fragile like the
afternoon

waste   the steeple placement
flesh too hot to last
or thin
no winner knows
the vulnerable victory arriving
dead between the baby hands
unlikely kindred
disappearing

cries around the brighter ravage
relegates an ear alone

an ear afflicted solitary
teach the hollow
formulate crude necrophilia
perhaps

or worse

the phony whining bones
disintegrate to tender tiny now
impossible and true

and true
impossible

In Love

in love

never tired of the forward to retreat
never stayed at the edges
imagining now the full

crack-wrung oblivion rolls
and roars a shifting
certainty

thorns to snare the stars
sea forest firm jaggedly cluster
hard-leaved
bird and bee brambling green
prickle hills of the earth rise
a ready thrust a foamchoke hushing
huge against the tides

galactic gallop leading darkness
to its flourish

indivisible the vision sounding
space enough

enough

affinity and I am
where we want to be

particular and chronic

What Would I Do White?

What would I do white?
What would I do clearly full
of not exactly beans nor
pearls my nose a manicure
my eyes a picture of your wall?

I would disturb the streets by
passing by so pretty kids
on stolen petty cash would look
at me like foreign
writing in the sky

I would forget my furs on any chair.
I would ignore the doormen at the knob
the social sanskrit of my life
unwilling to disclose my cosmetology,
I would forget.

Over my wine I would acquire
I would inspire big returns to equity
the equity of capital I am
accustomed to accept

like wintertime.

I would do nothing.
That would be enough.

Okay "Negroes"

Okay "Negroes"
American Negroes
looking for milk
crying out loud
in the nursery of freedomland:
the rides are rough.
Tell me where you got that image
of a male white mammy.
God is vague and he don't take no sides.
You think clean fingernails crossed legs a smile
shined shoes
a crucifix around your neck
good manners
no more noise
you think who's gonna give you something?

Come a little closer.
Where you from?

For Beautiful Mary Brown:
Chicago Rent Strike Leader

All of them are six
who wait inside that other room
where no man walks but many
talk about the many wars

Your baby holds your laboring arms
that bloat from pulling

up and down the stairs to tell
to call the neighbors: We can fight.

She listens to you and she sees
you crying on your knees or else
the dust drifts from your tongue and almost
she can feel her father standing tall.

Came to Chicago like flies to fish.
Found no heroes on the corner.
Butter the bread and cover the couch.
Save on money.

       Don't
tell me how you wash hope hurt and lose
don't tell me how you
sit still at the windowsill:

you will be god to bless you
Mary Brown.

Solidarity Day, 1968

      I

Down
between 2 monuments
the cameras and practically
balloons fried chicken cocktail
shrimp
a crayon poster megaphones
police

along the side as always
if you knew them
people

live like pigs

the children bruised and bare and brown
and big enough to know about a bitterness
from rats preoccupied
helpless competition

the fetter crazy male and female
blue green purple black revolving
slowly holy/brief
battalions limited to tear the entrails
clean like food
somebody grew

for garbage

2

american proximity a zebra

zoo the miserable journeyman
the jackass caravan

yeah yeah

show the sharks their carnage
look at that
humility in hunger

marks the moment of the mud

3

in the kitchen listening
a child sits at a table
steps away from basement stairs
his parents carry ashes
up
his parents rising from the cellar

hold on lug the heavy
heaving holdon lift
the buckets

carry through the ashes

    4

Resurrection died
but not like Jesus only
nailed and crucified

resurrection died
all during the rain
and right among the roses
and under wonderful trees

resurrection died
in full consideration of various
proposals here set forth
or there further considered
or in dedicated statements of nevertheless
never and no
in overweight in ties
in musical clock alarms
in uniform in limousines
in wellattended classrooms
and in ordinary church
from coast to coast

on holiday
on little more than grits
and other bits of boomerang bravado

resurrection went the way the money's spent
on *d, e, dash, dash, ashes.*

LBJ: Rejoinder

The President talks about peril
to Negroes talking about power
and all I want to say
to him The President
(no less)
until we sway as many
people as he can scare
until we tell
and compel as loud and
as much as The Lonestar
State is large:
"Don't warn me Big
Buddy you have kept me
in my peril long enough you
been pushing Hush My Mouth on me
my lips been black and very blue
but nothing
else than now but power now
and nothing else
will warn
or worry you."

He lost the peace so
he can keep the peril he
knows war is nothing like please.

Poem for My Family: Hazel Griffin and Victor Hernandez Cruz

Dedicated to Robert Penn Warren

I

December 15, 1811
a black, well-butchered slave
named George took leave of Old Kentucky – true

he left that living hell in pieces –
first his feet fell to the fire
and the jelly of his eyes lay smoking
on the pyre a long while –
but he burned complete
at last he left at least he got away.
The others had to stay there
where he died like meat
(that slave)

how did he live?

December 15, 1811

Lilburn Lewis and his brother
cut and killed somebody real
because they missed their mother:
Thomas Jefferson's sweet sister Lucy
Correction: Killed no body: killed a slave
the time was close to Christmas sent the poor
black bastard to the snow zones of a blue-eyed
heaven and he went the way he came like meat
not good enough to eat
not nice enough to see
not light enough to live
he came the way he went like meat

POEM FOR 175 Pounds
("Poor George")

2

Southern Kentucky, Memphis, New Orleans,
Little Rock, Milwaukee, Brooklyn, San Antonio,
Chicago, Augusta.
I am screaming
do you hear the pulse
destroying properties
of your defense against me and my life
now what are you counting

dollar bills or lives?
How did you put me down
as property?
as life?
How did you describe the damage?
I am naked
I am Harlem and Detroit
currently knives and bullets
I am lives
YOUR PROPERTY IS DYING
I am lives
MY LIFE IS BEING BORN
This is a lesson
in American History
What can you teach me?
The fire smells of slavery.

   3

Here is my voice the speed and the wondering
darkness of my desire is
all that I am here
all that you never allowed:
I came and went like meat not good enough to eat
remember no remember
yes remember me
the shadow following your dreams
the human sound that never reached your ears
that disappear
vestigial
when the question is my scream
and I am screaming
whiteman
do you hear the loud
the blood, the real hysteria of birth
my life is being born
your property is dying

4

What can you seize
from the furnace
what can you save?
America
I mean America how
do you intend to incinerate
my slavery?
I have taken my eyes from the light of your fires.
The begging body grows cold.
I see.
I see my self
Alive
A life

Uhuru *in the O.R.*

The only successful heart transplant, of the first
five attempts, meant that a black heart kept alive a
white man – a white man who upheld apartheid.

I like love anonymous
more than murder incorporated or
shall we say South Africa
I like the Valentine the heart the power
incorruptible but failing body
flowers of the world

From my death the white man
takes new breath he stands as
formerly he stood and he commands me
for his good he overlooks
my land my people
in transition transplantations
hearts   and power
beating beating beating beating

hearts in transplantation
power in transition

New like Nagasaki
Nice like Nicene

Out of the marketplace where
would I go?
Even Holy Communion and I met
my Host across the counter
there in Brooklyn High
Episcopalian
incense of expensive rites
I bowed my braided hair
and held my head as low
as all the rules

I believe the bedside
manner of the church
within the temples full of
gold I believe the gold the
body and the blood let in my name
as citizen belonging to the marketplace
I believe the sale and take the credit
as it comes

Jesus Christ
or God
the creed expands as progress moves
along in step like soldiers
marching everywhere at once
the unsung partners of the great
big bigger biggest button
manufacturers
more buttons for the uniform
shroud paring of the profits from
the boys who wear the flags and

off-days flip their zippers to half-
mast the boys who
fly the planes that kill
the children
over there.

I believe the boys the planes the
button for the uniform the gory raiment
I believe that anyone can be a Christian
like a camera let's
reverse morality read right
to left what else
besides the marketplace what else?
Where would I go? And think about it:

Why would I know your name?

Bus Window

bus window
show himself a
wholesale florist rose somebody
help the wholesale
dollar blossom spill to soil
low pile
on wanton windowsills
whole
saleflorists seedy
decorations startle   small

No Train of Thought

April 4, 1969

A year runs long enough
from force momentum trips
the memory

hard dark tracks

rush hatred hearts
nobody destination
home away

parallels to scare the starting place
start
tracks together
hard dark real long bloody tracks

pull pointless

killers
kill people pointless
killing (people) life
killing (people) love
killing (people)

partly (   )

killing

all of us (   )

Poem from the Empire State

Three of us went to the top of the city
a friend, my son, and I

on that day when winter wrote like snow
across the moonlike sky
and stood there breathing a heavy height
as wide as the streets to see
so poor and frozen far below
that nothing would change for you and me
that swallowing death lay wallowing still
with the wind at the bloat of piled-up swill.
And that was the day we conquered the air
with 100,000 tons of garbage.

No rhyme can be said
where reason has fled.

47,000 *Windows*

The Lower East Side of New York City offers, in itself, a
history of American contradiction, devotion to profit,
and the failure of environmental design for human life.
People had to pass a law in order that ventilation and
minimal, natural light be available to the immigrants
who had no money for decent housing. Instead of
tearing down the tenements that were unfit for human
habitation when they were first erected, the reformers
satisfied themselves by legislating phony windows
blasted into the bricks. That was a hundred years ago.
People still have to live in those Lower East Side
hellholes. This is a poem about the law that passed
some light and air into that deliberated slum.

1. There were probably more Indians alive
   than Jews and Italians in that whole
   early American place of New York
   when the city began being big:
   a perfect convergency confirmed
   congested with trade
   creating tolerance for trade requires
   abject curiosity or general indifference
   to anything that sells not well enough

to tell somebody else about it. And
at the beginning of New York
the world was selling well and so was
tolerance along with trade that
provocation to a polyethnic population
trading every bit of time for money
made the city made me take
your eye for mine according to extreme
prosperity and appetite.

2. In 1830 then the blurring crowd
    that overwhelming beggarly blur of people came
    they pushed into the seaport cornucopia of New York
    small many people forced
    from land from farms from food from family forced
    like seasons dictatorial
    the people fled
    political hostilities and hunger
    people fled
    that soon consuming triumph
    of elimination
    that machinery for triumph
    by a few.

3. Then in 1830 the Astors and the Vanderbilts left.
    They rode by carriage from the uproar
    trouble from arrival by the millions
    shoved their ships that wandered
    with the sea to make their glad delivery
    of travelers penniless and hellbent toward
    the welcoming coast of always America.

    Those other ones
    they came
    not trading things
    but lives.

4. Unskilled millions crammed old mansions
   broke apart large rooms and took a corner
   held a place a spot a bed a chair a box
   a looking glass
   and kept that space (except for death)
   a safety now for fugitives
   from infamy and famine
   working hard to live.

5. In place of land that street the outhouse
   tenement testimonies
   to a horrifying speculation that would quarter
   and condemn
   debase and shadow and efface
   the privacies of human being.

6. Real estate arose as profit spread
   to mutilate the multitudes and kill them
   living just to live.
   What can a man survive?
   They say: The poor persist.

7. O the Chinese and the Irish and the names!
   The names survived.
   Likewise some families.

8. 1867 after the first and only Civil War
   men looked at others
   men again
   not targets.
   Looked at latrines six stories high
   people paralyzed by penury immobilized
   and children docked
   and hopes untied and
   lying loose and less than skeleton
   at the dirty waters
   by the building of a dollarbill
   venality

near to nothing
at the doorway nothing
only life and speculation:
What can a man survive?

9. Men looked at other men again
   not targets
   and in 1869 they passed a law
   about the nightmare rising as they saw
   sick men and women nurse their babies
   although love
   is not enough to eat.

10. The Tenement Act of 1869
    was merciful, well-meant, and fine
    in its enforcement
    tore 47,000 windows out of hellhole
    shelter of no light.

   It must be hard to make a window.

What Happens

What happens when a dog sits on a tiger
when the fat man sells a picture of himself
when a lady shoves a sword inside her
when an elephant takes tea cups from the shelf

or the giant starts to cry
and the grizzly loses his grip
or the acrobat begins to fly
and gorillas run away with the whip

What happens when a boy sits on a chair
and watches all the action on the ground and in the air
or when the children leave the greatest show on earth
and see the circus?

Clock on Hancock Street

In the wintertime my father wears a hat
a green straw laundry shrunken hat
to open up the wartime iron gate
requiring a special key he keeps
in case he hears the seldom basement bell
a long key cost him seven dollars
took three days to make

around the corner

in the house no furniture remains
he gave away the piano
and the hard-back parlor couch the rosy rug
and the double bed
the large black bureau
china cups and saucers
from Japan

His suitcase is a wooden floor
where magazines called *Life*
smell like a garbage truck
that travels farther than he
reasonably can expect
to go

His face seems small or
loose and bearded in the afternoon

Today he was complaining about criminals:

They will come and steal the heavy red umbrella stand

from upstairs in the hallway
where my mother used to walk

and talk to him

Exercise in Quits

November 15, 1969

1

moratorium means well what
you think it means you
dense? Stop it means stop.

We move and we march sing songs
move march sing songs move march move

It/stop means stop.

hey mister man

how long you been fixing to kill somebody?
Waste of time
the preparation training

you was born a bullet.

2

we be wondering what they gone do
all them others left and right
what they have in mind

about us
and who by the way is "us"

listen you got a match you got the light
you got two eyes two hands
why you taking pictures of the people
what you sposed to be you
got to photograph the people?

you afraid you will (otherwise) forget
what people look like?

man
or however you been paying dues

we look like you

         on second thought
there is a clear resemblance to the dead
among the living so

go ahead go on
and take my picture

quick

A Poem for All the Children

The kind of place for sale big cities
where no gateways wide to greet
or terminate the staying there
persist

you keep it
we can corner what we need

The kind of place for sale the price tag
trees the price tag waters of the land the price
tag lighting of a life the cold cash
freeze on filth

                         o freedom days

The mind or face for sale insensate
supermarket ghostly frozen canned
wrapped-up well-labeled on the counter
always counter-top

The mind or face for sale delivers
hardhead hothouse whoring
homicidal mainly boring
laughter skull

take them things away
we got that   we got that

That place that mind that face
that hereditary rich disgrace

disturbs the triumph
turns the trust disgusting

books that lie and lullaby
schools of enemies and fools

the grownup grab thrownup
blownup

long live the child
love bless the wild

lord lord the older deadly life
the deadly older
lord lord

stale dues. no news. no sale

Cameo No. 1

Abraham Lincoln shit he never walked nowhere to read
a book tell all about it all about
the violation the continuous the fuck my face
the dark and evil dark is evil no good dark
the evil and continuous

the light the white the literature he read was
lying blood to leech the life away

believe the Abraham the Lincoln log the literature
the books he read the book he wrote down put
down
put you on the rawhide prairie
emancipated proclaiming
Illinois the noise
the boombang bothering my life
the crapcrashchaos print the words
the sprightly syllable destruction
nobody black black nobody black nobody
black
nobody

man

he no Abraham no kind
a president a power walk the miles and read the piles of
pages pale to murder real

                              no wonder he was so depressed

that character
cost me almost
my whole
future   times

Cameo No. 2

The name of this poem is

George Washington
somebody want me to think he bad

he bad

George Washington the father of this country
the most the first the holy-poly ghost
the father of this country
took my mother

anyway you want to take that

George the father hypocrite
his life some other bit
than freedom down to every man

George Washington he think he big
he trade my father for a pig

his ordinary
extraordinary human
slaves 300 people Black
and bleeding life beholden to the Presidential
owner underneath the powder of his wicked wig
he think he big

he pull a blackman from his pocket
put a pig inside the other one
George Washington

the father of this country
stocked
by declarations at the auction block

Prez Washington he say
"give me niggers
let me pay

by check"
(Check the father of this country
what he say:)

"I always pay for niggers
let them stay
like vermin
at Mount Vernon"

impeccable in battle
ManKill Number One
the revolutionary head
aristocratic raider at the vulnerable
slavegirl bed

Americanus Rex
Secretus Blanco-Bronco-Night-Time-Sex

the father of this country
leading privileges of rape and run

George Washington

somebody tell me how he bad he big

I know how he
the great great great great
great great proto-

typical

I Celebrate the Sons of Malcolm

I celebrate the sons of Malcolm
multiplying powerful
implicit
passionate and somber
                              Celebrate
the sons of Malcolm gather
black unruly as alive and hard

against the papal skirts the palace
walls collapsing
                          Celebrate
the sons of Malcolm hold my soul
alert to children building
temples on their feet to face the
suddenly phantom terrors
                          Celebrate
the sons of Malcolm fathering the person
destinies arouse a royal yearning
culminate magnificent
and new

In My Own Quietly Explosive Here

In my own quietly explosive here
all silence isolates
to kill the artificial suffocates
a hunger

Likely dying underground
in circles hold together
wings
develop still regardless

Of Faith: Confessional

silence polishing the streets to rain
who walk the waters
side by side

or used to dance apart
a squaretoe solo stunt
apart

ran stubbornly to pantomime
a corpse

show shadows of the deafman
yesterday the breathing broke
to blow some light against the walls

tomorrow drums the body into birth
a symbol of the sun
entirely alive

a birth to darkness

furnace rioting inside the fruit-rim ribs
dogeaten at the garden gate
but better than the other
early bones
that made the dog eat dog
that made the man smash man

catastrophe

far better
better bones

establishing

a second starting
history

a happiness

Poem to the Mass Communications Media

I long to fly vast feathers past your mouths on mine
I will to leave the language of the bladder

live yellow and all waste

I will to be

I have begun

I am speaking for

my self

Last Poem for a Little While

1

Thanksgiving 1969
Dear God I thank you for the problems that are mine
and evidently mine alone

By mine I mean just ours
crooked perishable blue like blood
problems yielding to no powers
we can muster we can only starve or stud
the sky the soil the stomach of the human hewn

2

(I am in this crazy room
where people all over the place
look at people all over the place.
For instance Emperors in Bronze Black Face
Or Buddha Bodhisattva sandstone trickled old and dirty
     into inexpensive, public space.)

Insanity goes back a long time I suppose.
An alien religion strikes me lightly
And I wonder if it shows
then how?

3

Immediately prior to the messed-up statues that inspire
monographs and fake mistakes
the Greco-Roman paraplegic tricks
the permanently unbent knee
that indoor amphitheater that celebrates the amputee –

Immediately prior to the messed-up statues
just before the lucratively mutilated choir
of worthless lying recollection

There the aged sit and sleep;
for them museum histories spread too far too deep
for actual exploration

(aged men and women) sit and sleep
before the costly exhibition can begin

to tire what remains of life.

4

If love and sex were easier
we would choose something else
to suffer.

5

Holidays do loosen up the holocaust
the memories (sting tides) of rain and refuge
patterns hurt across the stranger city
holidays do loosen up the holocaust
They liberate the stolen totem tongue

The cripples fill the temple
palace entertainment under glass
the cripples crutching near the columns swayed
by plastic wrap

disfiguring haven halls or veils the void
impromptu void
where formerly
Egyptian sarcasucker or more recently
where European painting
turns out nothing
no one
I have ever known.

These environments these
artifacts facsimiles these
metaphors these
earrings vase that sword
none of it
none of it
is somehow what I own.

6

Symbols like the bridge.
Like bridges generally.
Today a flag a red and white and blue new flag
confused the symbols in confusion
bridge over the river
flag over the bridge
The flag hung like a loincloth flicked in drag.

7

Can't cross that bridge. You listen
things is pretty bad
you want to reach New Jersey
got to underslide the lying spangled banner.
Bad enough New Jersey.
Now Songmy.
Songmy. A sorry song. Songmy.
The massacre of sorrow songs.
Songmy. Songmy. Vietnam.
Goddamn. Vietnam.

I would go pray about the bridge.
I would go pray a sorrow Songmy song.
But last time I looked the American flag was flying
from the center of the crucifix.

8

"Well, where you want to go?"
he asks. "I don't know. It's a long
walk to the subway."
"Well," he says, "there's nothing at home."
"That's a sure thing," she answers.
"That's a sure thing: Nothing's at home."

9

Please pass the dark meat.
Turkey's one thing I can eat
and eat.
eeney eeney meeney mo
It's hard to know
whether I should head into
a movie
or take the highway to the airport.
Pass the salt.
Pass the white meat.
Pass the massacre.
o eeney eeney myney mo.
How bad was it, exactly?
What's your evidence?
Songmy o my sorrow
eeney meeney myney mo
Please pass the ham.
I want to show
Vietnam how we give thanks
around here.
Pass the ham.
And wipe your fingers on the flag.

10

Hang my haven
Jesus Christ
is temporarily off
the wall.

11

American existence twists
you finally
into a separatist.

12

I am spiders
on the ceiling of a shadow.

13

Daumier was not mistaken.
Old people sleep with their mouths open
and their hands closed flat
like an empty wallet.

So do I.

∞ 1974

New Days

POEMS OF EXILE AND RETURN

For Christopher, and all of my family

∽ CONDITIONS FOR LEAVING

May 1, 1970

My Fellow Eggs and Apples
rising acid
from the rotten barrel belly
of the drunken killer whale

Here am I
a darkspot on
the underwear of ivory snow

Buggered by
this tricky mildew problem

How to clean out Mr. Clean
(I mean
Macbeth among the cherry blossoms)

Out!
The Moral laxative is working.
Quick! Fresh air! Fresh air!

We must prepare
for Operation Total Victory

Step One

Shave and a haircut FREE
for Miss America

On the Twenty-fifth Anniversary of the United Nations: 1970

1

Of the world so beautiful the men and women
easy like the waters interchange and changing
make for change for children

An ordinary struggle through the day ignores
the natural tide below the waking crust
the one and simple earth before the breaking
of the waters
birth or separation from an early
urgent trust a solid continental
walkland for the one and simple walking
life

And yet we do go on

There are ways to count the trees
before they fall
and death is not the time for ceremony.
All before the end is all.

2

Light is history in flames.
Let us forget about the light.
Can anyone define
the darkness that defines the star?
We need to know about the darkness where
dreams go and where we are.

3

In the universe of many names love
fails like silence when the word is
love.

And like the first the onward screaming
of the witness
human soul will only listen when
the witness takes a stand.

Memo to Daniel Pretty Moynihan

You done what you done
I do what I can

Don't you liberate me
from my female black pathology

I been working off my knees
I been drinking what I please

And when I vine
I know I'm fine
I mean
All right for each and every Friday night

But you been screwing me so long
I got a idea something's wrong
with you

I got a simple proposition
You takeover my position

Clean your own house, babyface.

∽ POEMS OF EXILE

Roman Poem Number One

1

Only my own room is gray

from morning on
those high those closing windows
may divide

to make an open wall

(that's maybe nine or ten feet tall)

and when you pulley up the wooden blinds
the outdoor cypress trees
confront
consume
caress the (relatively) small and starving eyes
that mark your face

for love

2

How old is Jesus?

for example well

the dark bronze fountain boy

(behold him)

wet
perpetual

the running water slides his belly loose
the snake around his arm
supplies the slick delectable

the difference

the dry parts where his hard
fat fingers never reach

the area where early light
or late

the boy is there alone

and listening to a sound that is

not his

Roman Poem Number Two

I

Toward the end of twenty minutes
we come to a still standing archway
in the city dump
nearby the motorcycle the treetrunk garbage
on the heavy smelling ground

as laurel bay leaves
(grecian laurel) break into

a heavy smell

Nicholas and Florence sharp last night
in life without an urban crisis that be-
longs to you

no demon in the throat of them
but sometimes just a harping on
the silence

No.

"What do you mean, *the subject?* That
has nothing to do with it."

"Listen I teethed on the Brooklyn Bridge"
she will insist her

refugee brown eyes and
hair showing artificial yellow

One can see how color is particularly hard
to manage in a personal way.

"I know every lamppost," she goes on.

Her husband adds another ending
to the movie we
Americans watched in American English
smack in the middle of this wonderful
Italian little Italian slum

"Let's put your money in the bank
– the retarded movie hero – he
would have been smiling at the heroine.
And that would have been," her husband continues
he repeats himself, "That would have been
a wonderful ending."

At this point his wife interrupts his
improvisation.

At the next evening table over espresso

the young woman married to a
well-educated employee
a first-rate worker in the First
National Bank Abroad

exclaims

"I have spent 3 days by myself!
Can you imagine?"

    2

On that day exactly when
Christ was born
where the children sprawl and laugh out loud
where the disappearing churchclock only
bells from twelve to two
where I could break my cup of coffee
throwing wakeup at the knowing nuns
where we sit so close we see
each other sideways

the cobblestones turned black
with holy oil

but now ten lire
would be hard to find

and some of us seem
lost

Roman Poem Number Three

"I am so sorry to say this but
our poor are not as poor
as yours.
In Italy you will never see the
terrible
sad face the hopelessness
and very dry eyes of America."
And now
my teacher turns to bargain

for three small handkerchiefs
to send to Wisconsin for Christmas.

Roman Poem Number Four

The tiny electrical coffee pot
takes a long time to make
toy bubbles of hot water while
we wait we laugh a lot in a stiff
and a stuffy chair jokes about the world
the war the regular material for
belly laughing through
and "By the way
do you know anyone in Greece? I have/
I had some friends who went there after
the coup. But they have not
written suddenly
for several months and the telephone
operator says that no
such persons as
The Cacoullos
exist."

    – "If you give me the stamps
I will write to somebody who can find out
if your friends are still alive or what."
I hand over the stamps.
It is a good thing sometimes
to buy a few extra.

Roman Poem Number Six

You walk downstairs
to see this man who moves so
quietly in a dark room

where there are balancing
scales on every table.
Signore D'Ettore can tell
you anything about
communications if you mean
the weight the price
of letters
packages
and special post cards.
Hunch-back
short
his gray hair always groomed
meticulous
with a comb and just a touch
of grease
         for three months
he has worn the same well
tailored suit
a gray suit quite unlike
his hair.
      I find it restful
just to watch him making
judgments all of us accept.
"But are you sad?" he asks
me looking up.

"The world is beautiful
but men are bad," he says in
slow Italian.
I smile with him but still the problem
is not solved.
The photographs of Rome
must reach my father but the big
official looking book seems blank
the finger-nail of Signore D'Ettore
seems blind and wandering
from line to line among the countries
of a long

small-printed list.
"Jamaica? Where is Jamaica?"
I am silent. My Italian
is not good enough to say, "Jamaica
is an island where you can find
calypso roses sunlight and an old man
my father
on his knees."

Roman Poem Number Seven

After dinner we take to the streets
let the alleys lead us as they will
into darkness and doorways
regardless
we scratch through the city hot
with wine
our feet our legs as steady
as a kiss on the wall.
In the dress shop
dirty dresses hang idle while
the owner rearranges her own
wool embroidered
heavy legs and plays with the jewelry
someone must have died
to give away.
Her companions make themselves
comfortable with sweat
in the little store
                    hustlers
curling sideburns royal
blue wide
wale corduroys packed
smooth in the high
black patent leather boots.
"These jewelry, they are very old.

From Paris. You will like them."
And she hands around the shoebox
graciously.

Two of the men begin to wrestle
each other.
              "Wait!" calls the third.
There is a piece of lint
on the back-slash pocket
of his friend.

Roman Poem Number Eight

He ordered a beer
She ordered a beer
I asked for apricot
yoghurt
              "You know this game?
Nothing personal. For instance
June is all bird
but you," he spoke
to my rival, "You
are half-horse-half-
butterfly."
              "Why
do you say I'm a bird?"

"Always up in the head
thinking
far from the earth."

I had been counting
the hairs on his wrist
but today
since he has been really
riding his horse

I venture to startle
the hairs of his arm
and listen to the thick
crackling
of his
persistent sex.

Roman Poem Number Nine

Return is not a way of going forward
after all
or back. In any case it seems
a matter of opinion how
you face although
the changing bed the different voice
around the different room
may testify to movement
entry exit it
is motion takes you in
and memory that lets you out again.
Or
as my love will let me say
the body travels faster than the keeping
heart will turn away.

Roman Poem Number Ten

Quarter past midnight and the sea
the dark blue music
does not belong to me

an elephant desire
heavy speeding whisper phantom
elephantom atmosphere

the heart rip hurts me
like the let go at the cliff

fell down shadow
loose and cold

let go
let go

Roman Poem Number Eleven

Spring has not arrived
and we already share
a beach that is a bed
where I can reach the worry
of his sometimes staring light blue
sometimes indecipherable
head
     (To reach is not to know
     or solve.
     A bed is not a beach
     exactly
     but the elements lie down the same.)
Outside
the cold and golden air
will strip my holding legs
bare on the back of his own red
motorcycle
but
I am warm my
arms my body most remember
from the night before
free
igneous
and he is there
between the memories
to take me.

Roman Poem Number Twelve

Tim and Johnny run by hoping
to play
off dope "a whole
week
clearing our heads you know
reading science fiction" now
eating an orange not
political
with a magic marker fist
Tim drew on it and
afterward
we move out on the afternoon
a sharing overflow we
play
soccer with a partly broken
pine cone "Hey
man
is that a regulation pine cone?"
"Yeah. God has done it again."

Roman Poem Number Thirteen

For Eddie

Only our hearts will argue hard
against the small lights letting in the news
and who can choose between the worst possibility
and the last
between the winners of the wars against the breathing
and the last
war everyone will lose
and who can choose between the dry gas
domination of the future
and the past
between the consequences of the killers

and the past
of all the killing? There
is no choice in these.
Your voice
breaks very close to me my love.

Roman Poem Number Fourteen

believe it love
believe

      my lover
lying down he
lifts me up and high
and I am
high on him

believe it love
believe

the carnage scores around
the corner

o believe it love
believe

the bleeding fills the carnage cup
my lover lifts me
I am up
      and love is lying down

believe
believe it

crazies wear a clean shirt to the fire
o my lover
lift me higher higher

crazies take a scream and
make a speech they talk and
wash their mouths in dirt
no love will hurt
me lover lift me lying down

believe
believe it
carnage crazies
snap smash more more
(what you waiting for?)

you own the rope knife rifles the whole list
the searing bomb starch brighteners
the nuclear family whiteners

look the bridge be fallen down
look the ashes from the bones turn brown
look the mushroom hides the town
look the general wears his drip dry red
drip gown

o my lover nakedly
believe my love

believe
believe it

Roman Poem Number Fifteen

For Greg

Palm Sunday

(we)
duck underneath umbrellas
covering a snug an ugly
light of the wonderdreadful
faces that the watering streets
the concrete textures of transition
literal to rain like faulty colors
strip away
to livid blameful coloring
a wet a temporary
ransack through the earlier
when the rain started up so
unreasonable like one
child as the whole house
atmosphere
the separate bodies
separated
dry when no one will
try
the umbrella
no one will try
anything
anymore

Roman Poem Number Sixteen: Sightseer

Next to me a boy is wearing
a red brocaded velvet jacket

and ragged trousers

in the window
a raw lamb's head
hangs
eyes still in the skull

down the street

we find the Cathedral of Naples
under
extreme repair
twisted marble with mosaic
jewels glinting in a cold belt
for a corpse

dwarf women
blowing kisses to the golden altarpiece
or standing
in cheap green cardigans
lace headkerchief
and kissing the wood of the seats
where the faithful
tithe
at the feet of statues
stupid with age

the church delivers the people
from the streets
outside
narrow

a man embraces a sterling silver
pitcher as he emerges from
a grocery store
a girl carries eggs and flowers
children
struggle under boxloads
of
decaying vegetables

humpbacked men and women
limping
overweight
toothless
purulent eyelids
pastry colored cheeks

we
were leaving the church when he said
smiling
"I have a great respect
for the dead. Don't you?"

I didn't answer him.
He must have been speaking
about
his own self-
respect

and
God help him
God
help all of us.

Roman Poem Number Seventeen

In their tomb paintings the Greeks reveal
what was important to them
pitchers of wine
supine repose
flute music
leisure
sex
and love

the homosexuals with lyre
one reaching his arm around the other's
head and into his hair his hand
the other boy reaching to caress the
breast of his man
the languid grace
thick lips
sloe eyes

the really comic book depiction
of a man stiffly
diving from a cliff
into water

Hippocrates wrote of birth as a breaking
down of the roadway
so that things could move more easily

we may have to die
again
before we can understand
the grace of the dead
but
it may not be worth
the destruction
of a second birth.

Roman Poem Number Five

For Millen and Julius
and for Peter and for Eddie

I

This is a trip that strangers make
a journey ending on the beach where things
come together like four fingers on his

rather predictable
spine exposed by stars and
when he said this
has never happened before he
meant something
specific to himself because he could not
meet me anywhere inside but
you know
we were both out of the water
both out of it
and really what we wanted was
to screw ourselves into
the place

Pompeii
the Sarno River to the south
the mountain of Vesuvius to the north
the river did not burn
none of the records indicate
a burning river

        of all that went before the earth
        remembers nothing

                everywhere you see
        the fertility of its contempt
        the sweet alyssum blooming
        in the tomb

        an inward town
well suited to the lives
unraveled and undone
despite the secretly coloring
interior of their suddenly blasted
walls

Vesuvius created and destroyed
            WHOLE TOP OF THE MOUNTAIN

BLOWN OFF
you can hum some words
catchy like the title of a song
(a little song)
WHOLE TOP OF THE
MOUNTAIN
BLOWN OFF
                    (play it again sam)

Pompeii
the mountain truly coming to the men
who used to walk these streets these
sewer drains (the difference is
not very clear)

            juniper and cypress trees
            inspire the dark the only definite the trying
            forms on the horizon sky and sea and the Bay
            of Naples
            single trees
            against abstraction
            trees

the mainstreet moves directly
to the mouth the mountaintop
a vicious puckering

                This is a place where all the lives
                are planted in the ground
                the green things grow
                the other ones
                volcanic victims of an overflow
                a fireflushing tremble
                soul unseasonal
                in rush and rapture
                well they do not grow
                they seed the rest of us
                who prowl

with plundersucking polysyllables
to rape the corpse
to fuck the fallen down and died
long time ago
again.

his hand removes some of the sand on my neck
with difficulty

did the river did the river burn

Pliny the Younger who delivered the volcano
who arrested the eruption into words
excited arrogant terrific
an exclusive
elegant account of mass destruction
79 A.D. that Johnny-on-the-spot say nothing
much about the river and
but eighteen is not too old to worry
for the rivers of the world
                              around the apple flesh and fit
loves holds easily
the hard skin soft enough
                        picture him sweet but cold
                        above the eyebrows
                        just a teenage witness with his pencil
                        writing down disaster
some say
put that apple into uniform
the tree itself wears buttons
in the spring
              VISITING DISASTER IS A WEIRD IDEA
              WHETHER YOU THINK ABOUT IT OR
              NOT

for example limestone the facade the statues the limestone statues
of the everyone of them dead and dead and dead and no more
face among the buried under twenty-seven feet of limestone other

various in general all kinds of dust covering the dead the finally comfortable statues of the dusty smell today the nectar fragrance the sun knocks down my meter taking notes the wheel ruts gutter drains the overhanging upperstories the timber superstructure the dead the very dead the very very dead dead farmland pasture dead potato chip dead rooms of the dead the no longer turbulent blazing the no longer glorious inglorious the finish of the limestone building limestone statues look at the wild morning glories red and yellow laughter at the dying who dig into the death of limestone hard to believe

the guide leads people to the public baths I Bagni di Publicci to talk about slaves and masters and how many sat at table he explains the plumbing where men bathed and where the women (bathed) hot water cold where the wall has a hole in it or where there is no hole in the wall and the tourists listening and nobody asks him a question how about the living and the dead how about that

Pompeii
and we are people who notice the mosaic decorations
of a coffin

we claim to be ordinary men and women or
extraordinary
elbows touching
cameras ready
sensible shoes
architects archaeologists classical
scholars one poet
Black and White and Jewish and Gentile and partly young
and married and once or twice married but
why do we follow
all
inquisitive
confessional or
necrophilomaniac or anyhow
alone

I am not here for you and I will stay there
we are disturbing the peace of the graveyard and
that is the believable limit of our impact
our intent
no
tonight he will hold me hard on the rocks of the ground
if the weather is warm and if
it doesn't rain

2

KEEP MOVING KEEP MOVING

the past is practically
behind us

half skull and teeth
knocked down running an
extreme tilt jerk tilted skull
stiff on its pole plaster cartilage
the legs apart like elbows
then the arms themselves the mouth
of the dead man tense defending still
the visitors peruse these plaster
memories of people
forms created in the cinders
living visitors admire the poise
of agony the poise of agony is
absolute
and who would call it sculpture
raise your own hand to the fire

IN THE VILLA DEI MISTERI
THERE ARE BLACK WALLS

another plaster person
crouched into his suffocation

yes well in the 14th century B.C.
they had this remarkable
bedroom where
they would keep one bed
or (some authorities say)
two beds
maybe it was the 15th

            Pompeii
            the unfamiliar plain
            the unfamiliar guilt
            annihilated men and women who
            most likely
            never heard of archaeology of
            dusty lust

all the possible homes were never built
(repeat)

"What's that?"

"That's a whorehouse, honey."

freckle hands chafing together
urbane
he tells the group that in
the declinium
women stayed apart with their loom
(in the declinium

occasional among the rocks the buttercups
obscure until the devil of the land)

            Perhaps Aristotle said the size
            of a city
            should take a man's shout to ears
            even on the edge
            but size never took anything

much no matter what the porno
makes believe but
what will take in the
scream of a what will
take it in?

current calculations postulate the
human beings half the size of the market
place

BEES
LIZARDS

walls plus walls inhibit action on the lateral
or
with all them walls now how
you gone get next to me
                    the falling of ashes
                    rolling lava

the way the things be happening
that garden story figleaf it belong
on top your head
                    they had these industries these
                    wool and fish sauce
                    ways to spend the
                    fooler

                    even the moon is dark among us
                    except for the lights by the mountainside
                    except for the lights

20,000 people
subject
to Vesuvius in natural violence blew
up the handicrafted
fortress spirit of Pompeii
the liquid mangling

motley blood and lava
subject
20,000 people

KEEP MOVING KEEP MOVING

to them the theater was "indispensable"
seats for 5,000 fabulous acoustics
what
was the performance of the people
in surprise
the rhythm chorus speaking
rescue
multitudes to acrobat survival
one last action on that last
entire stage
                today the cypress tree tips dally
                wild above the bleachers

when it happened what is happening to us

to hell with this
look at the vegetables blue
in the moonlight

                a pinetree colonnade
                the wall just under
                and the one man made

come to Pompeii
touch my tongue with yours
study the cold formulation of a fearful fix
grid patterns to the streets
the boundaries "unalterable"

the rights of property in stone
the trapezoidal plot the signals
of possession

laughter
(let's hear it loud)
the laughing of the lava
tell me
stern
rigid
corpulent
stories

the mountains surround the wastebasket bricks of our inquiry

in part
the waters barely stir with poison or with fish

I think I know
the people who
were here
where I am

3

my love completely and
one evening anywhere
I will arrive
the right way
given
up to you
and keep no peace

my body sings the force
of your disturbing legs

WHAT DID YOU SAY?
NO THANKS.
WHAT DID YOU SAY?

Vesuvius
when Daddy Adam did what he did

the blame the bliss beginning
of no thanks
this is a bad connection
are you serious?

        the river did not burn

the group goes on
among the bones we travel
light into a new
starvation

        Pompeii was yesterday
here is Herculaneum
a second interesting testimony
to excuse me but how
will you try to give testimony
to a mountain?

        there it is baby there it is
        FURTHER EXCAVATION INTO
        HERCULANEUM
        ARRESTED TODAY BY RESSINI living
        inhabitants impoverished the non-
        descript Ressini town on top the
        ruins of

amazing Herculaneum
constructed on an earlier rehearsal flow
of lava maybe
courage or like that a seashore
a resort the remnant spread the
houses under houses
tall trees underlying grass the
pine and palm trees spring toward
Ressini grass retaining walls against the water
where there is no water and the sound of children
crying from which city is it Ressini is it

Herculaneum that
does not matter does it is it
the living or the visited the living or
the honored ERCOLANO

                    SUCK
                    SUCK HARD

"Here's where they sold spaghetti"
the leafy sound the feel
of the floor the tile
the painting of a wineglass
a wineglass on the wall unprecedented
turquoise colors would
the red walls make you warm
in winter
          INFORMATION
          WAS
          NOT AVAILABLE
          THE POOR
          OF RESSINI
          REFUSE
          TO COOPERATE
          WITH AUTHORITIES

you better watch out
next summer
and Ressini gone slide
                    down inside them fancy
                    stones
                    and stay there
                    using
                    flashlight
                    or whatever

NOBODY BUDGE
KEEP MOVING KEEP MOVING

cabbages cauliflower broccoli
the luminous leaves on the land

4

yesterday and yesterday
Paestum dates from four
hundred fifty years before the Christ
a fertile lowland calmly naked
and the sky excites the rubble flowers
in between
the mountains and the water
bleaching gentle
in the Middle Ages
mountainstreams came down
and made the meadow into marsh
marble travertine deposits when
the mountains left the land
the memory
deranged the water
turned the plants
to stone

this is the truth the people left this place alone

        we are somewhere wounded by the wind
        a mystery
        a stand deserted by the trees

drizzling rain
destroys the dandelion
and your lips enlarge the glittering
of silence

        Paestum dedicated temples dedicated
        to the terra cotta figurines of trust
        the women in becoming mother of the world

the midwives hold her arms
like wings

the river does not burn

delivering the life

the temple does not stand
still

PERMISSION GRANTED TO PRESENT STONE SEX THE ECSTASY OF PAESTUM

4 main rows of
six in front
the tapering the girth the groove
the massive lifted fit of things
the penis worshipping
fecundity
fecundity
the crepis
stylobate
the cella
columns in entasis
magic
diminution
Doric
flutes
entablature
the leaning
curvilinear
the curve
the profile
magic
elasticity
diameter
effacement

THE TEMPLE IS THE COLOR OF A LIFE

ON STONE THE SUN CONTINUES
BLISTERING THE SURFACE
TENDERLY

WHAT TIME IS IT?

as we approach each other
someone else is making
a movie
there are horses
one or two beautiful men
and
birds flying
away

POEMS OF RETURN

May 27, 1971: No Poem

blood stains Union Street in Mississippi

so now there will be
another investigation to see
whether or not
the murder of the running young girl
by drunken whiteboys
was
a Federal offense
                    "of some kind"

there are no details to her early death
her
high school graduation
glory
yellow dress
branded
new the rolled-up
clean
diploma
certifying ready
certifying aim
certifying shot
by bathtub whiskey hatred by
a bloody .22 let loose
at her life

Joetha Collier she was
killed

at eighteen only
daughter
born to Mr. and Mrs. Love
the family
Black love wracked

by outside hogstyle hatred
on the bullet fly

Joetha Collier she was
young and she
was Black and she was
she was
she was

and

blood stains Union Street in Mississippi

Realizing That Revolution Will Not Take Place by Telephone

I

It's morning. We get up old
and then
discovering the waters of the bay
changed
in the night towards a world of water
waves
whitecaps posing at the windows
wild
ducks beside both doors
swimming calmly
and the wind
smash rushing thrust push shaking
ancient tower trees the kitchen walls
our confidence
in staying
anywhere

(discovering the transformation
we moved slowly so

reluctant to transform ourselves
although
I guess my son could be an elegant
canoe
and I could try to be a dark blue
sail)

    2

We thought we got up (old)
but we were different
in a sudden thoroughgoing difference
a highly irregular
a natural
storm
surrounded the table and the breakfast
was an absentminded
habit up against
the closing shock of danger
outdoors
racing nearer
raising water three to seven feet
of water free
great rhythms
               racing nearer
high
over the whole flat marshland
                       fish
came by amazed by drowning grass
and we

we called the Weather Bureau

    3

They said we knew
the ocean and the bay the sky and
northeast blasting

45 to 60 mile per hour winds
beat non-stop breaking eardrums

They said

Good Morning
Weather Forecast for Nassau and Suffolk County
precipitation probability
barometer thermometer

warnings
flood

winds
heavy rains

They said
                GET OFF THE TELEPHONE

OVERNIGHT
ALL THINGS HAVE CHANGED
THE CHANGES ARE THE THINGS YOU KNOW.
THE WEATHER AND THE WORLD ARE WHERE
    YOU ARE.
TOMORROW MORNING
WHEN YOU WAKE UP
WILL
YOU WAKE UP?

            PLEASE GET OFF THE PHONE!

On the Spirit of Mildred Jordan

After sickness and a begging
from her bed
my mother dressed herself

gray lace-up oxfords
stockings baggy on her shrunken legs
an orange topper
rhinestone buttons
and a powder blue straw
hat with plastic
flowers

Then
she took the street
in short steps toward the corner

chewing gum
no less

she let the family laugh
again

she wasn't foxy
she was strong

After Reading the Number One Intellectual American Best Seller, Future Shock, All about Change Is Where We're At

Well
Number Two
Baby
Is That Change Ain' Nowhere
You Can Hold On

Now Read That
Now Read This

            gone
            gone

Eddie
gone
Greg
gone
Julius
Millen
Peter
Alice
Frances
Terri
gone
Aunt
Uncle
Cousins
Niece and Nephew
Father
Mother
Son
GONE
GONE
Dale
Primus
Clarence
Ross
GONE
GONE
Damn. Don'
give me no garbage
about
DIS IS DUH FUTURE
speed up
travel
turn around
make it mobile
hit the road

shit
I'm just tired saying good-bye

On Holidays in the Best Tradition

Thanksgiving is a good time to stuff
a T.W.A. Ambassador turkey flight
to Las Vegas
now leaving
   the family
   the friends

at 500 miles per hour
the pilot explains that
      "knowledge of this procedure
       will definitely expedite survival"

(so that's cool)

now leaving
   the family
   the friends

to fasten your eyes
on the positively most
enormous
high billboard signal calls
for HELP

now leaving
(for)
  money money
  money money money

neon names and neon numbers
neon blink blank

here is a store on the street in Las Vegas
"Selling Indian Jewelry Since 1957"
but

here are no Indians in Las Vegas
since you know
the other people have arrived
the hearts spades clubs and diamonds
mixed up
alone and gambling
everybody stretched out on the dark
felt wheel
fuzzy cowboys teachers Black folks white folks
almost
all the American stuffing
of the all American turkey
tricked out lonely
gambling
ringading ding
ringading dingdong
dingaling
money
money

now leaving
   the family
   the friends

For C.G., Because David Came in Hot and Crying from the News

He was still here the friend
the legend
of a good song given
huge
after the commonplace reporting of his death

The film of his smooth
high
outward motion

blurred
the eyelids of the people
who
kept loving him
a
movie in the selfish heart
that will not close
the cameras
        do not record
        a final take
        on living.

On Your Love

Beloved
where I have been
if
you loved me more than your own
and God's
soul
you could not have lifted me
out of the water
or
lit even one of the cigarettes I stood
smoking alone.

Beloved
what I have done
if
you discounted the devil
entirely
and rejected the truth as a rumor
you
would turn from the heat of my face
that burns
under your lips.

Beloved
what I have dreamed
if
you ended the fevers and riot
the claw and the wail and the absolute
furious
dishevel of my unkempt mind
you
could never believe the quiet
your arms
make true around me.

In your love I am sometimes redeemed
a stranger
to myself.

About Enrique's Drawing

She lies down a mess
on white paper under glass
a long and a short leg a twisted
arm one good and even
muscular
an okay head
but body in a bloat
impossible

"NO! Not impossible," he says
standing.
"It is
a body.
It is
a structure
that   is not
regular.
Do you see?
No?

Listen:
          ONE
          ONE
          ONE TWO
          THREE FOUR
          ONE
          ONE
          ONETWOTHREE
          ONETWOTHREE
          ONE TWO
          ONETWOTHREE
          ONE TWO
          THREE FOUR
          ONE
          ONE..."

Enrique's body
has become the structure
of a dance. He is real.
And she
the woman lying down a mess
she
has become
mysterious.

About Merry Christmas/Don't Believe the Daily News

I had a good time in New York City
visiting
the hothouse for "ratpacks"
"junkies" "weirdos"
"crazies" "straights"
and simpleminded
victims of the
What They Calling It These Days?
Anyway

I had a good time there.
Walked down the avenue
shook hands and hugged
a guy I used to know
then
went to the movies with my friend
and caught this flick
called
DESPERATE CHARACTERS
showing you the urban truth that
indoors and outdoors and daylight
and evening and westside and east
and downtown if
it's New York City
it's a terrible trick
to scare you way WAY out your mind
so
we watched the movie
digging on its realistic dangers
and the popcorn
then
I left my wallet
in that theater that city in that hothouse
jungleland of
terror crime and loneliness
and
you know what
a man named Mr. Atkins, Jr.
found my wallet
picked it
up
and mailed it back to me

It's like I said.
I had a good time in the city.

Poem about the Sweetwaters of the City

the subway comes up
for air
a quick one
two stops rattle rusted short
above ground
where the letters tell me
PLEASE KEEP HANDS OFF DOORS
(Or near there)
you assume the buildings and
the smallprint roadways and
the cornered accidents
of roof and oozing tar and ordinary concrete
zigzag. Well.
It is not beautiful.
It never was.
These are the shaven
private parts
the city show
of what somebody means
when he don't even bother
just to say
"I don't give a goddamn"
(and)
"I hate you."

West Coast Episode

Eddie hung a light globe with the best electric
tape
he could find in
five minutes

then he left the room where he lives

to meet me

(in Los Angeles)

Meanwhile the light globe fell and
smashed glass everywhere

(the waterbed
was dangerous
for days)

but we used the paper bag that hid
the dollar-twenty-nine-California-Champagne
to hide
the light bulb
with a warm brown atmosphere

and that
worked really well

so there was no problem
except
we had to walk like feet
on broken seashells
even though
the color of the rug was green
and out beyond the one room
of our love
the world was mostly
dry.

From an Uprooted Condition

In the house of my son I am hiding myself
who will not tell anybody
that love lies behind or before

this need when no one
is near to her

sometimes the poem tends to repeat itself
the subject is screaming and sad
and the hours do not belong or allow

Pitiless
she watches the stranger
she thinks that at least he
comes from someplace
that gave him permission to leave

She is taking small steps
and making small noises that melt in the air
easily
easily
there is nowhere that she can go
and her hands are frozen hard
in this
absolutely new
position
                more or less
we know the attitude the forms
of childbirth and of dying

what
is the right way the womanly expression
of the infinitive that fights
infinity

to abort?

Poem for Angela

Outside tonight the moon is not a fantasy
At last again the moon moves full and dark
with color in the universe
where nothing terrifies the truth
where light is known as energy
and cherished

Too many many days and nights
have choked back
unlit paralyzed and tortured clockwork
regulating savagely against
the heartbeat of the prisoner

The heavies poised themselves on fat feet
running backwards after her
the one they named The Number One

They have taken away the woman who loved the people.
They have hunted the moon in its honesty.
They think they have captured the moon in a closet.

But
children know that the moon is used to the night.
She has returned

And now we can see more clearly
the prisoners of this electrified hell
And now we can see more clearly
ourselves
in the teachings of darkness
that liberate the beauty of the moon

On the Black Poet Reading His Poems in the Park

For Clarence and Sharyn

knit together firm a short triangular
full body holding lust but
tender then the words
grope wild to ask
around the woman
he loves do you
hear me am I
yours am
I

so he sounds uncertain
and the night-time
questions of his
poetry compel
the answers
from her
heart
that

comes and comes and comes and comes

On the Black Family

we making love real
they mining the rivers

we been going without trees and going
without please and growing on –
on make-dos and breakthroughs to baby
makes three's a family
ole Charlie knows nothing
about out there
where

he burning the leaves and firing the earth
and killing and killing

we been raising the children
to hold us some love for tomorrows
that show how we won our own wars
just to come in the night
Black and Loving
Man and Woman
definitely in despite
of
all the hurdles that the murdering
masterminds threw up to stop
the comings of
Black Love

we came
we came and we come in a glory of darkness
around the true reasons for sharing
our dark and our beautiful
name
that we give to our dark and our beautiful
daughters and sons
who must make the same struggle
to love

and must win

against the tyrannical soldierly sins
of the ones who beatify plastic and steel
and who fly themselves high on the failure to feel

     — they mining the rivers
     we making love real

For David: 1972

Hello.
I was watching the war
on color television
Channel 2
when your letter came.

How can anybody stay high
on anti-personnel bombing missions
twenty-six times a day?

It's not the same as fucking
all night long.

Is it?

Anyway
your letter reads like the nightmare
I keep having when I try to sleep.

It's all about blowing up a family

or a slow parade of people
African and Irish
and Chinese and folks from Brooklyn
under the palm trees
of an open space

then a portable TV
a big one
a Black and White receiver
turns the war on right
over our heads
and when we look up
we
disintegrate

It's crude. The nightmare.
Obvious. I know.
That seems to be the living color trick
today. A nightmare.
Crude.
And I wish I knew something else to say
besides
be well and please
take care.

On Declining Values

I

In the shadows of the waiting room
are other shadows
beaten
elderly women or
oldfolk bums
depending on your point of view

but
all depending

formerly mothers formerly wives
formerly citizens of some acceptable
position
but
depending and
depending

now exposed unable and unwashed
a slow and feeble crawling through the city
varicose
veins bulging
while the arteries the intake systems
harden

wither
shrivel
close
depending and depending

    2

She will leave Grand Central Station
and
depending
spend two hours in St. Patrick's
if the guards there
if the police ignore the groveling length
of time it takes
a hungry woman
just to pray

but here
she whispers
with an aging boyfriend
fugitive and darkblue suited out
for begging who
has promised her a piece
of candy or an orange or an apple
if
they meet tomorrow
if the cops don't chase them separated
wandering under thin
gray hair

    3

meanwhile
cops come quick
knockbopping up the oakwood benches
BANG
BOP
"GET OUTAHERE," they shout around
the ladies women sisters dying old and all

the formerly wives and mothers
shuffle soft
away
with paper shopping bags beside them

almost empty
and a medium young man
comes up
to ask a question:
"Tell me, I mean, seriously,
how does it feel to be beautiful?"

And I look back at him
a little bit alarmed
a little bit amused
before I say:

"It all depends too much
on you."

It's about You: On the Beach

You have
two hands absolutely lean and clean
to let go the gold
the silver flat or plain rock
sand
but hold the purple pieces
atom articles
that glorify a color
yours is orange
oranges are like you love
a promising
a calm skin and a juice
inside
a juice

a running from the desert
Lord
see how you run
YOUR BODY IS A LONG BLACK WING
YOUR BODY IS A LONG BLACK WING

On the Paradox in Rhyme

When he comes on top of me
I am high as I can be.

About the Reunion

"I am rarely vindictive but
this summer I have taken great
pleasure in killing mosquitoes"

He says that to me
It is quite dark where we sit
and difficult to see

or tells me of work he will do
films of no end no beginning
and pours more wine
or takes another cigarette

And I know that is probably true
of his life of our love not to begin
not to end not be ugly or fine

But there is this history of once
when his hands and the length of his legs
came suddenly
to claim me all
bone and all flesh forcing away

the wall and the image of the wall
in one
fast meeting of amazement

And that was another year and somewhere
else

Here we talk outside
or do not talk

almost asleep in separated
wood chairs as hard as the time
between us
and
I admit
you are not as tall as the trees around me
your eyes are not as open as surprising
as the sea
but I watch for your words any changing
of your head
from a deadspot in the darkness
to a face

and finally you move

"I have to get in touch with
some other people"
you say
after so much silence

and I do not move

and
you leave.

Of Nightsong and Flight

There are things lovely and dangerous still

the rain
when the heat of an evening
sweetens the darkness with mist

and the eyes cannot see what the memory will
of new pain

when the headlights deceive
like the windows wild birds believe to be air
and bash bodies and wings
on the glass

when the headlights show space
but the house and the room and the bed and your face
are still there

while I am mistaken
and try to drive by

the actual kiss
of the world everywhere

After All Is Said and Done

Maybe you thought I would forget
about the sunrise
how the moon stayed in the morning
time a lower lip
your partly open partly spoken
mouth

Maybe you thought I would exaggerate
the fire of the stars
the fire of the wet wood burning by
the waterside
the fire of the fuck the sudden move
you made me make
to meet you
(fire)

BABY
I do not exaggerate and
if
I could
I would.

Shortsong from My Heart

Within our love the world
looks like a reasonable easy plan
the continents the oceans
are not harder/larger than the dreams
our dreams
so readily embrace
and time is absolute newspace
beginning where you are
the sex of family and clear
far goal at once
beginning where you are
I am beginning to belong/be free
Let me be borne into the mystery
with you
Let me come home

Onesided Dialog

OK. So she got back the baby
but what happened to the record player?

No shit. The authorized appropriation
contradicts my falling out of love?

You're wrong. It's not that I gave away my keys.
The problem is nobody wants to steal me or my house.

Poem for My Love

How do we come to be here next to each other
in the night
Where are the stars that show us to our love
inevitable
Outside the leaves flame usual in darkness
and the rain
falls cool and blessed on the holy flesh
the black men waiting on the corner for
a womanly mirage
I am amazed by peace
It is this possibility of you
asleep
and breathing in the quiet air

About Long Distances on Saturday

he calls me from his house and
the timing seems bad
and I offer to call him back
later
but he says "no"
I'm about to split for the weekend

so
call me yeah
early next week or
sometime
and the answer is
that the question
is

(isn't it)

where are you going
baby

without me?

On Divine Adaptation to an Age of Disbelief

Watch out.
God is on the TV and the color
and the sex the role
the performance
the everlasting omnipotent
advertised
trial
product
cannot de-code
cannot deny
            (Him)
WATCH OUT.

God is on the TV
watching you
and watching me

we

better be

good

On My Happy / Matrimonial Condition

last time I got married was
yesterday (in
bed)
we stayed there
talking it over
nobody
shook
hands
but
the agreement
felt
very good
as a matter of fact
so
that was what
will be
the absolute
last time I ever
get
married

Calling on All Silent Minorities

HEY

C'MON
COME OUT

WHEREVER YOU ARE
WE NEED TO HAVE THIS MEETING
AT THIS TREE

AIN' EVEN BEEN
PLANTED
YET

No Poem Because Time Is Not a Name

But beyond the
anxiety
the
querulous and reckless intersecting
conflict
and the trivial misleading banal
and separating fences every scrim
disguise each mask and feint
red herrings broadside poor
maneuvers of the
begging
hopeful
heart that wants and waits the
head that works against the minute
minute
There are pictures/memories of
temperature or cast or tone
or hue and vision
pictures of a dream
and dreams of memories and
dreams of gardens dreams of film
and pictures
of the daring
simple
fabulous
bold

difficult
and distant
inextricable
main
nigger
that I love
and
this is not
a poem

∽

Fragments from a Parable

Paul was Saul. Saul got on the road and the road
and somebody else changed him into somebody else
on the road.

The worst is not knowing if I do take somebody's
word on it means I don't know and you have to believe
if you just don't know. How do I dare to stand as
still as I am still standing? Arrows create me.
And I despise directions. I am no wish.
After the lunging still
myself is no sanctuary
birds feed and fly inside me shattering
the sullen spell of my desiring and the
accidental conquest.
Eyeless wings will
twist and sting
the tree of my remaining
like the wind.
Always there is not knowing, not knowing everything
of myself and having to take whoever you are at your
word. About me.

I am she.

And this is my story of Her. The story is properly yours to tell. You
have created Her, but carelessly. As large as a person, she never-
theless learns why she walks and the aim of her gaze and the force
of her breath from you who coax her to solve independently the
mystery of your making: Her self.

Your patterns deny parenthood; deny every connection suggesting
a connection; a consequence. She cannot discover how she began
nor how she may begin. She seeks the authority of birth. Her fails.

Launched or spinning politely she fails to become her as self unless
you allow her a specialty she will accept as her reason for being.

Perhaps you allow her a skill like mercy or torment. The particular means nothing. Your approval matters like life and death. She is who I am.

I am.

My name is me. I am what you call black. (Only I am still. Arrest me. Arrest me any one or thing. If you arrest me I am yours. I am yours ready for murder or am I yours ready to expose any closed vein. Which is not important. Am I matter to you? Does it? You will try when. But now I am never under arrest. Meanwhile that slit allows me concentration on the bricks black between the windows. I am one of those suffering frozen to the perpetual corrosion of me. Where is the stillness that means?)

Here am I holding a pen with two fingers of frenzy of stream of retreat of connection and neurons. Supposedly there is a synapse between things like this: A difference:

between
beyond
beneath

illusions

At least a space without pulse. Without illusion: Only I am still: Only I am remaining. I repeat: I am not still: I repeat: Arrest me! You would say mine is a monotone if I could keep my tongue in my fist and my fist in my mouth and my mouth in a glass and that glass in my eyes. But monotony resonates: That would prove how merely am i a complicated position. Or riveted respectably with foot to the ground ignoring the drum and the furnace, the seeds and the water then could I say I am still pretending to be still.

But that complicated position is not. I was simply conceived by something like love. I was simply conceived during the war. My mother was the most beautiful woman in the world. My father was a macro-sperm of lust for that woman painfully asleep on the battlefield. This lust, this loving uncertainty seized three hundred soldiers who paused at her silence as she lay. They made their rabid inquiry and left her.

For almost a year she wandered. For almost a year she wandered with a great song of hatred troubling her lips. She became deranged, an idiot, and everyone adored my mother. Certainly, her song amused them.

At last she struggled to be rid of me. Among the minerals she lay. Silently among the stones of sand she lay. There where the waters begin, like the most elemental mammal she lay. She lay down alone: a small whale. And at the impossible poise between absolute flux and accidental suspense, the most beautiful woman in the world became my mother. But as nothing is absolute nor accidental: I only exchanged equilibria: I was not particularly born.

For days I suckled on the blood of my delivery. Later she learned to ease her breasts and civilized my mouth with milk. No. I played with porpoises. No. Already there is progress. So. Not even then. Not even when beginning. Then is it the beginning not the stillness that means.

If I could eclipse the commencement of the moon. Skip the schedule. Be lunatic and always plunging. Then would I evade the agony of origin. Nor would I suffer an initiation. I would be just an actress, automatic to an action. And that must be how easy. The streets seem mine if I merge with a motion I do not determine. (The fireman slides down a pole. Yes and a siren controls him. There are no obstacles. He attaches himself to the vehicle carrying him. He follows the rules and there are rules how to approach a fire.)

But this is the matter of one step. If I pretend a paralysis am i not seeing? Am I not seeing white cranes idle tonight on the disappearing sidewalk, an empty truck tapered to a spoon that makes the sidewalk disappear, hatchet grass that punctures the pavement, careless carpentry to conceal an incomplete facade, a stairway almost destroyed? But I have reached this random excrement and already my eyes begin a building here at this place of pretended paralysis.

I AM NOT STILL AS i stand here like a phony catatonic:
    aggressively resisting. I am not, it is not important
    am i an impermeable membrane. This resistance
    provokes the madness of enumeration:
        I am insensible to a,b,c,d,e,f,g, –
    And the gamble of elimination:
              $A^x, B^x, C^x-.$
    The energy this resistance requires is itself an
    alteration of temperature, at least.
    So I surrender. I surrender and I multiply:
    Polyblot:

Sponge.

Now am I leaning on a lamppost with metal leaves and a foundation of dung. Details obliterate within this light. But I become corpuscular. I AM SEEKING THE CAPITAL INTRODUCTION TO THE VERY FIRST WORD OF MY MIND. I WANT TO DESTROY IT. I KNOW THAT THE VERY LAST WORD IS NOT ME.

But I am this moment and corpuscular. I am that horizontal line laughing at the bottom of the wall.

I might be the palace protected by the wall. But I refuse protection: I am better laughing at the bottom of the wall.

Within this kingdom of the wall is there a king and a palace gullible to light; gullibility to light despite the infinite opacities of active men opaque and infinite within this kingdom of the wall.

The forced stones spread. The town begins to grow among the bones.

My father came to sanctify my birth; to sanctify the birth of Her. He came to name my mother, His. He came to tame my mother and to shelter her. I am supposing.

We will stabilize the sand, he said. We will contain the waters. We will close the sky. We will squeeze the wind, he said.

Build me a wall!

he said that.

He said: We will call this construction by a holy name. The syllable almost subdued him but he mastered his invention: masterfully then he said: The House.

My mother was His. The proud scheme of protection completely included her. And it was only after he had protected my mother from experience that he became afraid of the experience of living with her labyrinthine illusions. Soon he seldom stayed in what he called The House.

At first such room as he created strangulated us. Then my mother began to vanish: security is not a color. Paralysis is not an exercise.

I was learning my father. My father was innocent perhaps: He wanted me to participate in his perseveration of himself: he wanted me to pursue the circle of his escape. And so I left The House and went to walk with him to what he called *the corner of The Wall*.

In that crude culmination, there where the exploitation of silence looks like a cobweb, he taught me the way of The Wall.

Worship this thing, he said. Esteem this enemy of impulse. Let the wall become a sacred system for you, the fundamental lie you will believe.

Outside, inside, against, beside The Wall you will hover or hide, or climb, or penetrate, or withdraw. Whatever you choose, your deed will blunder as a dumb show on THE WALL. The absurd, insensible, arbitrary, obstacle qualities of The Wall will annihilate your mind. In this place of The Wall you will discover no necessity to act. The immovable of your awareness is The Wall. You and what you do are optional. That is the secret, he said, that is the secret of your tragic spontaneity. Be glad you are optional, he told me. His voice was deep. His eyes were shut.

But here am I. Not there. Where am I is there where I am. Here am I. Am I there where nothing is here where nothing is NOW? *I am not here for you and I will stay there.* Now there is nothing but now which is why am I here?

              Look at the cloud on the circle.
                   I am full suddenly full of light.

          My father said: There shall be shadow.
            I am shining shadows on The Wall.

And my father was only a shadow. His shadow of flesh divulged me: I was an apology of bone.

Anyone is of no consequence. How am I my one?

If I am, I am If in the middle of The Way. The Way leads neither north nor south with possibilities.

Possibilities preclude a wall.

The Way lies between two walls.

                    These are the ways of first and last reality. These are the ways of populous, foul, vertiginous, predatory, vicious, liquidating, lavatory truth. The Way is not a transformative via, nor a road for flight from arrival nor the rhythmic gesture of a street. The Way reveals only the curb.
    It is an intestinal trap: a trick coiled labyrinthine and guttural. I am in the middle of the way.
    I am in the middle of a dirty line squeezed by bricks of the wall precluding possibility. But I am not if I am in the middle clearly. If I am clearly then am I in the way of nothing.

But I am not alive nor dead.
    I am not alive nor dead nor gray nor anything absolute but I am

black. That may mean that gamma rays or brown or turd is another word that may mean brown inside this intestinal trap. Brown may mean negro. Negro may mean nothing. I am in the middle of delusion. I am in the way of nothing. But I am in the way.

My father loved the delusion he sired. The fundamental dream of my mother, her unnatural ignorance refreshed him and he surrounded her with new unnecessaries; things that do not matter, have no matter like The Wall. He gave to her. He gave of himself to her. He gave gold to her. He told her stories of herself. He told her the myth of the mirror. He made her the mirror of myth. He said to my mother many nouns. He said face and sky and ear and emerald and eye, but then he said grass. He said she was grass.

My mother wondered what she was. And so he opened the house.
He gave evening to her and winter.
He gave her alternative illusions.
He gave her a glimpse of endless, enjoyable illusion.
My father opened the house with windows.

I asked my father where was grass Or is there more than my mother as a metaphor. Around me was my mother and The Wall and the words my father used to call her as a sound
        I asked my father is there no grass in The House

While we live in The House he said there is no grass
When you have done with living in The House then
when you leave The Wall
when you stop your self
people carry you over THE WALL and bury you under the grass

Sometimes my father said smiling at me sometimes people bury you under the grass near an evergreen tree
        I was happy to think of the burial place and I asked my father to tell me a word for my first dream
        He held me on his lap as he gave me the word for my dream
Cemetery was what he whispered in my ear.

I would like to live in that cemetery of trees and grass but he told me I must go with him struggling for survival until I finally have done with living in The House

Then will I be taken to the cemetery And this my father called A Promise

> gulls fly along a shoulder
> I am baffled by
> your neck concealing
> flight

It does not do to say it. And I would not but I cannot do. You will not let me more than words. I wish that this word were less than I. I will to be more than this word. You will laughing let me try. For example, flight.

Three million molecules and marrow but still I will not rise and am I still. But is there that word. Desire has its sound but is there a stillness that means. There are wings between my teeth. Or my mouth consumes some cumulae fuming near my eyes striated from the hours of the day or garbanzo is a chick-pea. Still I am still.

Touch my tongue with yours.

I would swallow the limbs of your body and refuse to Write Down and disturb the magic of my engorgement

Let me more than words: I would be more than medium or limestone. I would be more than looking more than knowing more than any of these less than looking less than knowing (*words*)

On the dirt and stones between us was my hand that lay between us like a word between my eyes

On the dirt and stones between us was my hand that lay between us like another stone. Desire has no sound.

I looked the length of more than light at you away from me
Things were hanging   Rosebush maid and mirror hung.
Wires screws hooks and rope were there   Rope no longer
green is there in that very long room

I have heard the rope of your throat
I have heard the rope in your throat ready to squeeze
me into the syntax of stone
The sound of my life is a name you may not remember
I am losing the touch of the world to a word
You must have said anything to me

On the Murder of Two Human Being Black Men, Denver A. Smith and His Unidentified Brother, at Southern University, Baton Rouge, Louisiana, 1972

What you have to realize is about private property
like
for example do you know how much the president's
house weighs in at

do you know that?

But see it's important because obviously
that had to be some heavy building some kinda
heavy heavy bricks and whatnot
dig
the students stood outside the thing
outside of it
and also
on the grass belonging to somebody else (although
who the hell can tell who owns the grass)
but
well the governor/he said the students
in addition
to standing outside the building that was

The House of The President
in addition to that and in addition to
standing on the grass that was growing
beside that heavy real estate
in addition (the governor said) the students
used
quote vile language unquote and
what you have to realize about quote
vile language unquote
is what you have to realize about private property
and
that is
you and your mother and your father and your
sister and your brother
you
and you and you
be strictly lightstuff on them scales
be strictly human life
be lightstuff
weighing in at zero
plus
you better clean your language up

don't be be calling mothafuckas *mothafuckas*
pigs *pigs*
animals *animals*
murderers *murderers*
you
weighing less than blades of grass the last
dog peed on
less than bricks smeared gray by pigeon shit
less than euphemisms for a mercenary and
a killer
you be lightstuff
lightstuff on them scales

look out!

For My Brother

Teach me to sing
Blackman Blacklove
sing when the cops break your head
full of song
sing when the bullets explode in the back
you bend over me
Blacklove Blackman
sing when you empty the world
to fill up the needles that kill
needles killing you
killing
you
teach me to sing
Blackman Blacklove
teach me to sing.

Poem for My Pretty Man

the complexity is like your legs
around me
simple
an entanglement
and strong
the ready
curling
hair
the brownskin tones of action
quiet
temporarily
like listening
serene
and passionate
and
slowly closer

slowly
closer
kissing

inch by inch

Poem to My Sister, Ethel Ennis, Who Sang "The Star-Spangled Banner" at the Second Inauguration of Richard Milhous Nixon, January 20, 1973

gave proof through the night
that our flag was still there

on his 47th inauguration of the killer king
my sister
what is this song
you have chosen to sing?

and the rockets' red glare
the bombs bursting in air
my sister
what is your song to a flag?

to the twelve days of Christmas
bombing when the homicidal holiday shit tore forth
pouring from the B-52 bowels loose over Hanoi and the skin
and the agonized the blown limbs the blinded eyes the
silence of the children dead on the street and the
incinerated homes and Bach Mai Hospital blasted and
drowned by the military the American shit vomit
dropping down death and burying the lives the people
of the new burial ground
under the flag

for the second coronation of the killer king
what is this song
you have chosen to sing?

my sister
when will it come finally clear
in the rockets' red glare
my sister
after the ceremonial guns salute the ceremonial rifles
saluting the ceremonial cannons that burst forth a choking
smoke to celebrate murder
will it be clear
in that red that bloody red glare
my sister
that glare of murder and atrocity/atrocities
of power
strangling every program
to protect and feed and educate and heal and house
the people

(talking about *us*/you and me talking
about *us*)

when will it be clear to you

which night will curse out the stars with the blood
of the flag
for you
for enough of us

by the rockets' red glare
when will it be clear
that the flag that this flag is still there is still
here and will smother you smother your songs

can you see
my sister
is the night
and the red glaring blood clear at last
say

can you see
my sister

say you can see
my sister

and sing no more of war

On Moral Leadership as a Political Dilemma

Watergate, 1973

I don't know why but
I cannot tell a lie

I chopped down the cherry tree
I did
I did that
yessirree
I chopped down the cherry tree

and to tell you the truth
see
that was only in the morning

which left a whole day and part
of an evening (until suppertime)
to continue doing what I like to do
about cherry trees

which is

to chop them down

then pick the cherries
and roll them into a cherry-pie circle
and then

stomp the cherries
stomp them
jumping up and down

hard and heavy
jumping up to stomp them
so the flesh leaks and the juice
runs loose
and then I get to pick at the pits
or else I pick up the cherry pits
(depending on my mood)
and then
I fill my mouth completely full
of cherry pits
and run over to the river
the Potomac
where I spit
the cherry pits
47 to 65 cherry pits spit
into the Potomac
at one spit

and to tell you the truth some more
if I ever see a cherry tree
standing around no matter where
and here let me please be perfectly clear
no matter where
I see a cherry tree
standing around
even if it belongs to a middle-American of
moderate means with a two-car family
that is falling apart in a respectable
civilized
falling apart
mind-your-manners manner

even then

or even if you happen to be
corporate rich or
unspeakably poor or famous
or fashionably thin or comfortably fat
or even as peculiar as misguided as
a Democrat

or even a Democrat

even then
see
if you have a cherry tree
and I see it
I will chop that cherry tree down
stomp the cherries
fill my mouth completely with the pits to
spit them into the Potomac
and I don't know why
it is
that I cannot tell a lie

but that's the truth.

For Michael Angelo Thompson

October 25, 1959–March 23, 1973

So Brooklyn has become a holy place

the streets have turned to meadowland
where
wild
free
ponies
eat among the wild
free

flowers
growing there

                        Please do not forget.

A tiger does not fall or stumble
broken by an accident.
A tiger does not lose his stride or
clumsy
slip and slide to tragedy
that buzzards feast upon.

                        Do not forget.

The Black prince Michael Black boy
our young brother
has not "died"
he
has not "passed away"

the Black prince Michael Black boy

our young brother

                        He was killed.
                        He did not die.

It was the city took him off
(that city bus)
and smashed him suddenly
to death
deliberate.

It was the city took him off
the hospital
that turned him down the hospital
that turned away from so much beauty
bleeding

bleeding
in Black struggle
                just to live.
It was the city took him off
the casket names and faces
of the hatred spirit
stripped the force the
laughter and the agile power
of the child

                He did not die.
                A tiger does not fall.
                Do not forget.

The streets have turned to meadowland
where
wild
free
ponies
eat among the wild
free
flowers
growing there

and Brooklyn
has become a holy place.

Getting Down to Get Over

                Dedicated to my mother

    I

MOMMA MOMMA MOMMA
momma momma
mammy
nanny

granny
woman
mistress
sista

luv

blackgirl
slavegirl

gal

honeychile
sweetstuff
sugar
sweetheart
baby
Baby Baby

MOMMA MOMMA
Black Momma
Black bitch
Black pussy
piecea tail
nice piecea ass

hey daddy! hey
bro!
we walk together (an')
talk together (an')
dance and *do*
(together)
dance and do/hey!
daddy!
bro!
hey!
nina nikki nonni nommo nommo

momma Black
Momma

Black Woman
Black
Female Head of Household
Black Matriarchal Matriarchy
Black Statistical
Lowlife Lowlevel Lowdown
Lowdown and *up*
to be Low-down
Black Statistical
Low Factor
Factotum
Factitious Fictitious
Figment Figuring in Lowdown Lyin
Annual Reports

Black Woman/Black
Hallelujah Saintly
patient
smilin
humble
givin thanks
for
Annual Reports and
Monthly Dole
and
Friday night
and
(*good* God!)
Monday mornin: Black and Female
martyr masochist
(A BIG WHITE LIE)
Momma Momma

What does Mothafuckin mean?
WHO'S THE MOTHAFUCKA

FUCKED MY MOMMA
messed yours over
and right now
be trippin on my starveblack
female soul
a macktruck
mothafuck
the first primordial
the paradig/digmatic
dogmatistic mothafucka who
is he?
hey!
momma momma

dry eyes on the
shy/dark/hidden/cryin Black
face
of the loneliness
the rape
the brokeup mailbox
an' no western union roses
come inside the kitchen
and no poem
take you through the whole night
and no big
Black
burly
hand
be holdin yours
to have to hold onto
no
big Black burly hand
no nommo
no Black prince
come riding from the darkness
on a beautiful black horse
no bro
no daddy

"I was sixteen when I met my father.
In a bar.
In Baltimore.
He told me who he was
and what he does.
Paid for the drinks.
I looked.
I listened.
And I left him.
It was civil
perfectly
and absolute bull
shit.
The drinks was leakin waterweak
and never got down to my knees."

hey daddy
what they been and done to you
and what you been and done
to me
to momma
momma momma
hey
sugar daddy
big daddy
sweet daddy
Black Daddy
The Original Father Divine
the everlovin
deep
tall
bad
buck
jive
cold
strut
bop
split

tight
loose
close
hot
hot
hot
sweet SWEET DADDY
WHERE YOU BEEN AND
WHEN YOU COMIN BACK TO ME
HEY
WHEN YOU COMIN BACK
TO MOMMA
momma momma

And Suppose He Finally Say
"Look, Baby.
I Loves Me Some
Everything about You.
Let Me Be Your Man."
That reach around the hurtin
like a dream.
And I ain' never wakin up
from that one.
momma momma
momma momma

2

Consider the Queen

hand on her hip
sweat restin from
the corn/bean/greens' field
steamy under the pale/sly
suffocatin sky

Consider the Queen

she fix the cufflinks
on his Sunday shirt
and fry some chicken
bake some cake
and tell the family
"Never mind about the bossman
don' know how a human
bein spozed to act. Jus'
never mind about him.
Wash your face.
Sit down. And let
the good Lord bless this table."

Consider the Queen

her babies pullin at the nipples
pullin at the momma milk

the infant fingers gingerly
approach caress the
soft/Black/swollen/momma breast

and there
inside the mommasoft
life-spillin treasure chest
the heart
breaks

rage by grief by sorrow
weary weary
breaks
breaks quiet
silently
the weary sorrow
quiet now the furious
the adamant the broken
busted beaten down and beaten up
the beaten beaten beaten

weary heart beats
tender-steady
and the babies suck/
the seed of blood
and love glows at the
soft/Black/swollen momma breast

Consider the Queen

she works when she works
in the laundry *in jail*
in the school house *in jail*
in the office *in jail*
on the soap box *in jail*
on the desk
on the floor
on the street
on the line
at the door
lookin fine
at the head of the line
steppin sharp from behind
in the light
with a song
wearing boots
or a belt
and a gun
drinkin wine when it's time
when the long week is done
but she works when she works
in the laundry in jail
she works when she works

Consider the Queen

she sleeps when she sleeps
with the king in the kingdom
she

sleeps when she sleeps
with the wall
with whatever it is who happens
to call
with me and with you
(to survive you make
do/you explore more and more)
so she sleeps when she sleeps
a really deep sleep

Consider the Queen

a full/Black/glorious/a purple rose
aroused by the tiger breathin
beside her
a shell with the moanin
of ages inside her
a hungry one feedin the folk
what they need

Consider the Queen.

3
Blackman
let that white girl go
She know what you ought to know.
(By now.)

4
MOMMA MOMMA
momma momma
family face
face of the family alive
momma
mammy
momma
woman

sista
baby
luv

the house on fire/
poison waters/
earthquake/
and the air a nightmare/
turn
turn
turn around the
national gross product
growin
really gross/turn
turn
turn the pestilence away
the miserable killers
and Canarsie
Alabama
people beggin to be people
warfare on the welfare
of the folk/
hey
turn
turn away
the trickbag university/the
trickbag propaganda
trickbag
tricklins of prosperity/of
pseudo-"status"
lynchtree necklace
on the strong
round
neck of you
my momma
momma momma
turn away
the f.b.i./the state police/the cops/

the/everyone of the
infest/incestuous investigators
into you
and Daddy/into us
hey
turn
my mother
turn
the face of history
to your own
and please be smilin
if you can
be smilin
at the family

momma momma

let the funky forecast
be the last
one we will ever
want to listen to

And Daddy see
the stars fall down
and burn a light
into the singin
darkness of your eyes
my Daddy
my Blackman
you take my body in
your arms/you use
the oil of coconuts/of trees and
flowers/fish and new fruits
from the new world
to enflame me in this otherwise
cold place
please

meanwhile
momma
momma momma
teach me how to kiss
the king within the kingdom
teach me how to t.c.b./to make do
and be
like you
teach me to survive my
momma
teach me how to hold a new life
momma
help me
turn the face of history
to your face.

from *Things that I Do in the Dark*

Dedicated
to the liberation of all my love
and
to the memory of Granville I. Jordan
who fathered many dreams
and
to the memory of Mildred M. Jordan
whose sacrifice I hope to vindicate
and
to life itself

∽ FOR MY OWN

July 4, 1974

Washington, D.C.

At least it helps me to think about my son
a Leo/born to us
(Aries and Cancer) some
sixteen years ago
in St. John's Hospital next to the Long Island
Railroad tracks
Atlantic Avenue/Brooklyn
New York

at dawn

which facts
do not really prepare you
(do they)

for him

angry
serious
and running through the darkness with his own

becoming light

For My Jamaican Sister a Little Bit Lost on the Island of Manhattan

small
and glowing in this cold place
of brick
  cement
   dry sand
   and

```
            broken glass
where there are waters
of the earth
flowing like love alive
you will make them warm
waters
hot (even)
like the delicate sweat
of tiger lilies
blowing about
barely in flame
                at sunrise
```

Poem for Granville Ivanhoe Jordan

November 4, 1890–December 21, 1974
Dedicated to Stephen Henderson

I

At the top of your tie
the dressy maroon number
with one/small
gravy stain
remaining

the knot is now too narrow for your neck

a ridiculous a dustfree/shiny box confines
your arms and legs
accustomed to a boxer's hunch a wrestler's hauling
energies at partial rest

3 or 4 A.M. a thousand nights
who stubbornly retrieved your own
into
illumination

bright beyond blindfiling of
a million letters at the Post Office which
never forwarded even one
of a hundred
fantasies
your kitchenkept plans
keeping you awake

West Indian in kitchen exile
alone between the days
and studying the National Geographic magazines
white explorations and
excitement
in the places you were forced to leave

                                        no shoes
                                        no teeth

but oxlike shoulders
and hazel eyes that watered
slightly
from the reading you did teach yourself to do

West Indian in kitchen exile
omnivorous consumer of thick
kitchen table catalogs
of seeds for sale
for red
bright flowers

seeds

slick and colorful
on the quick
lush pages
advertising pear and
apple trees

or peaches
in first bloom

        who saved for money orders
        for the flowers
        for the trees
        who used a spade
        and shovel
        heavily and well
        to plant the Brooklyn backyard
        innocent of all
        the succulent
        the gorgeous schemes
        you held between your fingers
        like a simple
        piece of paper

Jesus, Daddy
what did you expect

an orange grove
a eucalyptus
roses
from the cities that despised the sweet calypso
of your trust?

   2

Who stole the mustache from your face?
It's gone.
Who took it away?
Why did you stop there

        on your knees

at eighty-four

        a man

down on your knees

in inconceivable but willing
prayer/your life
God's baby in gray hair

What pushed you from your own two feet?

my father

3
To this you have come

a calm a concrete pit
contains your corpse
above the spumespent ending of the surf
against the mountain trees and fertile pitch
of steeply clinging dirt

"Sleep on Beloved
Take Thy Rest"

the minister
eyes bare beneath the island light
intones a feeling mumbo jumbo

"ashes to ashes
dust to dust"

the village men
wrists strained to lumped up veins and cartilage
(from carrying the casket)
do not pray
they do not sing

"A-bide with me,
fast falls the eventide"

It's afternoon
It's hot
It's lit by sun that cannot be undone

by death

Ah, Momma

Ah, Momma,

Did the house ever know the night-time of your spirit: the flash
and flame of you who once, when we crouched in what you called
"the little room," where your dresses hung in their pallid color-
ings – an uninteresting row of uniforms – and where there were
dusty, sweet-smelling boxes of costume jewelry that nevertheless
shone like rubies, gold, and diamonds, once, in that place where
the secondhand mirror blurred the person, dull, that place with-
out windows, with doors instead of walls, so that your small-space
most resembled a large and rather hazardous closet, once, in there
you told me, whispering, that once, you had wanted to be an
artist: someone, you explained, who could just boldly go and sit
near the top of a hill and watch the setting of the sun
Ah, Momma!
You said this had been your wish when you were quite as young as
I was then: a twelve- or thirteen-year-old girl who heard your con-
fidence with terrified amazement: what had happened to you and
your wish? Would it happen to me too?

Ah, Momma:
"The little room" of your secrets, your costumery, perfumes, and
photographs of an old boyfriend you did not marry (for reasons
not truly clear to me as I saw you make sure, time after time, that
his pictures were being kept as clean and as safe as possible) –
"the little room" adjoined the kitchen, the kitchen where no mys-
tery survived, except for the mystery of you: woman who covered
her thick and long, black hair with a starched, white nurse's cap

when she went "on duty" away from our home into the hospital I came to hate, jealously, woman who rolled up her wild and heavy, beautiful hair before she went to bed, woman who tied a headrag around the waving, kinky, well-washed braids, or lengthy, fat curls of her hair while she moved, without particular grace or light, between the table and the stove, between the sink and the table, around and around and around in the spacious, ugly kitchen where she, where you, never dreamed about what you were doing or what you might do instead, and where you taught me to set down plates and silverware, and even fresh-cut flowers from the garden, without appetite, without excitement, without expectation

It was not there, in that obvious, open, square cookery where you spent most of the hours of the days, it was not there, in the kitchen where nothing ever tasted sweet or sharp enough to sate the yearnings I began to suspect inside your eyes, and also inside the eyes of my father, it was not there that I began to hunger for the sun as my own, legitimate preoccupation; it was not there, in the kitchen, that I began, really, to love you

Ah, Momma,

It was where I found you, hidden away, in your "little room," where your life and the power, the rhythms of your sacrifice, the ritual of your bowed head, and your laughter always partly concealed, where all of you, womanly, reverberated big as the whole house, it was there that I came, humbly, into an angry, an absolute determination that I would, one day, prove myself to be, in fact, your daughter

Ah, Momma, I am still trying

From The Talking Back of Miss Valentine Jones: *Poem # One*

well I wanted to braid my hair
bathe and bedeck my
self so fine
so fully aforethought for
your pleasure

see:
I wanted to travel and read
and runaround fantastic
into war and peace:
I wanted to
surf
dive
fly
climb
conquer
and be conquered
THEN
I wanted to pickup the phone
and find you asking me
if I might possibly be alone
some night
(so I could answer cool
as the jewels I would wear
on bareskin for your
digmedaddy delectation:)
"WHEN
you comin ova?"
But
I had to remember to write down
margarine on the list
and shoepolish and a can of
sliced pineapples in casea company
and a quarta skim milk cause Teresa's
gainin weight and don' nobody groove on
that much
girl
and next I hadta sort for darks and lights before
the laundry hit the water which I had
to kinda keep a eye on be-
cause if the big hose jumps the sink again that
Mrs. Thompson gointa come upstairs
and brain me with a mop don' smell too
nice even though she hang

it headfirst out the winda
and I had to check
on William like to
burn hisself to death with fever
boy so thin be
callin all day "Momma! Sing to me?"
"Ma! Am I gone die?" and me not
wake enough to sit beside him longer than
to wipeaway the sweat or change the sheets/
his shirt and feed him orange
juice before I fall out sleep and
Sweet My Jesus ain' but one can
left
and we not thru the afternoon
and now
you (temporarily) shownup with a thing
you say's a poem and you
call it
"Will The Real Miss Black America Standup?"

                              guilty po' mouth
                              about duty beauties of my
                              headrag
                              boozedup doozies about
                              never mind
                              cause love is blind

well
I can't use it

and the very next bodacious Blackman
call me queen
because my life ain' shit
because (in any case) he ain' been here to share it
with me
(dish for dish and do for do and
dream for dream)
I'm gone scream him out my house

be-
cause what I wanted was
to braid my hair/bathe and bedeck my
self so fully be-
cause what I wanted was
your love
not pity
be-
cause what I wanted was
your love
your love

∽ DIRECTED BY DESIRE

The Round of Grief

Like lonely fools our limbs do not combine.

In some long ago third solstice
      we met; shadows in heat
opening yearn the twinship mouth
      tasting with clean thorn tongue.

Your hand is bone and mine is skin.

Accidents blundered through our space
      falling swallowed behind our face:
the joyful eclipse of alien
      circles measured in assault.

Like lonely fools our limbs do not combine.

Pale with hiding from the burning higher
      than the tree we suckled fearful in the shade:
too late the twilight cooled our eyes
      already blind (believing blindness safe).

Your hand is bone and mine is skin.
Like lonely fools our limbs do not combine.

Poem in Celebration of the Recovery of Mrs. R. Buckminster Fuller, June 1967

only nothing limits the world
an intimate an interstitial
following together
from the darkness now
disarms the night
with love
and moves along to open

flights of holding
that will not be blown

One Minus One Minus One

> This is a first map of territory
> I will have to explore as poems,
> again and again

My mother murdering me
to have a life of her own

What would I say
(if I could speak about it?)

My father raising me
to be a life that he
owns

What can I say
(in this loneliness)

On a New Year's Eve

Infinity doesn't interest me

not altogether
anymore

I crawl and kneel and grub about
I beg and listen for

what can go away
                    (as easily as love)

or perish
like the children
running
hard on oneway streets/infinity
doesn't interest me

not anymore

not even
repetition your/my/eye-
lid or the colorings of sunrise
or all the sky excitement
added up

is not enough

to satisfy this lusting adulation that I feel
for
your brown arm before it
moves

MOVES
CHANGES UP

the temporary sacred
tales ago
first bikeride round the house
when you first saw a squat
opossum
carry babies on her back
opossum up
in the persimmon tree
you reeling toward
that natural
first
absurdity
with so much wonder still
it shakes your voice

the temporary is the sacred
takes me out

and even the stars and even the snow and even
the rain
do not amount to much
unless these things submit to some disturbance
some derangement such
as when I yield myself/belonging
to your unmistaken
body

and let the powerful lock up the canyon/mountain
peaks the
hidden rivers/waterfalls the
deepdown minerals/the coalfields/goldfields/
diamond mines close by the whoring ore
hot
at the center of the earth

spinning fast as numbers
I cannot imagine

let the world blot
obliterate remove so-
called
magnificence
so-called
almighty/fathomless and everlasting/
treasures/
wealth
(whatever that may be)

it is this time
that matters

it is this history
I care about

the one we make together
awkward
inconsistent
as a lame cat on the loose
or quick as kids freed by the bell
or else as strictly
once
as only life must mean
a once upon a time

I have rejected propaganda teaching me
about the beautiful
the truly rare

(supposedly
the soft push of the ocean at the hushpoint of the shore
supposedly
the soft push of the ocean at the hushpoint of the shore
is beautiful
for instance)
but
the truly rare can stay out there

I have rejected that
abstraction that enormity
unless I see a dog walk on the beach/
a bird seize sandflies
or yourself
approach me
laughing out a sound to spoil
the pretty picture
make an uncontrolled
heartbeating memory
instead

I read the papers preaching on
that oil and oxygen
that redwoods and the evergreens

that trees the waters and the atmosphere
compile a final listing of the world in
short supply

but all alive and all the lives
persist perpetual
in jeopardy
persist
as scarce as every one of us
as difficult to find
or keep
as irreplaceable
as frail
as every one of us

and
as I watch your arm/your
brown arm
just
before it moves

I know

all things are dear
that disappear

all things are dear
that disappear

Sunflower Sonnet Number One

But if I tell you how my heart swings wide
enough to motivate flirtations with the trees
or how the happiness of passion freaks inside
me, will you then believe the faithful, yearning freeze
on random, fast explosions that I place

upon my lust? Or must I say the streets are bare
unless it is your door I face
unless they are your eyes that, rare
as tulips on a cold night, trick my mind
to oranges and yellow flames around a seed
as deep as anyone may find
in magic? What do you need?

I'll give you that, I hope, and more
But don't you be the one to choose me: poor.

Sunflower Sonnet Number Two

Supposing we could just go on and on as two
voracious in the days apart as well as when
we side by side (the many ways we do
that) well! I would consider then
perfection possible, or else worthwhile
to think about. Which is to say
I guess the costs of long term tend to pile
up, block and complicate, erase away
the accidental, temporary, near
thing/pulsebeat promises one makes
because the chance, the easy new, is there
in front of you. But still, perfection takes
some sacrifice of falling stars for rare.
And there are stars, but none of you, to spare.

Lullaby

as suddenly as love

the evening burns a low
red

line occasional with golden glass
across the sky

i celebrate the color of the heat
you fill me with
the bloodbeat
you instill me with

as suddenly as love

For Ethelbert

if I cda known youd be real
back in them supreme court
gonna rule all evil out
days
I wda rushd to judgment
(lordy lord)
rushd thru
to the fiery seat itselve
and stayd there
cool as any momma madeup
her holy/everlastin min'
(chile *honey!*)
and sed
"sentence me, please,
to a long life long
enough
so's I gets to meet
what's comin afta (this mess)"
meanin'
you

You Came with Shells

You came with shells. And left them:
shells.
They lay beautiful on the table.
Now they lie on my desk
peculiar
extraordinary under 60 watts.

This morning I disturb I destroy the window
(and its light) by moving my feet
in the water. There.
It's gone.
Last night the moon ranged from the left
to the right side
of the windshield. Only white lines
on a road strike me as
reasonable but
nevertheless and too often
we slow down for the fog.

I was going to say a natural environment
means this or
I was going to say we remain out of our
element or
sometimes you can get away completely
but the shells
will tell about the howling
and the loss

On the Aluminum

on the aluminum shelf
The Religious Experience of Mankind
would slide into a pile of sweet
pickles

except for the glassplate
that separates the two
elu-
sively

upright and sleepy in this depart-
mental armchair
I can see the light surprise
or titillate the still naked trees
and then
your eyes
(My God, the darkness of the sky
around the stars
moves like the sea
incessantly)

love seems a matter of coincidence
at odds with the ending
of anyone/any two
                              at war with the boundaries
implied by
"I love you"

Minutes from the Meeting

Some would rather know volcanoes
rumble with roulette like
lava lastingly
compelled
to hot or cold
deliverance

Some would rather know the rules
be miserable but safe
a well-dressed certainty
that runs from rain

and other
unbid
possibilities

But as for me
who knows no one to claim
her or propose
a scanning of the universe
or excavations
of a kiss

it is all
out of my arms

Queen Anne's Lace

Unseemly as a marvelous an astral renegade
now luminous and startling (rakish)
at the top of its thin/ordinary stem
the flower overpowers or outstares me
as I walk by thinking *weeds* and *poison
ivy, bush* and *fern* or *runaway grass:*
You (where are you, really?) never leave me
to my boredom: numb as I might like to be.
Repeatedly
you do revive
arouse alive

a suffering.

Wasted

You should slice the lying tongue of your love
into a billion bits of bile you swallow
one bilious element at a time

while
scalding water trembles drop
by drop between
(you hope)
between your eyes because
you said you loved me
and you lied
you lied

All you wanted was to rid me of my pride
to ruin me for tenderness
you lied
to thrust me monstrous from the hurt
you fabricated claiming
all the opposites of pain
while maiming
me
the victim of your whimsical disdain

And I still love you like the river
in the rain
in vain
you lied
in vain.

For Dave: 1976

There wasn't any hot water for the teapot
so you came by to fix the furnace
and you found me
"very pretty" (you said)
underneath my worries

Leaving the wind behind the door you came
and when you left to sleep elsewhere
you left me ready to keep on
dancing by myself

I was accustomed to the Army cap that spills your
hair below those clean-as-a-whistle ears nobody
knows how to blow so you can hear them honest-to-
God
But I was a stranger to your hair let free your arms
around me
reading my lips then licking them gentle as a bear
sure that he hugs a honey tree not going anywhere
(which is true: for you

                      washing up with Ajax
leaving the rifle outside the way the Japanese
leave shoes
catching eels to smoke them good enough to eat
rebuilding a friend's house "after work")

Now you were lifting me as easily as we could laugh
between ourselves
you wanting to know what I was thinking about
me wanting to tell but unwilling to shout
at you (so you could hear me)

You arrive (red shirt
        new shoes
        the shower shining everywhere about you)
And I accept again
that there are simple ways of being joined
to someone
absolutely different from myself
And I admire the forthright
crocus first to mitigate the winter
with its thrust voluptuous/
on time

I mean to say
that it's not talk that brings us close together
and
thank god!

Meta-Rhetoric

Homophobia
racism
self-definition
revolutionary struggle

the subject tonight for
public discussion is
our love

we sit apart
apparently at opposite ends of a line
and I feel the distance
between my eyes
between my legs
a dry
dust topography of our separation

In the meantime people
dispute the probabilities
of union

They reminisce about the chasmic histories
no ideology yet dares to surmount

I disagree with you
You disagree with me
The problem seems to be a matter of scale

Can you give me the statistical dimensions
of your mouth on my mouth
your breasts resting on my own?

I believe the agenda involves
several inches (at least)
of coincidence and endless recovery

My hope is that our lives will declare
this meeting
open

⅏ AGAINST THE STILLWATERS

On the Loss of Energy (and Other Things)

no more the chicken and the egg come

one of them
before the other
both
be fadin (steady)
from the supersafeway/a&p/giant
circus

      uh-huh
      the pilgrim cornucopia
      it ain' a pot to pee in
      much
      (these days)

gas is gone
and alka seltza runnin gas
a close race
outasight/you
name it
      toilet paper
      halfway honest politicians
there's a shortage
folks/*please*
step right up)
a crisis
(*come in closer*)
A International Disaster
Definitely Takin Place
(give the little lady down in front some room)
and (*how about the brother in the back row/can*
you hear me brother?)
      WELL
      I SAID THE HOT AIR'S RUNNIN
      OUTASTEAM

I SAID
THE MEAT'S NOT GOOD
FOR KIDS TO EAT
TOO FULLAFAT
AND STUFF LIKE THAT
AND
IF YOU EAT MEAT
HOW YOU PLAN TO PAY THE RENT?
I SAID
THE OILWELLS DRIBBLIN
LOWER THAN A SNAKE
AND SOON WON'T BE NO HEAT
AND SO YOU MIGHT AS WELL EAT MEAT
EXCEPT THERE AINT NO
MEAT TO EAT
I SAID

BROTHER CAN YOU SPARE A DIME?

these things/they gettin more and more worse in
the time it takes to tell
you
how the country's bound to hell
you
first
if you be middlin poor or poor or Black or Black-and-poor
this profit-makin mess the worst
mess we been force to handle
since the civil war
close down the crackers
reconstructed
how the north won
into victory the crackers like to celebrate/a
reconstruction of the facts
on poor and Blackbacks
but
I am digressin/*folks*
please settle down and listen good

I say you know
you know
the affluent society
starvin high
on the hog as pigs can get
I say you know
we all been pigs
but mostly we been little pigs/I say
the big pigs
got the whole big pigpen
underneath some tasty big-pig pigs' feet
dynamite can move
where is the dynamite?
How come we tryin to cooperate
with this "emergency"/this faker/phony
ripoff
got you plannin
not to die and not to have a baby
on the weekends
not to do too much/
much less to start to die or start to have
a baby
on a Sunday
or on early Monday
got you/stiff and slow and hungry
on them lines the richboys laugh about/
Will somebody
real and prominent and smart
please stand
up here
and tell about inequities and big and little pigs
and other animals and birds/and fish
don't know a thing about no hog behavior/*where's*
the dynamite?
I say you know/I say
you know.
And so do I.

From Inside the Continuum

well then let it all go
to hell
or wherever it may
But let the movement
in general
and mine
in particular
keep the pace of the days
in decision
         by tomorrow I will
         resolve to kill somebody
and what can I show
for this sumptuous proof
of consistency
         breathing in
         saying the names of things

hello
I am the victim who kills
I am the killer intending
to punish the past
for my destiny
         why
         does it require
         so much effort
         just to close the circle?

Poem Against the State (of Things): 1975

I

wherever I go (these
days)
the tide seems low
(oh) wherever I go (these

days)
the tide seems very
very low

ATTICA!
ALLENDE!
AMERIKA!

Welcome to the Sunday School
of outfront machineguns
and secretive
assassinations

EVERYBODY WELCOME!

Put your money on the plate
your feet on the floor
and better keep a bodyguard
standing at the open door

EVERYBODY WELCOME!

Almighty
Multinational
Corporate
Incorporeal
Bank of the World
The World Bank
Diplomacy
            and Gold

This is the story:
This is the prayer:

Rain fell
Monday the thirteenth
1971
Attica

> coldstone covered by a cold moon-
> light hidden by the night
> when fifteen hundred Black
> Puerto Rican
> White (one or two)
> altogether Fifteen Hundred Men
> plus
> thirty-eight hostages
> (former keepers of the keys
> to the ugliest
> big
> house of them all)
> Fifteen Hundred and Thirty
> Eight
> Men
> lay sleeping in a long
> wait
> for the sun
> and not one with a gun
> not one with a gun

(oh) wherever I go
the tide seems low

> Fifteen Hundred and Thirty
> Eight
> prisoners in prison
> at Attica/they
> lay sleeping in a long
> long wait
> for the sun
> and not one with a gun
> not one with a gun

But they were not really alone:

> ATTICA!
> ALLENDE!

AMERIKA!

Despite
the quiet of the cold moon-
light on the coldstone
of the place
Despite
the rain that fell
transforming the D-yard
blankets and tents
into heavyweight, soggy
and sweltering hell

The Brothers were hardly alone:

on the roofs
on the walkways
in turrets
and tunnels
from windows
and whirlybirds

overhead

The State
lay in wait

Attica Attack Troops
wearing masks
carrying gas canisters
and proud to be white
proud to be doing
what everyone can
for The Man
Attica Attack Troops
lay armed
at the ready
legalized killers

hard
chewing gum
to master an all-American impatience
to kill
to spill blood
to spill blood of the Bloods

and not one with a gun

the State
lay in wait

Attica Attack Troops
carrying pistols and
big-game/.270 rifles and
Ithaca Model 37 shotguns
with double-o buckshot
and also
shotguns appropriate
for "antivehicle duty"
or shotguns appropriate
for "reducing a cement block wall
to rubble"
they were ready

for what?

(*oh*) *wherever I go* (*these*
days)
the tide seems low

Fifteen Hundred and Thirty Eight
Prisoners
lay waiting for the next
day's sun
Fifteen Hundred and Thirty Eight
Brothers
asleep

and not one with a gun
not one with a gun

2

Why did the Brothers revolt
against Attica?

why were they there?

What did they want?

the minimum wage
less pork
fresh fruit
religious freedom
and more than one shower a week

What did they want?

a response
recognition
as men
"WE are MEN!" They
declared:
"WE are MEN!
We are not beasts and do not
intend to be beaten
or driven as such."

ATTICA!
ALLENDE!
AMERIKA!

The State
lay in wait.

3

Black woman weeping at the coldstone wall
Rain stops. And blood begins to fall

"JACKPOT ONE!" was the animal
cry of The State
in its final
reply
            "JACKPOT ONE!!"
was the cry

9:26 A.M.
Monday the thirteenth
September 1971
Police
State Troopers
prison guards
helicopters/The Attica Attack Troops
terrified the morning
broke through
to the beasts within them
beasts
unleashed by the Almighty
Multinational
Corporate
Incorporeal
Bank of the World
Despoilers
of Harlem
Cambodia
Chile
Detroit
the Philippines
Oakland
Montgomery
Dallas
South Africa

Albany
Attica
Attica
The Attica Killers
The Almighty State shot/
murdered/massacred
forty three men
forty three men

The other Brothers/they
were gassed and
beaten
bleeding or not
still clubbed and beaten:

"Nigger! You should
have got it through the head!
Nigger! You gone wish that you were
dead!   Nigger!   Nigger!"

Monday the Thirteenth
September 1971
Attica
Blood fell on the Brothers: Not one with a gun.
Black women weeping into coldstone.

4

wherever I go (these
days)
the tide seems low
(oh) wherever I go (these
days)
the tide seems very
very low

God's love has turned away
from this Almighty place

But
I will pray
one prayer while He yet grants me
time and space:

NO MORE AND NEVER AGAIN!
NO MORE AND NEVER AGAIN!

A-men.
A-men.

I Must Become a Menace to My Enemies

Dedicated to the Poet Agostinho Neto, President of
The People's Republic of Angola: 1976

I

I will no longer lightly walk behind
a one of you who fear me:
                    Be afraid.
I plan to give you reasons for your jumpy fits
and facial tics
I will not walk politely on the pavements anymore
and this is dedicated in particular
to those who hear my footsteps
or the insubstantial rattling of my grocery
cart
then turn around
see me
and hurry on
away from this impressive terror I must be:
I plan to blossom bloody on an afternoon
surrounded by my comrades singing
terrible revenge in merciless
accelerating
rhythms

But
I have watched a blind man studying his face.
I have set the table in the evening and sat down
to eat the news.
Regularly
I have gone to sleep.
There is no one to forgive me.
The dead do not give a damn.
I live like a lover
who drops her dime into the phone
just as the subway shakes into the station
wasting her message
canceling the question of her call:

fulminating or forgetful but late
and always after the fact that could save or
condemn me

I must become the action of my fate.

2

How many of my brothers and my sisters
will they kill
before I teach myself
retaliation?
Shall we pick a number?
South Africa for instance:
do we agree that more than ten thousand
in less than a year but that less than
five thousand slaughtered in more than six
months will
WHAT IS THE MATTER WITH ME?

I must become a menace to my enemies.

3
And if I
if I ever let you slide
who should be extirpated from my universe
who should be cauterized from earth
completely
(lawandorder jerkoffs of the first the
terrorist degree)
then let my body fail my soul
in its bedeviled lecheries

And if I
if I ever let love go
because the hatred and the whisperings
become a phantom dictate I o-
bey in lieu of impulse and realities
(the blossoming flamingos of my
wild mimosa trees)
then let love freeze me
out.

I must become
I must become a menace to my enemies.

From The Talking Back of Miss Valentine Jones

THE WAR IS OVER:

And
the small fry
littlefolk
slant-eye devils
gooks
the fertile peril
yellow
fellow travelers

THEY'VE WON:

The victory
the liberation
of the Indo-Chinese peoples
apparently
belongs to pint-size
short
slight
runt-hard armies
not excluding ten-year-olds
boyandgirl
guerrilla fireflies
a multi-thousandfold
an army
marching on and on
in 69¢
single-thong slippers
thin
loose pyjamas
a military presence
fortified
by a handful of rice
wild fruit
and the indomitable
sexy
instinct sexy sting
of freedom

(WANT THAT THING
THAT MIGHTY
SWEET THING SO MY SOUL
CAN SING
WANT FREEDOM
        FREEDOM
        FREEDOM
WANT MY FREEDOM
NOW)

There go the imperial
big-nose
eagles
　　　flown and blown
　　　BACK
　　　where they come from

LOOK AT 'EM GO:

　　　　a-slippin and a-slidin
　　　　a-tippin and a-hidin
　　　　and hardly afloat
　　　　and doin a desperate
　　　　flip-floppin
　　　　wing-down
　　　　to the nearest Red Cross
　　　　rescue boat

LOOK AT 'EM GO:

The imperial
big-nose
eagles
flying low enough to crawl

　　　　　　crawl eagle crawl
　　　　　　wipe your weepy eyes
　　　　　　turn to the west my darlin
　　　　　　fly the friendly skies

"LONG DISTANCE IS CHEAPER THAN YOU THINK"

　　　　　LOOK AT 'EM GO!

　　　　　THE WAR IS OVER!

In Xuan Loc
Hanoi
Phnom Penh
and Ho Chi Minh City
there are no
>   people/babies/lovers/widows/mothers
>   brothers/in-laws/children
>   who belong to
>   who survive
>   who grieve for
>   the crewcut losers of the war

the eagle-eye
anti-personnel missionaries
took no
>   land/nation/village/school/hospital
>   home/gardenplot
>   or rice field
>   with them
>   when they split

However
authorities attribute
these remaining items
to the big-nose foreigners
>   five pounds: ground round
>   frozen orange juice
>   a watch that runs under water
>   filter tip cigarettes
>   and a case of Coca-Cola

>   *and that's all*
>   *think small*
>   *THE WAR IS OVER*

∞

This myopic personage
pimply where she

wish she bloomin freckles
tell me

smack in the middle of the giant cock-
eyed suckers
truckin us into the ground
squeezin heads to the size of the sides
of a dime
smack then
when everybody hurt
for open/
free meals an'
open/
free schools an'
open/
free ways to a job
an' open/
free dreams of the future

when
the men
drink whiskey from brown bags
on the daylong corner places they don'
never leave

(o i need me somethin i can do
need me somethin i can do
well i have some kinda shoes
but still i got the blues
well i have some kinda food
but it don' really taste too good)

Smack then and there
this myopic personage
she tell me

"They don't look like students!
They don't act like students!!
It drives me crazy.

They come
doo-wah-ooo-ooh
Oh-Oh-Ba-Bee
playing those Japanese portable
radios
loud
so you can't hear nothing
worthwhile
or think
or carry on a proper
conversation
or
(for Godssake)
read a book! That's why I
say, honestly, Valentine,
we have only ourselves to
blame. Blackfolk got only
themselves to blame. You
don't see no white kids
carrying no radios.
Do you?"

I say,
"Maybe they don't have no radio."

My man,
Emanuel Addis Addaba Boo
Owens,
he say,
"Maybe they don't have no
need to dance through
streets of fire: Lady,
buy a radio!
Turn it up
turn it on
on and on/on and on
turn it up

don' wanna hear you
or be near you
you the problem
you the dryspot in the holy water
you the freezeass/imitation enemy

He say,
"Lady, buy a radio!"

(*The Writings on the Wall*)

"Dear Somebody
        I am un-happy. My boy-
        friend is a creep. He
        makes me
        sick. What should I do?
        Nobody likes me be-
        sides him, either."

                    ∞

"You should talk
over with him how he's
a creep and tell him how
you feel about that. May-
be he thinks you're a creep, too.
How do you know? Find out."

                    ∞

"I am not a lesbian but
I would like to have a real
experience with a girl who
is. What should I do?"

                    ∞

"Believe it or not, Jesus
is the answer. Join the
church. The Lord will
save you a lot of

trouble and keep you
busy on the weekends."

∽

"Boycott the Bicentennial"

∽

"My man say if I don't give
him a baby
boy
he will throw me
out or beat
me to death."

∽

"Tell him to fuck himself.
Don't he like girls?"

∽

I'm tellin you baby
the war's not hardly over
for anyone like me

We got a long way to go
before we get to where we need to be

Don' have no work
(don' have no work)
Can' fin' no job

The streets is mean
(the streets is mean)
An' my ship ain' nowhere
to be seen

The war's not hardly over
                          (WANT THAT THING
                          THAT MIGHTY

SWEET THING SO MY SOUL
CAN SING
WANT FREEDOM
    FREEDOM
    FREEDOM
WANT MY FREEDOM
    NOW!

In Africa
in Mozambique
Angola
liberation lifts
the head of the young girl
formerly burdened by laundry
and yams

She
straps the baby to her back
and
she carries her rifle
like she means
means to kill

for the love

for the life
of us all

❧ TOWARDS A PERSONAL SEMANTICS

I Am Untrue Yet I

That fool myself
at yesterday collapsed apart
from ownership
new spine seduced by easier
caress
than thinking shadows
thoroughly
full
lingered objects
visibly bewildering loose lips
the folded eyes that yield
at yesterday
that never may exist
that fool
myself declining

On a Monday Afternoon

That's me.
I am there.
At the bottom of a closet
among old and used shoes
immobilized
folded at least
in half
in darkness
under old and used clothes
belonging to somebody else.

On a Thursday Evening

Colossal
The head of the dead
John Kennedy
overlooks all of the citizens
in between acts
drinking champagne
or soda
or anything with bubbles
that will die
fast.

Excerpts from a Verse Diary of Somebody Trying to Get into Gear

for weeks I have been wanting to write this poem
that would muffle my life with the horoscope
of flowers
that would join with rivers rushing along
that would bolt and break up
sentences mid-
bolt and break
impressively
like mid-air somersaults
from high-wire freedom
eyes can scarcely capture

to enrapture
whirling words and
abstract dervishes
asplash
      in gutland reappraisal
      of the light we barely share

because for weeks I have been wanting
to make my move
(as the saying goes)
but the travel agents advise
against traveling unarmed
and the route is dark with ideas
I can no longer
calmly
interpret

and this afternoon I noticed
there are more onions than garlic
underneath the sink

will a poem help

me

(*out?*)

For the Poet: Adrienne Rich

The pheasant arrives
Flemish coloring that burns:
. Your word for an eye

Some People

Some people despise me be-
cause I have a Venus mound
and not a penis

Does that *sound*
right
to you?

Ecology

When I came back after a few days away
my return terrified a huge
marsh hawk
his new nest next to my front door
Twice that happened:
He explodes with a powerful shuffling
of feathers
aimed in a 45-degree angle that leads
to the sky above the sea
If I go away again
(big as he is)
I wonder which one of us will be

the more surprised?

Passion

Dedicated to
Everybody scared as I used to be

Poem for Nana

What will we do
when there is nobody left
to kill?

∾

40,000 gallons of oil gushing into
the ocean
But I
sit on top this mountainside above
the Pacific
checking out the flowers
the California poppies orange
as I meet myself in heat
                    I'm wondering
where's the Indians?

                    all this filmstrip territory
                    all this cowboy sagaland:
                    not
                    a single Indian
                    in sight

40,000 gallons gushing up poison
from the deepest seabeds
every hour

40,000 gallons
while
experts international
while
new pollutants
swallow the unfathomable
still:

   no Indians

I'm staring hard around me
past the pinks the poppies and the precipice
that let me see the wide Pacific
unsuspecting
even trivial
by virtue of its vast surrender

I am a woman searching for her savagery
even if it's doomed

Where are the Indians?

∽

Crow Nose
Little Bear
Slim Girl
Black Elk
Fox Belly

the people of the sacred trees
and rivers precious to the stars that told
old stories to the night

how do we follow after you?

falling
snow before the firelight
and buffalo as brothers
to the man

how do we follow into that?

∽

They found her facedown
where she would be dancing
to the shadow drums that humble
birds to silent
　　　flight

They found her body held
its life dispelled
by ice
my life burns to destroy

Anna Mae Pictou Aquash
slain on The Trail of Broken Treaties
bullet lodged in her brain/hands
and fingertips
dismembered

who won the only peace
that cannot pass
from mouth to mouth

&

Memory should agitate
the pierced bone crack
of one in pushed-back horror
pushed-back pain
as when I call out looking for my face
among the wounded coins
to toss about
or out
entirely
the legends of Geronimo
of Pocahontas
now become a squat
pedestrian cement inside the tomb
of all my trust

as when I feel you isolate
among the hungers of the trees
a trembling
hidden tinder so long unsolicited
by flame

as when I accept my sister dead
when there should be
a fluid holiness
of spirits wrapped around the world
redeemed by women
whispering communion

∽

I find my way by following your spine

Your heart indivisible from my real wish
we
compelled the moon into the evening when
you said, "No,
I will not let go
of your hand."

∽

Now I am diving for a tide to take me everywhere

Below
the soft Pacific spoils
a purple girdling of the globe
impregnable

∽

Last year the South African Minister of Justice
described Anti-Government Disturbances as
Part of a Worldwide Trend toward the
Breakdown of Established Political and Cultural
Orders

∽

God knows I hope he's right.

Poem for the Poet Alexis De Veaux

The shadows of the body
blue and not blue
brown and not blue
blue and not brown
intimate
insist

deify
the thing within
all of it
within the body shadows
from the rose

herself

Current Events

He did not!
He did so!
He did not!
I'm telling you!
You lie!
Uh-unhh.
You're kidding me!
Cross my heart and hope to die!
Really?
No shit!
Yeah?
Yeah!
The What?
The Ayatollah Khomeini!
Getoutahere.
Square business!
The Who?

The Ayatollah Khomeini of Iran!
So?
So he said it!
Big deal.
That's what I'm saying:
Thursday
November 15th
1979
the headline reads:
IRAN SET TO
FREE WOMEN
AND BLACKS
Run that by, again!
Okay:
Thursday
November 15th
No! Not that part!
Just wait a second:
Thursday
November 15th
1979 and
this is the headline:
IRAN SET TO
FREE WOMEN
AND BLACKS:
See now
I told you it's a big deal!
How was I supposed to know?
Girl
you better keep up with the news!
Yeah, yeah:
I'm planning to!

Poem about The Head of a Negro

Painted by Peter Paul Rubens, 1577–1640

Up the shaken stairway
Back four hundred years
Before the meaningless emancipation
In an arbitrary corner
Of an old room
I find the face a tender contradiction
To the not entirely invisible bullet
Hole
The circling blush macabre as its history
Told into the left temple of the humbling skull

I find a man
the mother of mysterious crime
I find a man
the mother of me

The sweet the burden of the air around the head
that must look down
down
down into the flesh
down
down
down into the muscle of the flesh
down
down
down into the bleeding of the muscle
down
down
down into the candle of the blood

The Morning on the Mountains

The morning on the mountains where the mist
diffuses
down into the depths of the leaves
of the ash and oak trees
trickling toward the complexion of the whole lake
cold
even though the overlooking sky
so solemnly vermilion
sub-divides/the
seething stripes as soft
as sweet as the opening
of your mouth

The Rationale, or "She Drove Me Crazy"

"Well, your Honor,
it was late. Three A.M. Nobody on the streets.
And I was movin along, mindin my business when
suddenly there she was
alone
by herself
gleamin under the street lamp. I thought
'Whoa. Check this out?, Hey, Baby! What's
happenin?' I said under my breath.
And I tried to walk past but she was lookin
so good and
the gleam and the shine and
the beautiful lines of her
body sittin out there
alone
by herself
made me wild. I went wild. But
I looked all around to see where her
owner/where the man in her life could

probably be. But no show. She was out.
By herself. On the street:
As fine, as ready to go as anythin you could
ever possibly want to see so
I checked myself out: what's this?
Then I lost my control; I couldn't resist.
What did she expect? She looked foreign
besides and small and sexy
and fast
by the curb. So I lost my control and

I forced her open and I entered
her body and I poured myself
into her
pumpin for all I was worth
wild as I was
when you caught me

third time apprehended
for the theft of a Porsche."

Case in Point

A friend of mine who raised six daughters and
who never wrote what she regards as serious
until she
was fifty-three
tells me there is no silence peculiar
to the female

I have decided I have something to say
about female silence: so to speak
these are my 2¢ on the subject:
2 weeks ago I was raped for the second
time in my life the first occasion
being a whiteman and the most recent

situation being a blackman actually
head of the local NAACP

Today is 2 weeks after the fact
of that man straddling
his knees either side of my chest
his hairy arm and powerful left hand
forcing my arms and my hands over my head
flat to the pillow while he rammed
what he described as his quote big dick
unquote into my mouth
and shouted out: "D'ya want to swallow
my big dick; well, do ya?"

He was being rhetorical.
My silence was peculiar
to the female.

Poem of Personal Greeting for Fidel

On the occasion of his trip to the United Nations,
October 1979

When I thought about you hiding away up
in the hills below Miami it was
frequently/before and after errands
to the drugstore or a toddling promenade
to show my three-year-old the ways
of a river (filthy but nonetheless) headed south
where I pictured you hilarious
and stalwart
in a Robin Hood Bodega

Any regular Goliath
could pull apart that arsenal (I thought)
of leaves
sleeping bags

mosquitoes
individual canteen supplies of muddy water
scalding chocolate in tin cups
around the Girl Scout fires

But you arrived
inside the stadium
inside the multitudinous *caminos/avenidas*
de la libertad
filled by half a million hot compadres
like a tidal waving
over the formerly inert
dirt of the lovely
island

To amend the broken knees the incredulities
of Harlem/of myself apostate to all miracles
before you
you came looming indisputable
a very hirsute
Spanish-speaking hero
forcibly translated to the English *what*
goes around comes around: what comes through
Cuba goes around the world

20 years additional and now
my son (a man to whom I mail the clippings
from your visit to New York) walks quietly
high but invisible among the sandhills of Nebraska
thinking rather well of Sandinista possibilities
for patience and for
victory and
plotting to return by rail and route he must lay
down himself
against the isolating miles of flat America
and nonetheless now
el norteamericano media
disgrace the meaning the persevering heroics

of your moral pace among the humble
urgencies that scab the whole incorporated
planet/the media
dismiss the grace of your arithmetic
transliterating bullets into butter
hospitals and books for children
and

this is to let you know that nonetheless
that now
I will drink new wine
tilt the bottle toward Nebraska
lift a glass toward your bearded image on the screen
and I will say *bienvenido*
y salud
because *what*
goes around comes around: what comes through
Cuba goes around the world!

Newport Jazz Festival: Saratoga Springs and Especially about George Benson and Everyone Who Was Listening

We got to the point of balloons all of us
held aloft/a tender tapping at the skin
of coloring translucent
and
nothing was too deep but the incendiary/slow the rainy/
rainbow crowded surface did not keep
anybody from caring enough to undertake a random
openhanded sharing of much hefty
toke equipment/smoke
was passing by like kisses in the air
where little girls
blew bubbles

benedictory below the softly bloated
clouds

While the trumpets lifted sterling
curvilinear tonalities
to turn the leaves down low/well-
lit by glowing globes of candlelight
that man was singing
That man was singing
Baby
Baby if you come with me
I'll make you my own Dairy Queen
or if that's locked we'll find an all-night Jack-
in-the-Box steak sandwich/fried onion rings
blackcherry/strawberry/butterscotch/shake
blackcherry/strawberry/butterscotch
shake
blackcherry/strawberry/butterscotch
shake

Baby
if you come now Baby if you if you Baby if you come
now

Patricia's Poem

"Listen
after I have set the table
folded the scottowel into napkins
cooked this delicious eggplant stuffed
with bulghur wheat
then baked the whole thing under a careful
covering of mozzarella cheese
and
said my grace

don't you bring Anita Bryant/Richard
Pryor/the Justices of the Supreme Court/don't
you bring any of these people in here
to spoil my digestive process
and ruin
my dinner

you hear?"

"Hey, Baby: You married?"

Willie at The Golden Grill
came straight from work to drink tequila
and explain this to me at eleven
P.M.
around the corner of the jukebox
where we partially ignore
the music

planning "to
break into business here
in Saratoga
at the racetrack or
whatever"

at 25
he's got 5 years before a marriage
hits him although
it could happen to you sooner
than you plan or so he solemnly
agrees

We do a slowdrool dance
him thin underneath the regulation blue
baseball cap

peaked carefully above the pretty eyes
and not much taller than I am

"I didn't have time to change my clothes"
Willie tells me/smiling true
to the rhythm of the melody of his mouth
is thick

"Around here?" he continues: "The disco is
THE RAFTERS: The best lightshow the best
DeeJay in New York State! And
I'm the bouncer!"

I watch the directions Willie gives me
carrying his fingers casual across
the jukebox title cards
lit from below

"Come up to THE RAFTERS
any Wednesday/Friday/Saturday night"
he says
"And"
he emphasizes quietly
"It'll be on me!"

"Yeah?" I ask him.

"Yeah!" he answers me:
"Why not?!"

TV Is Easy Next to Life

Check out Sidney Poitier as Noble Savage
and there's Rock Hudson playing Bwana
see him shoot down Noble Savage/Former
Childhood Playmate in the Jungle/shoot his

wife and all the tribe be decimated
by All A Big Mistake co-starring
U.S. Army rifles and Colonial Lust
then Bwana chase him playmate/Sidney:
"Noble Savage and your baby son, don't run!"
Sidney halts. The cameras zoom to large
native eyes of the African man who cries out:
"No! You kill my wife you kill my people:
No more talking!" But
Rock is like a rock: "Don't be a fool!" he
shouts back: "That was a mistake. Let
me explain!"
Cut to this advertisement:
"Now! Before Africa goes up in flames –
You can own these magnificent gems that
are everyone's best friend these days
at only $8.95 a half carat
yes
genuine
natural diamonds

The world's diamond deposits will
soon be exhausted. With diamonds
increasing in value 4 times in 15 years
it seems reasonable to suppose the value
of these diamonds will rise even more sharply when
South Africa explodes into full-scale war (comma)
which it could to momentarily (period) But regardless
if war comes (comma) this is a risk-free (comma) in
fact (comma) brilliant purchase (period)
Get several as gifts (period)
But hurry (period)"

TV is easy next to life
Check out the Noble Savage adamant against
the conversation the dialog the seminar the National
Commission to Investigate the slaughtering of his
wife and people

Sidney runs. But Bwana
quite determined to discuss these matters takes
a bead on Noble Savage fells him
to the forest floor from which my brother man
will rise no more
Another accident: Behold the childhood playmate of
the jungle dying now
he's dead
and Bwana says he'll raise the baby boy survivor
by himself instead
                    to be a what
                    for whom?
Ah, questions! Questions!

1978

The woman who left the house this morning
more or less on her way to Mississippi more
or less through Virginia in order to pack and get back to
New York on her way to The People's Republic of
Angola
was
stopped in Washington D.C. by an undercover
agent for the C.I.A. offering to help her with
her bags

The woman who came to the house tonight with
her boy baby Ché on the way to Philly
for a showdown with Customs that wants to deport both
of them
to Venezuela because Ché's
father months ago ducked out
entirely
she
just offered to make me chickweed tea
for my runny nose cold

"You know what I have? A desk that's big enough," Sara
had said and which I could see now as we sat opposite
the bathtub in the kitchen of her newplace
where we talked away a good part of the afternoon re-
considering sex into a status satellite to dialog/work
hanging out/sport while another a third poet currently
doing what she does in Seattle came into the room
by cassette

"I have loved you assiduously" Trazana Beverly's voice
advertising *for colored girls* cracks me up on my
way to the airport/*assiduously* on the FM (yeah Zaki!) on
my way to pick up Louise wiped out by Cambridge where
she proved the muse is female on
paper
and
all this stuff going on and my lover wants to know
am I a feminist or what and what does the question
mean I mean
or *what?*

An Explanation Always Follows

Rose and ivory roses open among
us
at breakfast/the roses slope into the smoky
crystal of the silver-tipped vase

carved mahogany
chairs with weathered leather
seats
hold the sleepers upright

Slicing a small peach the older
man with steep
European accent

pops
a morsel of the peach into his mouth

savoring the fruit he
does not masticate the morsel
quite discreetly/I
must avert my eyes or
witness the entire process: tongue
teeth and peach enmeshed
degenerate

Now comes volunteer expatiation on allegedly
famous porn districts in Germany
(The Reeperbahn in Hamburg
brewer's yeast and potency
yesterday's sperm count)

the older man
before cracking into soft-boiled eggs
(and balancing the knife in his right
hand with only four of the five
fingernails apparently
clean)
looks up to query my
increasing reticence

"Why," he questions me: "Don't you want to be seduced?!"

Letter to the Local Police

Dear Sirs:

I have been enjoying the law and order of our
community throughout the past three months since
my wife and I, our two cats, and miscellaneous
photographs of the six grandchildren belonging to

our previous neighbors (with whom we were very
close) arrived in Saratoga Springs which is clearly
prospering under your custody

Indeed, until yesterday afternoon and despite my
vigilant casting about, I have been unable to discover
a single instance of reasons for public-spirited concern,
much less complaint

You may easily appreciate, then, how it is that
I write to your office, at this date, with utmost
regret for the lamentable circumstances that force
my hand

Speaking directly to the issue of the moment:

I have encountered a regular profusion of certain
unidentified roses, growing to no discernible purpose,
and according to no perceptible control, approximately
one quarter mile west of the Northway, on the southern
side

To be specific, there are practically thousands of
the aforementioned abiding in perpetual near riot
of wild behavior, indiscriminate coloring, and only
the Good Lord Himself can say what diverse soliciting
of promiscuous cross-fertilization

As I say, these roses, no matter what the apparent
background, training, tropistic tendencies, age,
or color, do not demonstrate the least inclination
toward categorization, specified allegiance, resolute
preference, consideration of the needs of others, or
any other minimal traits of decency

May I point out that I did not assiduously seek out
this colony, as it were, and that these certain

unidentified roses remain open to viewing even by
children, with or without suitable supervision

(My wife asks me to append a note as regards the
seasonal but nevertheless seriously licentious
phenomenon of honeysuckle under the moon that one may
apprehend at the corner of Nelson and Main

However, I have recommended that she undertake direct
correspondence with you, as regards this: yet
another civic disturbance in our midst)

I am confident that you will devise and pursue
appropriate legal response to the roses in question
If I may aid your efforts in this respect, please
do not hesitate to call me into consultation

Respectfully yours,

Found Poem

Three stars: "Flaming Feather"
(1952)
A band of vigilantes rides
to the rescue of a white woman
captured by a tribe
of renegade Indians.

(1 hr. 30 min.)

Poem about a Night Out: Michael: Goodbye for a While

For Michael Harper

There had been death   There had been fire
and you would recommend Irish
whiskey saying "It's better than bourbon
smoother than scotch" and if I
replied, saying "Michael
the smoke tree sports the most infinitesimal
and linear blossomings
plus
perfectly elliptical leaves" you
might very well remark
"Uh-huh" and then inquire (the way
you did when you were pulling out the Volvo
and I ran over to the car alarmed at that)
"D'you need anything?" (gesturing to the stuff
in the backseat) "Rilke's
Duino Elegies, or anything?" the same
way you said (down to the local
disco after this guy about gave
it away to the beat that was not
that big) "Tell me
when you want me to kill him. And
I will."
There had been death   There had been fire
And the last night began behind the Fleetwood
Cadillac which the disco lady owner mo-
mentarily held beside the curbstone
boxes up on Broadway and you (laughing)
dropped my letters into LOCAL
while Barbara and Sonia and Robert
yelled, "Michael!"
then the saturnine the extremely pregnant
waitress told our table "If
you want anything just wave"

while Peter rapped to me about Barbara
while Robert rapped to Barbara
about himself
while you never sat down
      you never sat down

the red rim of your ears
red throughout the whole earlier
dinnertime
red from the grieving/there had been
death there had been
fire
around the edges of your head
and here we were at five A.M. alive
alive
a silver lunacy flying small above a few
dark conifers but inside
the crowd of us was singing to the highway
well
you loved me
then you snubbed
me
now what can I do
I'm still in love with you
seeing the Japanese smoke among the mountains

then rolling into it
a u-turn on the highway
and the smoke among the mountains
and
didn't we sing
didn't we sing

Earth Angel
Earth Angel
Will you be mi-ine

and

didn't you never
never
sit down!

Poem about Police Violence

Tell me something
what you think would happen if
everytime they kill a black boy
then we kill a cop
everytime they kill a black man
then we kill a cop

you think the accident rate would lower
subsequently?

sometimes the feeling like amaze me baby
comes back to my mouth and I am quiet
like Olympian pools from the running the
mountainous snows under the sun

sometimes thinking about the 12th House of the Cosmos
or the way your ear ensnares the tip
of my tongue or signs that I have never seen
like DANGER WOMEN WORKING

I lose consciousness of ugly bestial rabid
and repetitive affront as when they tell me
18 cops in order to subdue one man
18 strangled him to death in the ensuing scuffle (don't
you idolize the diction of the powerful: *subdue* and
scuffle my oh my) and that the murder
that the killing of Arthur Miller on a Brooklyn
street was just a "justifiable accident" again
(again)

People been having accidents all over the globe
so long like that I reckon that the only
suitable insurance is a gun
I'm saying war is not to understand or rerun
war is to be fought and won

sometimes the feeling like amaze me baby
blots it out/the bestial but
not too often

tell me something
what you think would happen if
everytime they kill a black boy
then we kill a cop
everytime they kill a black man
then we kill a cop

you think the accident rate would lower
subsequently?

Sketching in the Transcendental

Through the long night the long trucks running the road

The wind in the white pines does not ululate like
that

Nor do the boreal meadowlands the mesopotamia
of the spirit does not sing

the song of the long trucks

The spirit differs
from a truck

a helluva lot

A Poem about Intelligence for My Brothers and Sisters

A few years back and they told me Black
means a hole where other folks
got brain/it was like the cells in the heads
of Black children was out to every hour on the hour naps
Scientists called the phenomenon the Notorious
Jensen Lapse, remember?
Anyway I was thinking
about how to devise
a test for the wise
like a Stanford-Binet
for the C.I.A.
you know?
Take Einstein
being the most the unquestionable the outstanding
the maximal mind of the century
right?
And I'm struggling against this lapse leftover
from my Black childhood to fathom why
anybody should say so:
E=mc squared?
I try that on this old lady live on my block:
She sweeping away Saturday night from the stoop
and mad as can be because some absolute
jackass have left a kingsize mattress where
she have to sweep around it stains and all she
don't want to know nothing about in the first place
"Mrs. Johnson!" I say, leaning on the gate
between us: "What you think about somebody come up
with an *E* equals *M C 2?*"
"How you doin," she answer me, sideways, like she don't
want to let on she know I ain'
combed my hair yet and here it is
Sunday morning but still I have the nerve
to be bothering serious work with these crazy
questions about

"*E* equals what you say again, dear?"
Then I tell her, "Well
also this same guy? I think
he was undisputed Father of the Atom Bomb!"
"That right." She mumbles or grumbles, not too politely
"And dint remember to wear socks when he put on
his shoes!" I add on (getting desperate)
at which point Mrs. Johnson take herself and her broom
a very big step down the stoop away from me
"And never did nothing for nobody in particular
lessen it was a committee
and
used to say, 'What time is it?'
and
you'd say, 'Six o'clock.'
and
he'd say, 'Day or night?'
and
and he never made nobody a cup a tea
in his whole brilliant life!
and
[my voice rises slightly]
and
he dint never boogie neither: never!"

"Well," say Mrs. Johnson, "Well, honey,
I do guess
that's genius for you."

verse from a fragmentary marriage

midtown manhattan
honk
beep
piss
shit

buzzbuzz
buzzbuzz
you
all over my mind and eyes

lilacs in starlight

midnight manhattan
you

all over
all over

for a while

1977: Poem for Mrs. Fannie Lou Hamer

You used to say, "June?
Honey when you come down here you
supposed to stay with me. Where
else?"
Meanin home
against the beer the shotguns and the
point of view of whitemen don'
never see Black anybodies without
some violent itch start up.
                              The ones who
said, "No Nigga's Votin in This Town...
lessen it be feet first to the booth"
Then jailed you
beat you brutal
bloody/battered/beat
you blue beyond the feeling
of the terrible

And failed to stop you.
Only God could but He
wouldn't stop
you
fortress from self-
pity

Humble as a woman anywhere
I remember finding you inside the laundromat
in Ruleville
> lion spine relaxed/hell
> what's the point to courage
> when you washin clothes?

But that took courage

> just to sit there/target
> to the killers lookin
> for your singin face
> perspirey through the rinse
> and spin

and later
you stood mighty in the door on James Street
loud callin:

> "BULLETS OR NO BULLETS!
> THE FOOD IS COOKED
> AN' GETTIN COLD!"

We ate
A family tremulous but fortified
by turnips/okra/handpicked
like the lilies

filled to the very living
full

one solid gospel
           (*sanctified*)

one gospel
         (*peace*)

one full Black lily
luminescent
in a homemade field

of love

Poem for South African Women

> Commemoration of the 40,000 women and
> children who, August 9, 1956, presented
> themselves in bodily protest against the
> "dompass" in the capital of apartheid. Presented
> at the United Nations, August 9, 1978.

Our own shadows disappear as the feet of thousands
by the tens of thousands pound the fallow land
into new dust that
rising like a marvelous pollen will be
fertile
even as the first woman whispering
imagination to the trees around her made
for righteous fruit
from such deliberate defense of life
as no other still
will claim inferior to any other safety
in the world

The whispers too they
intimate to the inmost ear of every spirit
now aroused they
carousing in ferocious affirmation

of all peaceable and loving amplitude
sound a certainly unbounded heat
from a baptismal smoke where yes
there will be fire

And the babies cease alarm as mothers
raising arms
and heart high as the stars so far unseen
nevertheless hurl into the universe
a moving force
irreversible as light years
traveling to the open
eye

And who will join this standing up
and the ones who stood without sweet company
will sing and sing
back into the mountains and
if necessary
even under the sea

we are the ones we have been waiting for

Notes on the Peanut

For the Poet David Henderson

Hi there. My name is George
Washington
Carver.
If you will bear with me
for a few minutes I
will share with you
a few
of the 30,117 uses to which
the lowly peanut has been put
by me

since yesterday afternoon.
If you will look at my feet you will notice
my sensible shoelaces made from unadulterated
peanut leaf composition that is biodegradable
in the extreme.
To your left you can observe the lovely Renoir
masterpiece reproduction that I have cleverly
pieced together from several million peanut
shell chips painted painstakingly so as to
accurately represent the colors of the original!
Overhead you will spot a squadron of Peanut B-52
Bombers flying due west.
I would extend my hands to greet you
at this time
except for the fact that I am holding a reserve
supply of high energy dry roasted peanuts
guaranteed to accelerate protein assimilation
precisely documented by my pocket peanut calculator;

May I ask when did you last contemplate the relationship
between the expanding peanut products industry
and the development of post-Marxian economic theory
which (Let me emphasize) need not exclude moral attrition
of prepuberty
polymorphic
prehensible skills within the population age sectors
of 8 to 15?
I hope you will excuse me if I appear to be staring at you
through these functional yet high fashion and prescriptive
peanut contact lenses providing for the most
minute observation of your physical response to all of this
ultimately nutritional information.
Peanut butter peanut soap peanut margarine peanut
brick houses and house and field peanuts *per se* well
illustrate the diversified
potential of this lowly leguminous plant
to which you may correctly refer
also

as the goober the pindar the groundnut
and ground pea/let me
interrupt to take your name down on my
pocket peanut writing pad complete with matching
peanut pencil that only 3 or 4
chewing motions of the jaws will sharpen
into pyrotechnical utility
and no sweat.
Please:
Speak right into the peanut!

Your name?

Unemployment Monologue

You can call me Herbie Jr. or Ashamah
Kazaam. It don' matter much. The thing
is you don' wan' my name you
wanna mug shot
young
Black
male
who scares you chickenshit just
standin on the street just lookin
at you pass me by.
But I ain' doin nothing I ain' goin nowhere an'
you
know it an'
if you call me "Herbie" I don' mind
or "Junior"/that's all right
or "Ashamah Kazaam"/that's cool.
I say it don' really matter much
and then again/see
I may call you sweetmeat

I may call you tightass I might
one night I might break the windows
of the house you live in/I
might get tight and take your
wallet outasight/I might
hide out in the park to chase
you in the dark/etcetera/it
don' matter/I
may stay in school or quit
and I say
it
don' matter much
you wanna mug shot
and the way I feel about it/well
so what?

you got it!

Toward a City That Sings

Into the topaz the crystalline signals
of Manhattan
the nightplane lowers my body
scintillate with longing to lie positive
beside
the electric waters of your flesh
and
I will never tell you the meaning of this poem:
Just say, "She wrote it and I recognize
the reference." Please
let it go at that. Although
it is all the willingness you lend
the world
as when you picked it up
the garbage scattering the cool
formalities of Madison Avenue

after midnight (where we walked
for miles as though we knew the woods
well enough to ignore the darkness)
although it is all the willingness you lend
the world
that makes me want
to clean up everything
in sight
(myself included)

for your possible
discovery

A Song of Sojourner Truth

Dedicated to Bernice Reagon

The trolley cars was rollin and the passengers all white
when Sojourner just decided it was time to take a seat
The trolley cars was rollin and the passengers all white
When Sojourner decided it was time to take a seat
It was time she felt to rest awhile and ease up
on her feet
So Sojourner put her hand out
tried to flag the trolley down
So Sojourner put her hand out
for the trolley crossin town
And the driver did not see her
the conductor would not stop
But Sojourner yelled, "It's me!"
And put her body on the track
"It's me!" she yelled, "And yes,
I walked here but I ain' walkin back!"
The trolley car conductor and the driver was afraid
to roll right over her and leave her lying dead
So they opened up the car and Sojourner took a seat
So Sojourner sat to rest awhile and eased up on her feet

Sojourner had to be just crazy
tellin all that kinda truth
I say she musta been plain crazy
plus they say she was uncouth
talkin loud to any crowd
talkin bad insteada sad
She just had to be plain crazy
talkin all that kinda truth

If she had somewhere to go she said
I'll ride
If she had somewhere to go she said
I'll ride
jim crow or no
she said *I'll go*
just like the lady
that she was in all the knowing darkness
of her pride
she said *I'll ride*
she said *I'll talk*
she said *A Righteous Mouth*
ain' nothin you should hide
she said she'd ride
just like the lady
that she was in all the knowing darkness
of her pride
she said *I'll ride*

They said she's Black and ugly and they said she's
really rough
They said if you treat her like a dog
well that'll be plenty good enough
And Sojourner said
I'll ride
And Sojourner said
I'll go

I'm a woman and this hell has made me tough
(Thank God)
This hell has made me tough
I'm a strong Black woman
and Thank God!

REFRAIN:

Sojourner had to be just crazy
tellin all that kinda truth
I say she musta been plain crazy
plus they say she was uncouth
talkin loud to any crowd
talkin bad insteada sad
She just had to be plain crazy
talkin all that kinda truth

Alla Tha's All Right, but

Somebody come and carry me into a seven-day kiss
I can' use no historic no national no family bliss
I need an absolutely one to one a seven-day kiss

I can read the daily papers
I can even make a speech
But the news is stuff that tapers
down to salt poured in the breach

I been scheming about my people I been scheming about sex
I been dreaming about Africa and nightmaring Oedipus the Rex
But what I need is quite specific
terrifying rough stuff and terrific

I need an absolutely one to one a seven-day kiss
I can' use no more historic no national no bona fide family bliss
Somebody come and carry me into a seven-day kiss

Somebody come on
Somebody come on and carry me
over there!

Nightletters

You said, "In Morocco they make
        deliberate mistakes."

Next to you I do nothing
to perfect my safety

How should I dispel
the soul of such agile excitation?

Let no violence despoil
the sweet
translucent reasons for
our meeting

Once again I am wrong
but honestly

You walk away
and I am left to a maundering
through liberties

Already this wild beat leads me
to a stillness
opening

We are dangerous and undeniable/incense
in the English ivy
leaves

Evidently Looking at the Moon Requires a Clean Place to Stand

The forest dwindling narrow and irregular
to darken out the starlight on the ground
where needle shadows
signify the moon a harsh
a horizontal blank that lays the land
implicit to the movement of your body
is
the moon

You'd think I was lying to you
if I described precisely
how
implicit to the feeling of your lips
are luminous announcements
of more mystery than Arizona
more than just the imperturbable
convictions
of the cow

headfirst into a philosophy
and

so sexy
chewing up the grass

Free Flight

Nothing fills me up at night
I fall asleep for one or two hours then
up again my gut
alarms
I must arise
and wandering into the refrigerator

think about evaporated milk homemade vanilla ice cream
cherry pie hot from the oven with Something Like Vermont
Cheddar Cheese disintegrating luscious
on the top while
mildly
I devour almonds and raisins mixed to mathematical
criteria or celery or my very own sweet and sour snack
composed of brie peanut butter honey and
a minuscule slice of party size salami
on a single whole wheat cracker *no salt added*
or I read César Vallejo/Gabriela Mistral/last year's
complete anthology or
I might begin another list of things to do
that starts with toilet paper and
I notice that I never jot down fresh
strawberry shortcake: never
even though fresh strawberry shortcake shoots down
raisins and almonds 6 to nothing
effortlessly
effortlessly
is this poem on my list?
light bulbs lemons envelopes ballpoint refill
post office and zucchini
oranges no
it's not
I guess that means I just forgot
walking my dog around the block leads
to a space in my mind where
during the newspaper strike questions
sizzle through suddenly like
Is there an earthquake down in Ecuador?
Did a T.W.A. supersaver flight to San Francisco
land in Philadelphia instead
or
whatever happened to human rights
in Washington D.C.? Or what about downward destabilization
of the consumer price index
and I was in this school P.S. Tum-Ta-Tum and time came

for me to leave but
No! I couldn't leave: The Rule was anybody leaving
the premises without having taught somebody something
valuable would be henceforth proscribed from the
premises would be forever null and void/dull and
vilified well
I had stood in front of 40 to 50 students running my
mouth and I had been generous with deceitful smiles/soft-
spoken and pseudo-gentle wiles if and when forced
into discourse amongst such adults as constitutes
the regular treacheries of On The Job Behavior
ON THE JOB BEHAVIOR
is this poem on that list
polish shoes file nails coordinate tops and bottoms
lipstick control no
screaming I'm bored because
this is whoring away the hours of god's creation
pay attention to your eyes your hands the twilight
sky in the institutional big windows
no
I did not presume I was not so bold as to put this
poem on that list
then at the end of the class this boy gives me Mahler's 9th
symphony the double album listen
to it let it seep into you he
says transcendental love
he says
I think naw
I been angry all day long/nobody did the assignment
I am not prepared
I am not prepared for so much grace
the catapulting music of surprise that makes me
hideaway my face
nothing fills me up at night
yesterday the houseguest left a brown
towel in the bathroom for tonight
I set out a blue one and
an off-white washcloth seriously

I don't need no houseguest
I don't need no towels/lovers
I just need a dog

Maybe I'm kidding

Maybe I need a woman
a woman be so well you know so wifelike
so more or less motherly so listening so much
the universal skin you love to touch and who the
closer she gets to you the better she looks to me/somebody
say yes and make me laugh and tell me she know she
been there she spit bullets at my enemies she say you
need to sail around Alaska fuck it all try this new
cerebral tea and take a long bath

Maybe I need a man
a man be so well you know so manly so lifelike
so more or less virile so sure so much the deep
voice of opinion and the shoulders like a window
seat and cheeks so closely shaven by a twin-edged
razor blade no oily hair and no dandruff besides/
somebody say yes and make
me laugh and tell me he know he been there he spit
bullets at my enemies he say you need to sail around
Alaska fuck it all and take a long bath

lah-ti-dah and lah-ti-dum
what's this socialized obsession with the bathtub

Maybe I just need to love myself myself
(anyhow I'm more familiar with the subject)
Maybe when my cousin tells me you remind me
of a woman past her prime maybe I need
to hustle my cousin into a hammerlock
position make her cry out uncle and
I'm sorry
Maybe when I feel this horrible

inclination to kiss folks I despise
because the party's like that
an occasion to be kissing people
you despise maybe I should tell them kindly
kiss my

Maybe when I wake up in the middle of the night
I should go downstairs
dump the refrigerator contents on the floor
and stand there in the middle of the spilled milk
and the wasted butter spread beneath my dirty feet
writing poems
writing poems
maybe I just need to love myself myself and
anyway
I'm working on it

Letter to My Friend the Poet Ntozake Shange

Just back from Minnesota/North Dakota
All my clothes into the laundry or
dry cleaners before I leave
again
for Oregon then California
and my agent calls to say your business
manager is sending me
a Christmas present
from you
by messenger
within the next two hours: will
I be home?

Jesus Christ (I think) getting nervous
about two hours housebound
under the circumstances

maybe
one of us
better slow down!

Legend of the Holy Night When the Police Finally Held Fire

For Gwendolen Hardwick

Small as a mustard seed
from the nile and nubile kingdom
where the young God secretly
created conga drums
from sapling trees and slender skin
then blew a breeze between
two new
tumescent
beech leaves
for the full lips
playing of the flute

Transplanted to the rigid terrors
firm like trigger to the gun
she runs
she runs for life
confronts the cops
she stops
she cocks her large eyes
lock into courageous
accusation

Mothafuckas: Shoot me
Can't you see
me?
Shoot me: Mothafuckas
What?

Even they can see the mustard seed
the trembling river and the totem
trees

They do not shoot/inside the kingdom
where you
come from

A Poem about Vieques, Puerto Rico

In Vieques
"The Ocean Is Closed on Mondays"

Frank the Bartender is full of information:
"So this guy, a guest, here at the hotel,
says to me, there aren't any face cloths.

So I said to him, 'Sit down.'

He sat down. Then I said to him, 'If
you were in Paradise
would you expect to find a face
cloth?'"

If you were in Paradise
would you expect to find the U.S. Navy
and the Marines bombing the hell
out of the land/mining the waters
and throwing indigenous birds indigenous
trees into extinction?

Where sugarcane and pineapples
and locust trees and mango and
where soursop/acacia palm
and lusciously
gardenias/amaropa/bougainvillea

grew so beautiful
in Paradise would
you expect to find the river gullies
dried down to the dustbone of the earth/
and all the grass turned into tinderstuff?

At the hotel
Frank the Bartender says: "Jamaica?
                              No. I never had the time!"

Helen and her husband Tom tell me:
"Isn't it interesting how
the Haitians are
compared to the other islander peoples
so incredibly artistic!
But do you know the story how that happened?
It was a Swede. A man named
– what was his name? *Olafson*
I'm sure: yes: Olafson.
He came, this Swede, to Haiti
and he saw the possibilities
for artistic expression among the natives
there. So he encouraged, he taught them
to do it
That's the story!"

In Vieques there are these words painted white
on the night road

Vieques Sí
Navy NO

Navy FUERA
(NAVY OUT)

y

Rádame Fidel Castro

At the Hotel
Frank the Bartender says:

> "So I'm with this girl down on the beach
> one night
> and I'm giving it to her
> I'm going for broke
> I'm working myself out
> pumping away
> up and down
> up and down
> and I say to her
> *Is it in?*
> And she says
> NO
> Put it in! I yell
> So I'm going on like crazy
> Is it in? I ask her again
> Yeah, she says
> Oh, for crissakes, I tell her:
> In that case, put it back
> put it back in the sand."

I am lying on the sand
trying to relax under the spectacular sky
the Hollywood clouds looking quite superlative
in blue
y
los hombres me llaman así:
Hey, honey
Hey, darling
ssswssssw ssswsssw!
(Entonces)
Hey, Black Gurrl!

Last night a horse followed me home
I kept feeling there was something behind me

And there was:
A horse

His ribs glittering silver
under the tight soft colored skin
of his body, and there
wasn't any drinkable water in sight
or sound
and I noticed the hills around us dry
to the point where even Ingmar Bergman
couldn't eke out sensuality
from that ground
from the figure of that animal
standing hungry on that ground
no sensuality

and you may get the idea that the United States'
military establishment is Humphrey Bogart
cracking up all over the screen or Henry
Fonda sorry or Burt Lancaster screwing
whatshername
in the klieglit surf

but last night
this horse followed me home
in Vieques
in Paradise

and he was starved out

and as a matter of fact
this movie: the horse and the children and the flowers and
the fish and the coconuts and
the sea itself in Vieques

Jesus Christ!
Put it back!

Put it back!
In the sand!

The point of this movie
is
a pretty rough fuck.

Inaugural Rose

Wanting to stomp down Eighth Avenue snow
or no snow where you might be so we
can takeover the evening by taxi
by kerosene lamp by literal cups of tea

that you love me

wanting to say, "Jesus, I'm glad. And I am not
calm: Not calm!" But I
am shy. And shy is short
on reach and wide on bowing
out. It's in:
against the flint and deep
irradiation of this torso listing
to the phosphorescence of French windows in
the bells/your hair/the forehead
of the morning of your face a clear
a calm decision of the light
to gather there

And you an obstinate an elegant
nail-bitten hand on quandaries of self-correction/
self-perfection as political as building your own
bed to tell the truth in
And your waist as narrow as the questions
you insist upon palpate/

expose immense not knowing any of the words
to say *okay* or *wrong*

And my wanting to say
wanting to show and tell *bells/*
okay because I'm shy
but I
will not lie

to you

En Passant

A white man tells me he told a white woman

You need to be fucked to death
You need a Black man

She said: What would my family say?

I say the same thing: What would my family
say
about that?

For Li'l Bit

Pointing to the middle of your forehead where a white
stripe (you say) marks the face of a demonic
destiny you (a Black woman without
any visible marking of the soft skin easily
exact easily covering the definite
image of the ambiguous skull) insist on knowing in advance
or after the fact of perhaps divinity perhaps a character
curse revealed by power or by pain astonishing
an afternoon/you emphasize the problem of

the stripe the white disfigurement above your
eyes: you finger the place of such thin
skin where the real scar shows itself through its
invisibility: I look but I can only see a swollen
vein of painful declaration leading to the clarity
the cradle songs crude histories invent

"My mother took this picture of me as a little girl.
You could see it. Right here it was: A white
stripe. And I held the picture in
my hands. I held the picture of me
in my hands. But now it's lost.
I don't know what happened.
To the photograph. But look. You can
still see the stripe: The mark."

You point to the middle of your forehead where a white
stripe (you say) marks the face of a stranger a problematic
destiny and I watch the trembling of your index finger

my own heart shaken as I watch you (only one
Black woman kneeling on the floor) attempt to trace
to feel (in small) the meaning of the forced
the barbarous amalgamation that enchains
you with such pain: my sister blamed by names
and blamed by body into far configurations love
cannot entirely control:

Stand up to sweat away the wound
Stand up to dance away the snow
Or
let me kneel
beside you

Niagara Falls

Dedicated to Leonard Bernstein

And in the first place the flowing of the river
went about its business like a hulking
shallows curling ankle deep to spume

and in the second place the flowing river
fell
and falling fell stupendous
down
a breakneck cliff invisible behind
the cataclysmic streaming burst apart
at bottom
into spray that birds
attempted to delay by calmly
playing in the serpentine formations
of the frothing aftermath

and then in my place stood a fool
surprised by power that wins only
peace as when the sliding clouds collide
into a new perfection

quietly

calling it quits

honey dripping rain through the spruce
tree blossoms sticky in the sun
after the storm
aftermath to hatred dissolute in bed
the storm
the teasing up of deepsea animals flung
to a brawling surface
skewered wild by wind and moonstone

torturing
the tides into a finicky
fulfillment

a mirage

now wanes the moon the ocean
slides away
my love collects
itself

apart from you

Poem toward the Bottom Line

Then this is the truth: That we began here
where no road existed even
as a dream: where staggered scream and grief inside
the howling air where hunched against
the feeling and the sounds of beast we moved
the left and then the right leg: stilted terminals
against infinity against amorphous omnivores
against the frozen vertigo of all
position: there we moved against
the hungering for heat for ease we moved
as now we move against each
other unpredictable around the corner
of this sweet occasion. Or as now the earth
assumes the skeletal that just the snow that just
the body of your trusting me can capture

tenderly enough.

Memoranda toward the Spring of Seventy-nine

The Shah of Iran was overthrown
by only several million mostly un-
armed/inside agitators.

∞

The Daily News reports that one American
among the first to be evacuated, Patsy
Farness of Seattle, said she somehow en-
joyed the whole thing. Coming off the plane
with two Persian cats and a poodle, she said:
"It was a lovely experience. I didn't want
to leave."

∞

The instruction booklet for cooking with a
Chinese wok declares as follows: "With use
your wok will acquire the blackened look of
distinction."

∞

Martin Luther King, Jr., is still dead.
The sponsor for the memorial program on
his birthday is The National Boat Show
at the Coliseum running January 13th through
the 21st and open to the public.

∞

If only I could stay awake until 3
then
on Channel Eleven
I could watch Part One of Adolf Hitler
but
then I'd be too tired to get up by 8
to watch Kaptain Kangaroo and Woody Woodpecker
on Channels 2 and 5.

The Shah of Iran was overthrown
by only several million mostly un-
armed/inside agitators.

There must be something else on television.

Martin Luther King, Jr., is still dead.

Dear Abby,

The idea is two dozen red roses
but
there isn't any form around the house.
Please advise.

A Short Note to My Very Critical and Well-Beloved Friends and Comrades

First they said I was too light
Then they said I was too dark
Then they said I was too different
Then they said I was too much the same
Then they said I was too young
Then they said I was too old
Then they said I was too interracial
Then they said I was too much a nationalist
Then they said I was too silly
Then they said I was too angry
Then they said I was too idealistic
Then they said I was too confusing altogether:
Make up your mind! They said. Are you militant

or sweet? Are you vegetarian or meat? Are you straight
or are you gay?

And I said, Hey! It's not about *my* mind.

Rape Is Not a Poem

1

One day she saw them coming into the garden
where the flowers live.
They
found the colors beautiful and
they discovered the sweet smell
that the flowers held
so
they stamped upon and tore apart
the garden
just because (they said)
those flowers?
They were asking for it.

2

I let him into the house to say hello.
"Hello," he said.
"Hello," I said.
"How're you?" he asked me.
"Not bad," I told him.
"You look great," he smiled.
"Thanks; I've been busy: I am busy."
"Well, I guess I'll be heading out, again,"
he said.
"Okay," I answered and, "Take care," I said.
"I'm gonna do just that," he said.
"No!" I said: "No! Please don't. Please
leave me alone. Now. No. Please!" I said.

"I'm leaving," he laughed: "I'm leaving you
alone; I'm going now!"
"No!" I cried: "No. Please don't do this to me!"
But he was not talking anymore and there was
nothing else that I could say
to make him listen
to me.

        3

And considering your contempt
And considering my hatred consequent to that
And considering the history
that leads us to this dismal place where (your arm
raised
and my eyes
lowered)
there is nothing left but the drippings
of power and
a consummate wreck of tenderness/I
want to know:
Is this what you call
Only Natural?

        4

My dog will never learn the names
of stars or thorns but
fully he
encounters whatever it is
shits on the ground
then finds a fallen leaf still holding
raindrops from the day and
there he stays
a big dog
(licking at the tiny water)
delicate as he is
elsewhere
fierce

You should let him teach you how
to come down

Memo:

When I hear some woman say she
has finally decided you can spend time with
other women, I wonder what she means: Her
mother? My mother?
I've always despised my woman friends. Even
if they introduced me to a man I found
attractive I have never let them become
what you could call my intimates. Why
should I? Men are the ones with the money and
the big way with waiters and the passkey
to excitement in strange places of real
danger and the power to make things happen
like babies or war and all these great ideas
about mass magazines for members of the weaker sex
who need permission
to eat potatoes or a doctor's opinion on orgasm after death
or the latest word on what the female
executive should do, after hours, wearing
what. They must be morons: women!
Don't you think?
I guess you could say
I'm stuck in my ways
as
That Cosmopolitan Girl.

What Is This in Reference To?
or We Must Get Together Sometime Soon!

Hello.
I'm sorry.
I can't talk to you.
I am unavailable.
I am out of the house.
I am out of town.
I am out of the country.
I am out of my mind.
I am indisposed.
The cat has my tongue.
Please do not hang up.
I know this is frustrating
              ridiculous
              solipsistic
              inconvenient
              mechanical
              and
              a pain in the ass
Please listen for the beep.
When you hear the beep
please leave a message as long as you like
or better still
please leave a brief message
or better yet
state your purpose in concise
readily decipherable terms and be sure
to leave your name your number
the time
the date
the place
and a list of the secret desires underlying this conventional
even hackneyed outreach represented
by

your call.
This is your dime.
Listen for the beep. Sucker.

Poem #2 for Inaugural Rose

Calling you from my kitchen to the one where you cook
for strangers and it hits me how we fall
into usefulness/change into steak or sausage or
(more frequently) fried chicken
like glut to the gluttonous/choosing a leg a poem
a voice and even a smile a breast/dark or light moments
of the mind: how
they throw out the rest or adjudicate the best of our
feeling/inedible because somersault singing in silence
will not flake to the fork at 425 or any kind of cue
will not do
and joy is not nice on ice: joy is not nice
But thinking about you over there at the stove
while I sit near the sink and we are not turkey/
I am not ham or bananas/nothing about you
reminds me of money or grist for the fist
and so on and so on but outside you know there is
rain to no purpose in the cockroach concrete of this
common predicament
and I find myself transfixed by the downpour un-
necessarily beating my blood up to the (something inside me
wants to say the *visual instinct of your face* or
sometimes I need to write Drums to Overcome the Terrors
of Iran but really
it's about the) grace the chimerical
rising of your own and secret eyes to surprise
and to surprise
and to surprise

me

Poem about My Rights

Even tonight and I need to take a walk and clear
my head about this poem about why I can't
go out without changing my clothes my shoes
my body posture my gender identity my age
my status as a woman alone in the evening/
alone on the streets/alone not being the point/
the point being that I can't do what I want
to do with my own body because I am the wrong
sex the wrong age the wrong skin and
suppose it was not here in the city but down on the beach/
or far into the woods and I wanted to go
there by myself thinking about God/or thinking
about children or thinking about the world/all of it
disclosed by the stars and the silence:
I could not go and I could not think and I could not
stay there
alone
as I need to be
alone because I can't do what I want to do with my own
body and
who in the hell set things up
like this
and in France they say if the guy penetrates
but does not ejaculate then he did not rape me
and if after stabbing him if after screams if
after begging the bastard and if even after smashing
a hammer to his head if even after that if he
and his buddies fuck me after that
then I consented and there was
no rape because finally you understand finally
they fucked me over because I was wrong I was
wrong again to be me being me where I was/wrong
to be who I am
which is exactly like South Africa
penetrating into Namibia penetrating into

Angola and does that mean I mean how do you know if
Pretoria ejaculates what will the evidence look like the
proof of the monster jackboot ejaculation on Blackland
and if
after Namibia and if after Angola and if after Zimbabwe
and if after all of my kinsmen and women resist even to
self-immolation of the villages and if after that
we lose nevertheless what will the big boys say will they
claim my consent:
Do You Follow Me: We are the wrong people of
the wrong skin on the wrong continent and what
in the hell is everybody being reasonable about
and according to the *Times* this week
back in 1966 the C.I.A. decided that they had this problem
and the problem was a man named Nkrumah so they
killed him and before that it was Patrice Lumumba
and before that it was my father on the campus
of my Ivy League school and my father afraid
to walk into the cafeteria because he said he
was wrong the wrong age the wrong skin the wrong
gender identity and he was paying my tuition and
before that
it was my father saying I was wrong saying that
I should have been a boy because he wanted one/a
boy and that I should have been lighter skinned and
that I should have had straighter hair and that
I should not be so boy crazy but instead I should
just be one/a boy and before that
it was my mother pleading plastic surgery for
my nose and braces for my teeth and telling me
to let the books loose to let them loose in other
words
I am very familiar with the problems of the C.I.A.
and the problems of South Africa and the problems
of Exxon Corporation and the problems of white
America in general and the problems of the teachers
and the preachers and the F.B.I. and the social
workers and my particular Mom and Dad/I am very

familiar with the problems because the problems
turn out to be
me
I am the history of rape
I am the history of the rejection of who I am
I am the history of the terrorized incarceration of
my self
I am the history of battery assault and limitless
armies against whatever I want to do with my mind
and my body and my soul and
whether it's about walking out at night
or whether it's about the love that I feel or
whether it's about the sanctity of my vagina or
the sanctity of my national boundaries
or the sanctity of my leaders or the sanctity
of each and every desire
that I know from my personal and idiosyncratic
and indisputably single and singular heart
I have been raped
be-
cause I have been wrong the wrong sex the wrong age
the wrong skin the wrong nose the wrong hair the
wrong need the wrong dream the wrong geographic
the wrong sartorial I
I have been the meaning of rape
I have been the problem everyone seeks to
eliminate by forced
penetration with or without the evidence of slime and/
but let this be unmistakable this poem
is not consent I do not consent
to my mother to my father to the teachers to
the F.B.I. to South Africa to Bedford-Stuy
to Park Avenue to American Airlines to the hardon
idlers on the corners to the sneaky creeps in
cars
I am not wrong: Wrong is not my name
My name is my own my own my own
and I can't tell you who the hell set things up like this

but I can tell you that from now on my resistance
my simple and daily and nightly self-determination
may very well cost you your life

Grand Army Plaza

For Ethelbert

Why would anybody build a monument to civil war?

The tall man and myself tonight
we will not sleep together
we may not
either one of us
sleep
in any case
the differential between friend and lover
is a problem
definitions curse
as *nowadays we're friends*
or
we were lovers once
while
overarching the fastidious the starlit
dust
that softens space between us
is the history that bleeds
through shirt and blouse
alike

the stain of skin on stone

But on this hard ground curved by memories
of union and disunion and of brothers dead
by the familiar hand
how do we face to face a man
a woman

interpenetrated
free
and reaching still toward the kiss that will
not suffocate?

We are not survivors of a civil war

We survive our love
because we go on

loving

Taking Care

Dedicated to the Poet Sekou Sundiata and to the
Students of SUNY at Stony Brook

I

Down on East Pratt Street in Baltimore
where the bar on the corner and the frozen foods
grocery store look alike: (They're both closed
on weekdays or open only to rats too lazy to keep up
with the newstuff in town)
even the couple the police separated when one
night either she was going to scream his head off or
he meant to knock her teeth down her throat
(because the regular the identical
conjugal argument of their evenings together
about a flirtation or a misinterpretation from eleven
years ago in a bar that was
unmistakably wide open when whatever went down that
they couldn't seem to forget about
except at the certain risk of boredom worse
than violent horseplay enough to wake the neighbors from
related habits of monogamous monotony) even that separated
couple stays married
where

two guys measure each other
to a grim finesse: one wants to continue
slashing the skin from the young tree the city
planted outside the small
brick house of the other and the guy with the knife
and the anger and the tree and the guy
with the expectation of a bigger and a bigger and
a bigger tree outside his narrow
brick house apparently feel mixed about whether
the disagreement of the moment merits attempted
or accomplished homicide
in Baltimore the point about the stone steps
the white stonestairs that women wash
as frequently as underwear
the point is what else
should you try
to take care of
East Pratt Street is not Whopping Hollow Road
and whopping hollow is not Telegraph Avenue
not telepathy
among the birds
and Baltimore not Bali Hai
although they sell a lot of that
in bottles
the city squats as sized down as regulated
as predictable as elementary
school classroom
buildings mostly
sacrilegious/sacramental
Baltimore   Baltimore

        2

The boss man tell you: "For the little woman
                       nothing is too much:

                       Promise her anything
                       but give her
                       Rhodesia"

3

I see people leaving Stony Brook
bound for Portland Oregon
Humboldt's current
God's will
ridiculous redwood memories
free coastline/any exponential
wilderness to yell out
loud I love where rising
tides flood land to action
uninhibited
harmonious
and singular

4

Even if the trail turns back to Baltimore
I figure we (become familiar
with mashed fingers
flatfeet and the deadpan and
become acquainted with the dervish possibilities
of freak and roll and glide inside
no space)

I figure we (amazing transmutations/heavyweight
deposits of the soul)
can body forth this ship together
keep it in the water
balancing
or take it out
as far as we can go
drydock

but deep

A Right-to-Lifer in Grand Forks, North Dakota

For Sandy Donaldson

We stayed.
Through finger drifts and drifts to bury trees.
Men frozen on the road home from town.
Babies dead because the doctor could not see
the house for the snow.
Women dead from death.
Children trained to trust the first door the nearest
hand.
River flood.
Mud.
Wind down from Canada.
Blizzards from hell.
Winter long as life.
We stayed.
After the Buffalo.
After the Indians.
After the westward hustling types.
After the sunrise.
We stayed.
On land big and empty as the entire sky.
We stayed.
Sugar beets.
Barley.
Sunflowers.
Wheat.
Potatoes.
Sure:
We stayed.
Right to life?
Hell, yeah!
What you suppose this trouble's been
all about?

From America: A Poem in Process

Dedicated to Christopher David Meyer

ST. PAUL, MINNESOTA

Ice
Between me and the earth itself it's ice
between me and the single runners single
houses single cars slid wide on ice
it's ice
between me and the breath I need to melt
the frozen mouth of something soft
something mud
something conversational perhaps
it's ice

I walk across the roots of trees
enormous elm tree shelters from the faraway
firing stars
elm trees scribbling a confusion of dark branches
that must mystify the simple
sky stretched into cloudy scar
tissues torn by snow and sleet interruptions
of a wan and waning
moan

I hear no whispering no shout no scream

I walk particular to keep upright the whole head cold
stung tight; It's pick and toe to cross the ice
the massive avenues a fascist scale a
monumental holding action under gossamer
and glossy hoar frost assault

sweet home
sweet home
oh lord: I wonder
if I'm ever gone get
home

Carrying paperbag provisions from a supermarket
and the wolves leap closer howling
from the corners of a formal place
where little moves besides the moon
I am too small
to change anything at all
I am too small
to change anything at all
where little moves besides the moon

GRAND FORKS, NORTH DAKOTA

Around March and the crows
come back
flying low over the bodies when
the drifts melt down
flying low
looking for the eyes
where eight miles straight ahead
or seven miles behind
it's just the same in January
side to side
the same.
It's white.
It's flat.
(If you stood on top a beer can you could probably see
Mexico.)

One year a country wife went crazy from the winter
all that white around her up above
and underfoot the white was everywhere
too much: She hid away inside her mud
home on the prairie
and her husband just to please
her one day painted up the mud walls white
That lady killed herself

And in the beginning
was the buffalo

(How long does an epiphany take?)

The Red River and The Red Lake River
become The Red River North flowing North
The land becomes the reason why the world
is flat but infinite
Ice becomes the snow becomes the snirt (the topsoil blown
berserk but softly blown)
Sky becomes much more than left or right eyes can pretend
to comprehend even
incorrectly
Cars become the trunk filled with emergency supplies of candles
granola bars and plastic garbage bags against the oneway wind
Time becomes two minutes to pneumonia two minutes to death
of flesh in 45 degrees below
The face becomes remote from comedy and open to whatever heats
the heart
The mind becomes a cantilever: fair is
fair: "There's peace and quiet in
Grand Forks," he told me: "There's the
Air Force and the missile bases too: Fair
is fair," he
shrugs.

LEXINGTON, KENTUCKY

I wish I was a horse
had me a groom
a stable boy a jockey
and a master starve himself
to buy me hay
I wish I was a horse
had me plantations full of grass
for grazing and a swimming pool
and one helluva pretty city

upside down to watch me race
some other horse
every now and then

I wish I was a horse
couldn't read about nothing
couldn't read about some local boy
the daily papers
said they asked him what kind of school he'd
like
the boy said he'd "rather just
be hit by a truck" what
kind of a fool boy is that
in Lexington Kentucky
there's a railroad crossing
holds down traffic to a lengthy idle
while
the coal cars trundle through
The Burlington Northern
coal cars weighing 200,000 pounds each
coal car carrying its weight again 200,000 pounds
of coal: I reckon takes good track to carry that
a heavy rail

I hear they throw on up to three of them high-
powered engines each one 450,000 pounds at ¾ of a million
dollars each to pull 100 coal cars taking the goodies
out of Eastern Kentucky
where the only respite for the two-legged
variety of inhabitant is serious or fatal
injury
where
in relationship to The Red River North and The Red
Lake River flowing North
am I
too small
to change anything at all?

Black children traveling north from Tuscaloosa
Alabama into Lexington sing *Sweet*
Home
Sweet Home
O Lord
I wonder if I'm ever
gone get home
where
in relationship to The Burlington Northern Railroad
is
that song?

My own child tells me: "You
walk past
any railroad siding
and you hear the engines: just purring away"

Living Room

dedicated to the children of Atlanta and to the
children of Lebanon

dreams
arms
doors
air

ash

dreams
arms
doors
air

From Sea to Shining Sea

I

Natural order is being restored
Natural order means you take a pomegranate
that encapsulated plastic looking orb complete
with its little top/a childproof cap that you can
neither twist nor turn
and you keep the pomegranate stacked inside a wobbly
pyramid composed by 103 additional pomegranates
next to a sign saying 89 cents
each

Natural order is being restored
Natural order does not mean a pomegranate
split open to the seeds sucked by the tongue and lips
while teeth release the succulent sounds
of its voluptuous disintegration

The natural order is not about a good time
This is not a good time to be against
the natural order

(voices from the background)

*"Those Black bitches tore it up! Yakkety
yakkety complain complaints couldn't see
no further than they got to have this
they got to have that they got to have
my job, Jack: my job!"*

*"To me it was Black men laid us wide open for the cut.
Busy telling us to go home. Sit tight.
Be sweet. So busy hanging tail and chasing
tail they didn't have no time to take a good
look at the real deal."*

"Those macho bastards! They would rather blow
the whole thing up than give a little: It was
vote for spite: vote white for spite!"

"Fucken feminists turned themselves into bulldagger
dykes and scared the shit out of decent
smalltown people. That's what happened."

"Now I don't even like niggers but there they were
chewing into the middle of my paycheck
and not me but a lot of other white people
just got sick of it, sick of carrying
the niggers"

"Old men run the government: You think that's
their problem?
Everyone of them is old and my parents and the old
people get out big numbers of them, voting for the dead"

"He's eighteen just like all the rest.
Only thing he wants is a girl and a stereo
and hanging out hanging out. What
does he care about the country? What
did he care?"

Pomegranates 89¢ each

   2

Frozen cans of orange juice.
Pre-washed spinach.
Onions by the bag.
Fresh pineapple with a printed
message from the import company.
Cherry tomatoes by the box.
Scallions rubberbanded by the bunch.
Frozen cans of orange juice.
Napkins available.
No credit please.

3

This is not such a hot
time for you or for me.

4

Natural order is being restored.
Designer jeans will be replaced by the designer
of the jeans.
Music will be replaced by reproduction
of the music.
Food will be replaced by information.
Above all the flag is being replaced by the flag.

5

This was not a good time to be gay

Shortly before midnight a Wednesday
massacre felled eight homosexual Americans
and killed two: One man was on his way
to a delicatessen and the other
on his way to a drink. Using an Israeli
submachine gun the killer fired into the crowd
later telling police about the serpent in the garden
of his bloody heart, and so forth.

This was not a good time to be Black

Yesterday the Senate passed an anti-busing
rider and this morning the next head
of the Senate Judiciary said he would work
to repeal the Voter Registration
Act and this afternoon the Greensboro
jury fully acquitted members of the Klan
and the American Nazi party in the murder
of 5 citizens and in Youngstown Ohio and in
Chattanooga

Tennessee and in Brooklyn and in Miami
and in Salt Lake City and in Portland Oregon
and in Detroit Michigan
and in Los Angeles and in Buffalo
Black American women and men
were murdered and the hearts
of two of the victims were carved
from the bodies of the victims, etcetera.

This was not a good time to be old

Streamliner plans for the Federal Budget
include elimination of Social Security
as it exists; and similarly Medicare and Medicaid
face severe reevaluation, among other things.

This was not a good time to be young

Streamliner plans also include elimination
of the Office of Education and the military
draft becomes a drastic concern as the national
leadership boasts that this country will no longer
be bullied and blackmailed by wars for liberation
or wars
for independence elsewhere on the planet, and the like.

This was not a good time to be a pomegranate ripening on a tree

This was not a good time to be a child

Suicide rates among the young reached
alltime highs as the incidence of child
abuse and sexual abuse
rose dramatically across the nation.
In Atlanta Georgia at least twenty-eight Black
children have been murdered, with
several more missing and all of them feared dead, or
something of the sort.

This was not a good time to be without a job

Unemployment Compensation and the minimum
wage have been identified as programs
that plague the poor and the young
who really require different incentives
towards initiative/pluck and so forth.

This was not a good time to have a job

Promising to preserve traditional
values of freedom, the new administration
intends to remove safety regulations
that interfere
with productivity potential, etcetera.

This was not a good time to be a woman

Pursuing the theme of traditional values of freedom
the new leadership has pledged its
opposition to the Equal Rights Amendment
that would in the words of the President-elect
only throw the weaker sex into a vulnerable
position among mischievous men, and the like.

This was not a good time to live in Queens

Trucks carrying explosive nuclear wastes will
exit from the Long Island Expressway and then
travel through the residential streets of Queens
en route to the 59th Street Bridge, and so on.

This was not a good time to live in Arkansas

Occasional explosions caused by mystery
nuclear missiles have been cited
as cause for local alarm, among
other things.

This was not a good time to live in Grand Forks North Dakota

Given the presence of a United States nuclear
missile base in Grand Forks North Dakota
the non-military residents of the area feel
that they are living only a day by day distance
from certain
annihilation, etcetera.

This was not a good time to be married

The Pope has issued directives concerning
lust that make for difficult interaction
between otherwise interested parties

This was not a good time not to be married.
This was not a good time to buy a house
at 18% interest.
This was not a good time to rent housing
on a completely decontrolled
rental market.
This was not a good time to be a Jew
when the national Klan agenda targets
Jews as well as Blacks among its
enemies of the purity of the people
This was not a good time to be a tree
This was not a good time to be a river
This was not a good time to be found with a gun
This was not a good time to be found without one
This was not a good time to be gay
This was not a good time to be Black
This was not a good time to be a pomegranate
or an orange
This was not a good time to be against
the natural order

                          – Wait a minute –

6

Sucked by the tongue and the lips
while the teeth release the succulence
of all voluptuous disintegration
I am turning under the trees
I am trailing blood into the rivers
I am walking loud along the streets
I am digging my nails and my heels into the land
I am opening my mouth
I am just about to touch the pomegranates
piled up precarious

7

This is a good time
This is the best time
This is the only time to come together

Fractious
Kicking
Spilling
Burly
Whirling
Raucous
Messy

Free

Exploding like the seeds of a natural disorder.

"in the february blizzard of 1983"

in the february blizzard of 1983
this boy asking me do I know why
this is Black history month I
go sure I know
it's because of the snow

Des Moines Iowa Rap

So his wife and his daughters could qualify
Lester Williams told the people he was gonna try suicide:
suicide.
He promised the papers he would definitely try
so his wife and his babies could qualify for welfare
in the new year.
Welfare.
In the new year.

I wanna job so bad I can taste it I won't waste it
Wanna job so bad

36 years old and home from the Navy
Take my blood, he said, and my bones, he said
for the meat and the gravy/I'm a vet from the Navy!
Take my meat. Take my bones.
I'm a blood, he said.

Tried suicide. Tried suicide.

Lester Williams made the offer and the offer made news
Wasn't all that much to dispute and confuse
Wouldn't hide in no closet and under no bed
Said he'd straightaway shoot himself dead instead
Like a man
Like a natural man
Like a natural man wanna job so bad he
can taste it
he can taste it

Took the wife in his arms. Held the children in his heart.
Took the gun from his belt. Held the gun to his head.
Like a man.
Like a natural man.
Like a natural man wanna job so bad gotta waste it.
Gotta waste it.

Tried Suicide.
Tried Suicide.

A poem for Jonathan

Land cloven by the water
fall and rush the pushed
down slabs of wetbelly
slate rocks crashing up

This place so steep the trees
brake deep against the edges
of a lifelong avalanche held
more than momentarily by maple
or by cedar roots against this excitable
mountain slide
into lagoon and proliferating
tiny flowers wild
as Jonathan stands gentle
as the stars that follow tall
above it all
saying, "Yes:
This is a wilderness."

Poem for Nicaragua

So little I could hold the edges
of your earth inside my arms

Your coffee skin the cotton stuff
the rain makes small

Your boundaries of sea and ocean slow
or slow escape possession

Even a pig would move towards you
dignified from mud

Your inside walls a pastel stucco
for indelible graffiti:

movimiento del pueblo
unido

A handkerchief conceals the curling
of your outlaw lips

A pistol calms the trembling
of your fingers

I imagine you among the mountains
eating early rice

I remember you among the birds
that do not swallow blood

First poem from Nicaragua Libre: Teotecacinte

Can you say Teotecacinte?
Can you say it,
Teotecacinte?

Into the dirt she fell
she blew up the shell
fell into the dirt the artillery
shell blew up the girl
crouching near to the well of the little house
with the cool roof thatched on the slant
the little girl of the little house fell
beside the well unfinished for water
when that mortar

shattered the dirt under her barefeet
and scattered pieces of her four
year old anatomy
into the yard dust and up
among the lower branches of a short tree

Can you say it?

That is two and a half inches of her scalp there
with the soft hairs stiffening
in the grass

Teotecacinte
Can you say it,
Teotecacinte?

Can you say it?

Second poem from Nicaragua Libre: war zone

On the night road from El Rama the cows
congregate fully in the middle and you
wait
looking at the cowhide colors bleached
by the high stars above their bodies
big with ribs

At some point you just have to trust
somebody else the soldier
wearing a white shirt the poet
wearing glasses the woman
wearing red shoes
into combat

At dawn the student gave me a caramel
candy and pigs and dogs ran into the streets

as the sky began the gradual
wide burn and towards the top
of a new mountain I saw
the teen-age shadows of two sentries
armed with automatics
checking the horizon
for slow stars

Third poem from Nicaragua Libre: photograph of Managua

The man is not cute.
The man is not ugly.
The man is teaching himself
to read.
He sits in a kitchen chair
under a banana tree.
He holds the newspaper.
He tracks each word with a finger
and opens his mouth to the sound.
Next to the chair the old V-Z rifle
leans at the ready.
His wife chases a baby pig with a homemade
broom and then she chases her daughter running
behind the baby pig.
His neighbor washes up with water from the barrel
after work.
The dirt floor of his house has been swept.
The dirt around the chair where he sits
has been swept.
He has swept the dirt twice.
The dirt is clean.
The dirt is his dirt.
The man is not cute.
The man is not ugly.
The man is teaching himself
to read.

Fourth poem from Nicaragua Libre: report from the frontier

gone gone gone ghost
gone
both the house of the hard dirt floor and the church
next door
torn apart more raggedy than skeletons
when the bombs hit
leaving a patch of her hair on a piece of her scalp
like bird's nest
in the dark yard still lit by flowers

I found
the family trench empty
the pails of rainwater standing full
a soldier whistling while thunder invaded
the afternoon
shards
shreds
one electric bulb split by bullets
dead hanging plants
two Sandinistas riding donkeys
a child sucking a mango
many dogs lost
five seconds left above the speechless
tobacco fields
like a wooden bridge you wouldn't
trust
with the weight of a cat

Safe

The Río Escondido at night
in between
jungle growing down to the muddy

edges of deep water possibilities
      helicopter attacks
      alligator assault
      contra confrontations
      blood sliding into the silent scenery
where I sat cold and wet
but surrounded by five
compañeros
in a dugout canoe

Directions for Carrying Explosive Nuclear Wastes through Metropolitan New York

Enter the Long Island Expressway at Brookhaven.
Proceed West. Exit at Hoyt Street in Astoria.
Turn left onto Astoria Boulevard. Trundle
under the elevated tracks there. Turn
right to ramp for the 59th Street Bridge.
Cross the Bridge. Follow local streets traveling
West until Amsterdam Avenue. At Amsterdam
turn right. Proceed North.

SPECIAL NOTE TO DRIVERS OF TRUCKS CARRYING
EXPLOSIVE NUCLEAR WASTES THROUGH
METROPOLITAN NEW YORK:

Check oil levels every five miles.
Change fan belt every thousand.
Check tire pressure every morning.
Change tires.
Buy radials.
Check shocks every fifty miles.
Change shocks every hundred.
Check rearview mirror and sideview mirror
incessantly.
Keep eyes on road.

Grant all other vehicles and each pedestrian
the right of way.
Do not pass.
Do not drive in the rain.
Do not drive in the snow.
Do not drive in the dark.
Signal.
Use headlights on high beam.
Go slow.
Do not brake suddenly or
otherwise.
Think about your mother
and look out for the crazies.

Greensboro: North Carolina:

Dedicated to Constance Evans

We
studying the rule
you can
not say death to the Klan
you can
not say death to the Klan
       death to the Klan
you can
not say death to the Klan

We
answering the riddle
why the white
man will not give the black
man
a glass of water
why the white
man will not give
the black man

a glass of water why
the white
man will not give the black
man death to the Klan
you can
not say a glass of water
to a thirsty black man
you cannot
say
a glass of water
you cannot
say
death to the Klan

death to the Klan

Problems of Translation: Problems of Language

Dedicated to Myriam Díaz-Diocaretz

I

I turn to my Rand McNally Atlas.
Europe appears right after the Map of the World.
All of Italy can be seen page 9.
Half of Chile page 29.
I take out my ruler.
In global perspective Italy
amounts to less than half an inch.
Chile measures more than an inch and a quarter
of an inch.
Approximately
Chile is as long as China
is wide:
Back to the Atlas:
Chunk of China page 17.
All of France page 5: As we say in New York:

Who do France and Italy know
at Rand McNally?

2

I see the four mountains in Chile higher
than any mountain of North America.
I see Ojos del Salado the highest.
I see Chile unequivocal as crystal thread.
I see the Atacama Desert dry in Chile more than the rest
of the world is dry.
I see Chile dissolving into water.
I do not see what keeps the blue land of Chile
out of blue water.
I do not see the hand of Pablo Neruda on the blue land.

3

As the plane flies flat to the trees
below Brazil
below Bolivia
below five thousand miles below
my Brooklyn windows
and beside the shifted Pacific waters
welled away from the Atlantic at Cape Horn
La Isla Negra that is not an island La
Isla Negra
that is not black
is stone and stone of Chile
feeding clouds to color
scale and undertake terrestrial forms
of everything unspeakable

4

In your country how
do you say copper
for my country?

5

Blood rising under the Andes and above
the Andes blood
spilling down the rock
corrupted by the amorality
of so much space
that leaves such little trace of blood
rising to the irritated skin the face
of the confession far
from home:

I confess I did not resist interrogation.
I confess that by the next day I was no longer sure
of my identity.
I confess I knew the hunger.
I confess I saw the guns.
I confess I was afraid.
I confess I did not die.

6

What you Americans call a boycott
of the junta?
Who will that feed?

7

Not just the message but the sound.

8

Early morning now and I remember
corriendo a la madrugada from a different
English poem,
I remember from the difficulties of the talk
an argument
athwart the wine the dinner and the dancing
meant to welcome you

you did not understand the commonplace expression
of my heart:

the truth is in the life
la verdad de la vida

Early morning:
do you say *la mañanita?*
But then we lose
the idea of the sky uncurling to the light:

Early morning and I do not think we lose:
the rose we left behind
broken to a glass of water on the table
at the restaurant stands
even sweeter
por la mañanita

Independence Day in the U.S.A.

I wanted to tell you about July 4th
in northamerica and the lights computerized
shrapnel in white
or red or fast-fuse blue
to celebrate the only revolution
that was legitimate
in human history

I wanted to tell you about the baby
screaming this afternoon where the park
and the music of thousands who eat
food and stay hungry or homicidal
on the subways or the windowsills of the city
came together loud
like the original cannon shots
from that only legitimate revolution
in human history

I wanted to tell you about my Spanish
how it starts like a word aggravating the beat
of my heart then rushes up to my head
where my eyes dream Caribbean
flowers and my mouth waters
around black beans
or coffee that lets me forget
the hours before morning

But I am living inside the outcome
of the only legitimate revolution
in human history
and the operator will not place my call to Cuba
the mailman will not carry my letters to Managua
the State Department will not okay my visa
for a short-wave conversation
and you do not speak English

and I can dig it

I am the fallen/I am the cliff

After the last building the black and green river
pearls into darkness
Beyond the bars on my window the wind bangs every
bridge into the tree tops
Even the city sky becomes unspeakable
as flesh
See the white horse missing from the poem

To Sing a Song of Palestine

For Shula Koenig (Israeli Peace Activist)

All the natural wonders that don't grow there
(Nor tree nor river nor a great plains lifting grain
nor grass nor rooted fruit and
vegetables) forever curse the land
with wildly dreaming schemes
of transformation
military magic
thick accomplishments of blood.

I sing of Israel and Palestine:
The world as neither yours nor mine:
How many different men will fit
themselves how fast
into that place?

A woman's body as the universal
shelter to the demon or the sweet as paradigm
of home that starts and ends with face
to face surrendering to the need
that each of us can feed or take
away
amazing as the space created
by the mothers of our time
– can we behold ourselves
   like that
the ribs the breathing muscles and the fat
of everything desire requires
for its rational abatement?

I write beside the rainy sky
tonight an unexpected an American
cease-fire to the burning day
that worked like war across my
empty throat before I thought to try this way
to say I think we can: I think we can.

Poem on the Road; for Alice Walker

1. ON THE ROAD

Once in a while
it's like calling home long distance but nobody
lives there anymore

2. NEW HAMPSHIRE

White mountains or trout
streams or rocks sharp as a fighter plane
simply afloat
above the superhighways

Almost by herself
(trying to "live free or die")
a white girl twitching white tears
unpolluted under the roar
of Pease Air Force Base immortalized
by flyboys taking out Hiroshima
but now
real interested just to take her out
anywhere at all

This is not racist

3. BROOKLYN

Running imagery through the arteries of her
pictures posted up against apartheid
what does a young Black poet do?
What does a young
Black woman poet
do
after dark?

Six dollars in her backpack
carrying the streets like a solitary

sentinel possessed by visions
of new arms new
partners

what does she do?

What does the Black man
in his early thirties
in a bomber jacket
what does the Black man do about the poet
when he sees her?

After he took the six
dollars
After he punched her
down
After he pushed for pussy
After he punctured her lungs with his knife
After the Black man
in his early thirties
in a bomber jacket
After she stopped bleeding
After she stopped pleading
(*please don't hurt me*)

what was the imagery running
through the arteries of the heart
of that partner?

This is not racist

4. NEW BEDFORD

The lady wanted to have a drink
The lady wanted to have two drinks

Four men dragged the lady to the table
Two men blocked the door

All of them laughing
Four men
Two men
All of them laughing
A lot of the time the lady could not
breathe
A lot of the time the lady wanted
to lose consciousness

Six men
One lady

All of them Portuguese

This is a promise I am making
it here
legs spread on the pool
table of New Bedford

I am not racist

I am raising my knife
to carve out the heart
of no shame

5. ON THE ROAD

This is the promise
I am making it here on the road
of my country

I am raising my knife
to carve out the heart
of no shame

The very next move is not mine

July 4, 1984: For Buck

April 7, 1978–June 16, 1984

You would shrink back/jump up
cock ears/shake head
tonight
at this bloody idea of a birthday
represented by smackajack explosions
of percussive lunacy and downright
(blowawayavillage) boom boom
ratatat-tat-zap

Otherwise any threat would make you stand
quivering perfect as a story
no amount of repetition could hope to ruin
perfect as the kangaroo boogie you concocted
with a towel in your jaws and your tail
tucked under and your paws
speeding around the ecstatic circle
of your refutation of the rain
outdoors

And mostly you would lunge electrical
and verge into the night
ears practically on flat alert
nostrils on the agitated sniff
(for falling rawhide meteors) and laugh
at compliments galore and then
teach me to love you
by hand
teach me to love you
by heart

as I do now

Poem for Dana

1

Back in Minneapolis I became convinced
that swimming in the hotel pool with none of the water
over my head and all of the water warm as tea
was maximal security

Back and forth across the lovely public
tub I used my backstroke while I
counted up the blizzard clouds
above the low glass roof
above my nose

Any other city you'd see vast erratic downtown
tracts of wasting space specific as the blowing
garbage or the car parts turned to rust
on stony rubble swelling as now
the shadows slight
those planted trees as delicate as the surrounding
snow
stuck to steel construction cranes that red
and yellow sway
intentional across the frozen ground

2

Into Iowa and I
flying arms folded cold against the view
of trees extremely occasional below on flatland
unresponsive to the everywhere bending sky
I
did not expect you suddenly large suddenly
close beside me in a car or elevator
miles of heat away from outdoor details
like the stalks of pig corn sturdy on the light
blue dirt or rosy hogs loose in late

morning or the rooted quadrupeds the black
clump cattle paralyzed on rounded sightlines icy
as the earth itself

   3

who can move from space to flesh
who can knit her own wool cap to wear
who can make the coffee makes the rest of it seem
easier

   4

adding the strawberries
adding the cream

   5

Willow
Salix (species unknown)
who names the tree poor at the end of the Union
Footbridge bounced under my body absorbing the night
like birch
bark harboring stars in the heavyweight
snowstorm circling
the lips the eyelashes
river making the ice move
under me
the Iowa river making ice move

33,000 feet high and over one wing of the Ozark
DC-9 Fan
Jet I
look for the place to build you a house
only of snow

A Song for Soweto

At the throat of Soweto
a devil language falls
slashing
claw syllables to shred and leave
raw
the tongue of the young
girl
learning to sing
her own name

Where she would say
     water
They would teach her to cry
      blood
Where she would save
     grass
They would teach her to crave
       crawling into the grave
Where she would praise
     father
They would teach her to pray
       somebody please do not take
      him away
Where she would kiss with her mouth
       my homeland
They would teach her to swallow
      this dust

But words live in the spirit of her face and that
sound will no longer yield to imperial erase

Where they would draw
     blood
She will drink
    water

Where they would deepen
                        the grave
She will conjure up
                        grass
Where they would take
                        father and family away
She will stand
                        under the sun/she will stay
Where they would teach her to swallow
                        this dust
She will kiss with her mouth
                        my homeland
and stay
with the song of Soweto

stay
with the song of Soweto

Atlantic Coast Reggae

see what the man have done
                        done
see how the red blood run
                        run

From Tokyo Rose to the Eskimos
the battleship travels
wherever he goes like Vanilla Attila
the Hun

see what the man have done
                        done

Stop lunch for the kids
then decide over brunch
how many old folks should die
by the gun

see what the man have done
                      done

If you get sick you better get better
real quick
or the illness will cost you
a ton

Hari Kari was worried about
whom he should marry
but then he married a nun

see what the man have done
                      done

Work like a jerk and your job
just becomes a statistical quirk
there's damned little work left
under the sun

see how the red blood run
                      run

Grandita Banana gets stuck
in Havana for reasons of
Bradstreet and Dun

see what the man have done
                      done

Murder and pillage through city
and village
raping a tree is not easy
but fun

see what the man have done
                      done

see how the red blood run

　　　　　　　　run

Poem for Etel Adnan Who Writes:

"So we shall say: Don't fool
yourselves.
Jesus is not coming.
We are alone"
—1983

1

I am alone
I am not coming not coming to Jesus not coming to
the telephone
not coming to the door not coming to my own true
love I am alone
I am not coming

2

Jesus forgot
Jesus came and then he left but then he forgot
He forgot why he came
He forgot to come back
And this is written in the water by the dolphins
flying like rice-paper submarines
Jesus forgot

3

Nobody died to save the world

4

Come

5

Let us break heads together

Richard Wright Was Wrong

Richard Wright was wrong
because Bigger Thomas was a whiteman
yes he was
the one does it to you
did it to Fatima Ghazzawi
17 year old Palestinian whose leg
the real Bigger Thomas blew into infinity
he's the one teaching his children to kill
for the Klan
he's the one shot off the arm of 15 year old
Brenda Rocha in the land of the Sandinistas
FORGET THE METAPHORS
                        Black man in white girl's bedroom
                        Black man at furnace
                        Black man sawing off the head
the real Bigger Thomas don't fool around
with literature
FORGET THE METAPHOR
the real Bigger Thomas
don't sleep
don't hide
don't sweat
the real Bigger Thomas
allocates this
appropriates that
incinerates
assassinates
he hates he hates he hates
he intervenes
never means what he says
he means what he does

he does it to you
he's a whiteman
he's the Grand Duke Dragon of the Ku Klux Klan
he rules Chicago
he over-rules New York
he turns the Atlantic into a floating latrine
he looks at the stars and dreams about wars
he's mean
he's the trickytreating face in the pumpkin
the inventor of sin
the skull with the candles of hell
flaming inside
he's race purity race pride
he's son of Adolph Hitler in a Ferrari
roars into the tree that grew by mistake
in the way
he's the reason poor Richard Wright was wrong
all along
he's the real Bigger Thomas
the real Bigger Thomas
was a white man who does what he does
yes he was
yes he does it to you
yes he does

Easter Comes to the East Coast: 1981

Don' you worry about a thing
Mr. President and you too
Mr. Secretary of the State: Relax!
We not studying you guys:
NO NO NO NO NO!
This ain' real!
Ain' nobody standing around
We not side by side
This ain' no major league rally

We not holding hands again
We not some thousand varieties of one fist!
This ain' no coalition
This ain' no spirit no muscle no body to stop the bullets
We not serious
NO NO NO NO NO!
And I ain' never heard about El Salvador;
I ain' never seen the children sliced
and slaughtered at the Sumpul Riverside
And I ain' never heard about Atlanta;
I ain' never seen the children strangled in the woods
And I ain' never seen marines state troopers or the police
out here killing people
And I ain' never heard about no rage no tears
no developing
rebellion
I ain' never felt no love enough to fight what's hateful
to my love

NO NO NO NO NO!
This is just a fantasy.
We just kidding around.

You watch!

Song of the Law Abiding Citizen

so hot so hot so hot so what
so hot so what so hot so hot

They made a mistake
I got more than I usually take
I got food stamps food stamps I got
so many stamps in the mail
I thought maybe I should put them on sale
How lucky I am

I got food stamps: Hot damn!
I made up my mind
to be decent and kind
to let my upright character shine
I sent 10,000 food stamps
back to the President (and his beautiful wife)
and I can't pay the rent
but I sent 10,000 food stamps
back to the President (and his beautiful wife)
how lucky I am
hot damn
They made a mistake
for Chrissake
And I gave it away to the President
I thought that was legal I thought that was kind
and I can't pay the rent
but I sent 10,000 food stamps
back back back to the President

so hot so hot so hot so what
so hot so what so hot so hot

Trucks cruisin' down the avenue
carrying nuclear garbage right next to you
and it's legal
it's radioaction ridin' like a regal
load of jewels
past the bars the cruel
school house and the church and if
the trucks wipeout or crash
or even lurch too hard around a corner
we will just be goners
and it's legal
it's radioaction ridin' regal
through the skittery city street
and don't be jittery
because it's legal
radioaction ridin' the road

Avenue A Avenue B Avenue C Avenue D
Avenue of the Americas

so hot so hot so hot so what
so hot so what so hot so hot
so hot so hot so hot so what

October 23, 1983

for a.b.t.

The way she played the piano
     the one listening was the one taken
     the one taken was the one
         into the water/
         watching the foam
         find the beautiful boulders
         dark
         easily liquid
         and true as the stone
         of that meeting/molecular
         elements of lust
         distilled by the developing
         sound
         sorrow
         sound
         fused by the need of the fingers
         to note down
         to touch upon
         to span
         to isolate
         to pound
         to syncopate
         to sound
         sorrow
         sound
         among the waters

gathering
corpuscular/exquisite

constellations tuning among waves
the soul itself
pitched atonal but below
the constellations tuning among waves
the soul itself

a muscular/exquisite

matter of tactful
       exact
       uproarious
heart
collecting the easily dark
liquid
look
of the beautiful boulders

in that gathering
  that water

"look at the blackbird fall"

look at the blackbird fall
down
into the lake
split by white speedboats full of white people
loading the atmosphere with gasoline
and noise
now
you can't drink the water
of the lake
you must drive somewhere else to buy
bottles of water to drink

beside the lake that is ten miles
long
(what I need is a change of season
a snowmobile
or a springtime tomb
that takes me from birth to 55
in six seconds)
what I need is to adjust
to the tree
without the blackbird that fell
down
into the lake

March Song

Snow knuckles melted to pearls
of black water
Face like a landslide of stars
in the dark

Icicles plunging to waken the grave
Tree berries purple and bitten
by birds

Curves of horizon squeeze
on the sky
Telephone wires glide
down the moon

Outlines of space later
pieces of land
with names like Beirut
where the game is to tear
up the whole Hemisphere
into pieces of children
and patches of sand

Asleep on a pillow the two
of us whisper we know
about apples and hot bread
and honey

Hunting for safety
and eager for peace
We follow the leaders who chew up
the land
with names like Beirut
where the game is to tear
up the whole Hemisphere .
into pieces of children
and patches of sand

I'm standing in place
I'm holding your hand
and pieces of children
on patches of sand

Menu

We got crispy chicken
we got frisky chicken
we got digital chicken
we got Chicken Evergreen

We got chicken salad
we got chicken with rice
we got radar chicken
we got chicken in the first degree

but we ain't got no fried chicken.

We got Chicken Red Light
we got drive-in chicken

we got felony chicken
we got chicken gravy

but we ain't got no fried chicken.

We got half a chicken
we got 2 chickens
we got Chicken Tylenol
we got chicken on ice

but we ain't got no fried chicken.

We got King Chicken
we got chicken à la mode
we got no-lead chicken

We got chainsaw chicken
we got chicken in a chair
we got borderline chicken
we got Chicken for the Young at Heart

We got aerosol chicken
we got Chicken Guitar

but we ain't got no fried chicken.

We got Coast Guard Chicken
we got sixpack chicken
we got Chicken Las Vegas
we got chicken to burn

but we ain't got no fried chicken.

We got 10-speed chicken
we got atomic chicken
we got chicken on tape

We got day-care chicken
we got Chicken Mascara
we got second-hand chicken

but we ain't got no fried chicken.

We got dead chicken
we got chicken on the hoof
we got open admissions chicken
we got Chicken Motel

We got astronaut chicken
we got chicken to go

We got gospel chicken
we got four-wheel drive chicken
we got chain gang chicken
we got chicken transfusions

but we ain't got no fried chicken.

We got wrong turn chicken
we got rough draft chicken
we got chicken sodas
we got Chicken Deluxe

but we ain't
got
no

fried chicken.

Addenda to the Papal Bull

Dedicated to the Poet Nicanor Parra

The Pope thinks.
The Pope thinks all of the time.
The Pope thinks it is the duty of His
Holiness to think out loud.
The Pope thinks out loud.
The Pope thinks it is the duty of His
Holiness to publish His thoughts.
The Pope publishes His thoughts.
The Pope is thinking about peace.
He is in favor of peace.
The Pope is thinking about meat.
He is in favor of fish.
The Pope is thinking about women.
He thinks women can be acceptable.
These are the thoughts of the Pope on sex:
The Pope thinks that no sex is better than good.
The Pope thinks that good sex is better than sin.
The Pope thinks that sin happens
when sex happens when two people
want to have sex with each other.
The Pope thinks that is an example of lust.
The Pope thinks that lust is for the birds.
Marriage without sex without lust is permissible.
Remarriage is permissible only
without lackluster and lusty sex, both.
The Pope thinks that these thoughts
on peace and women and meat and sex
deserve our most obedient attention.
The Pope is thinking and thinking and thinking.
Who can deny the usefulness of His concern?

Poem for the Poet Sara Miles

Not quite enough starlight lets me write
this poem tonight without clicking the lamp
on the way the 42nd street billboard streams
electrode rumors right around the triangular
building based on that island where the U.S.
Armed Forces Recruiting Station
closed because it's raining
grants no shelter to the few pedestrians
while the big
bus boats by and taxis cruise through and cars
halt because the poet stands there
mid-river
moving words times square times words
because the cold rain
holds her thin to an ineradicable pinpoint
between traffic and inertia
searching out a Sunday flick they call The House
of All Evil while the guy who wears
the button with the one word SEX gawks
openmindedly to see the impact of minutiae
the music of such poetry that sways the racket
into sweet commotion
moving words times square times words
that pray this city
will not allow its living noise
to quiet now

for keeps

Poem for Guatemala

Dedicated to Rigoberta Menchú

No matter how loudly I call you the sound of your name
makes the day soft
Nothing about it sticks to my throat
Guatemala
syllables that lilt into twilight and lust
Guatemala
syllables to melt bullets

They call you Indian
They called me West Indian
You learned to speak Spanish when I did
We were thirteen
I wore shoes
I ate rice and peas
The beans and the rice in your pot
brought the soldiers
to hack off your arms

"Walk like that into the kitchen!
Walk like that into the clearing!
Girl with no arms!"

I had been playing the piano

Because of the beans and the rice in your pot
the soldiers arrived with an axe
to claim you guerrilla
girl with no arms

An Indian is not supposed to own a pot of food
An Indian is too crude
An Indian covers herself with dirt so the cold
times will not hurt her

Cover yourself with no arms!

They buried my mother in New Jersey.
Black cars carried her there.
She wore flowers and a long dress.

Soldiers pushed into your mother
and tore out her tongue
and whipped her under a tree
and planted a fly in the bleeding
places so that worms
spread through the flesh
then the dogs
then the buzzards
then the soldiers laughing
at the family of the girl
with no arms
guerrilla girl
with no arms

You go with no arms
among the jungle treacheries
You go with no arms
into the mountains hunting
revenge

I watch you
walk like that
into the kitchen
walk like that
into the clearing
girl with no arms

I am learning new syllables
of revolution

Guatemala
Guatemala
Girl with no arms

On the Real World: Meditation #1

5 shirts
2 blouses
3 pairs of jeans and the iron's on hot
for cotton:
I press the steam trigger to begin
with the section underneath the collar
from the inside out.
Then the sleeves. Starting with the cuffs.
Now the collar wrong way before it's right.
I'm not doing so good.
Around where the sleeve joins the shoulder looks
funny.
My hand stops startled.
New like a baby there's a howling on the rise.
I switch the shirt so that the iron reaches
the front panel easily.
That howling like a long walk by the Red
Brigades for twenty years between improbable
Chinese ravines with watercolor trees
poked into a spot as graceful as clouds
missing deliberate from a revolutionary land-
scape printed in Japan
ebbs then returns a louder howling cold
as the long walk towards the watery
limits of the whole earth blasted by the air
become tumescent in a lonely place
inhabited by the deaf or the invisible
but querulously looming victims of such speed
in spoken pain the louder howling large
as the original canvas containing that landscape
printed in Japan almost overloaded as the howling loses

even its small voice while I
bite my lips and lower my head
hard into the ferocity of that sound
dwarfing me into someone almost immaterial
as now I smell fire
and look down all the way to the shirt
pocket
skyblue and slightly burned

"the snow"

the snow
nearly as soft
as the sleeping nipple
of your left breast

Who Would Be Free, Themselves Must Strike the Blow

– Frederick Douglass

The cow could not stand up. The deadly river
washed the feet of children. Where the cows
grazed the ground concealed invisible
charged particles that did not glow or make
a tiny sound.

It was pretty quiet.

The cow could not stand up. The deadly clouds
bemused the lovers lying on the deadly ground
to watch the widening nuclear light
commingle with the wind their bodies set
to motion.

It was pretty quiet.

The cow could not stand up.
The milk should not be sold.
The baby would not be born right.
The mother could not do anything about the baby
or the cow.

It was pretty quiet.

A Runaway Li'l Bit Poem

Sometimes DeLiza get so crazy she omit
the bebop from the concrete she intimidate
the music she excruciate the whiskey she
obliterate the blow she sneeze
hypothetical at sex

Sometimes DeLiza get so crazy she abstruse
about a bar-be-cue ribs wonder-white-bread
sandwich in the car with hot sauce
make the eyes roll right to where you are
fastidious among the fried-up chicken wings

Sometimes DeLiza get so crazy she exasperate
on do they hook it up they being Ingrid
Bergman and some paranoid schizophrenic Mister
Gregory Peck-peck: Do
they hook it up?

Sometimes DeLiza get so crazy she drive
right across the water flying champagne bottles
from the bridge she last drink to close the bars she
holler kissey lips she laugh she let
you walk yourself away:

Sometimes DeLiza get so crazy!

DeLiza Spend the Day in the City

DeLiza drive the car to fetch Alexis
running from she building past the pickets
make she gap tooth laugh why don't
they think up something new they picket now
for three months soon it be too cold
to care

Opposite the Thrift Shop
Alexis ask to stop at the Botanica
St. Jacques Majeur find oil to heal she
sister lying in the hospital from lymphoma
and much western drug agenda

DeLiza stop. Alexis running back
with oil and myrrh and frankincense and coal
to burn these odors free the myrrh like rocks
a baby break to pieces fit inside the palm
of long or short lifelines

DeLiza driving and Alexis
point out Nyabinghi's African emporium
of gems and cloth and Kwanza cards and clay:
DeLiza look.

Alexis opening the envelope to give DeLiza
faint gray copies of she article on refugees
from Haiti and some other thing on one white
male one
David Mayer
sixty-six
a second world war veteran
who want America to stop atomic arms
who want America to live without the nuclear death
who want it bad enough to say he'll blow
the Washington

D.C. Monument into the southside of the White House
where the First White Lady counting up she
$209,000 china plates and cups and bowls
but cops blow him away
blow him/he David Mayer
man of peace
away
Alexis saying, "Shit.
He could be Jesus. Died to save you,
didn't he?"
DeLiza nod she head.
God do not seem entirely to be dead.

DeLiza Questioning Perplexities:

If Dustin Hoffaman prove
a father be a better mother than a mother

If Dustin Hoffaman prove
a man be a better woman than a woman

When do she get to see
a Betterman than Hoffaman?

November

Given those leaves why should I complain
That is not Machu Picchu to my left
Under my feet the trees deposit lives at last
in color not dividing into class or coronation
of any kind

The slave lives in my mouth
White gates to the dark throat of my name
at fifty miles an hour I visualize a profile

leading to another language I am cowardly
to understand

A woman my age lying down at the top
of the outdoor stairs delivers her vote
her face to the stone of voice and makes
the awkward leadership swerve resolute around
her fallen body

In my room the boy stammering they
promised me a job they promised me they
do not hear the edge to the stutter
the gun under stultimultistultifying
failures of the scream

I prophesy the same unto the same
an imagery to overflow the frame
beyond the tombstone straight ahead
beyond the monologue of living normal
with the dead

Verse after Listening to Bartók Play Bartók a Second Time, or Different Ways of Tingling All Over

now

and then

unexpectedly
unexpectedly
unexpectedly

(praying)

then

and now

Poem towards a Final Solution

In a press conference this afternoon the Secretary
of Space Development confirmed earlier reports
of a comprehensive plan nearing completion
in his Office.

Scheduled to meet with the President later
this week, Mr. Samuel B. Fierce the Third
jokingly termed the forthcoming package of proposals
"A Doozy."

The following represents a news team summary
of his remarks:

His Office will issue findings of a joint survey
of all National Parks conducted in cooperation with
the Department of the Interior in an effort to delimit
unnecessary vegetation.

His Office will recommend installation of nuclear
reactors inside low-growth residential areas of American
cities in order to encourage voluntary citizen re-
location at estimated savings to the Federal Government
of more than 2 billion dollars, yearly.

At the same time, Mr. Fierce suggested that he will
recommend
quick phasing out of Federal programs for
land reclamation
described by the Secretary at one particularly
light-hearted

moment during the press conference as
"Neanderthal nostalgia
for the little flowers that grow."

In addition, the Secretary indicated he will call
for the computation of food stamps as income so that,
for example, a legitimate Welfare recipient in Mississippi
will have exactly $8 a month as disposable cash.

Finally, Mr. Fierce alluded to a companion proposal
that will raise the rent for subsidized housing by 20%.

These various initiatives can be trusted to contribute
significantly to the President's economic goals and to
the development of more space, coast to coast. They
will furthermore establish the Office of
Space Development
as an increasingly powerful factor in budget-conscious
policymaking.

An unidentified reporter then queried the Secretary as to
whether this plan could fairly be translated as take
down the trees, tear up the earth, evacuate the urban poor,
and let the people hang, generally speaking.

Mr. Fierce dismissed the question as a clear-cut attempt
at misleading and alarmist language deliberately obtuse
to the main objective of economic recovery for the nation.

Pending official release of his recommendations to
the President, the Secretary refused to comment on
the snow
falling on the stones of the cities everywhere.

1981: On Call

And even as you light
the cigarette or turn the page
blood flows from the throat of the scream

Every standing tree is quiet at night
and mute to the flood
but part of the dream

Silence will nothing redeem
into body or bud
for the actual fight

3 for Kimako

Kimako Baraka
1936–1984

She loved garlic
sometimes I thought she was altogether garlic
cloves small as they are thinskinned stones

She loved silk
sometimes I thought the sinews of her body
intimated silk at the atomic level of a hand

She loved poetry
sometimes I thought that she would take the words
and eat them carefully as filaments of saffron

She loved commotion
sometimes I thought a movement created Kimako
but sometimes (I thought) she created a movement

∽

ASSAILANT: ANTONIO MOORE

You were hungry and she
let you into her life

You grabbed her by the throat
you stabbed her in the throat
you stabbed her in the chest
you stabbed her in the back
you beat her eyes out
you beat her ears off
you smashed her skull
you busted her nose
you tore away her clothes
you tore apart her mouth

you said thank you
the only way you knew how

And I only wish for you
exactly what you deserve
for that
exactly what you deserve

∾

It should not be the death
        not that we should gather now
        remembering that laugh between her teeth
                that spine behind the curtain
                that Egypt prize of window eyes

        not that we should tremble now
        remembering what we forgot
the glory gone
the old shoes on the street
the hand out for the handout

not that we should rally now
remembering the glitter of the tricks she lit
the horns
the drums
the stage

It should be the dance
It should be the dance she danced
with death

A Reagan Era Poem in Memory of Scarlett O'Hara

who said, in *Gone With the Wind,*
something like this:

"As God is my witness, so help me God:
I'm going to live through this
And when it's over
If I have to lie, steal, cheat, or kill,
I'll never go hungry again."

The poem says:
"Amen!"

Apologies to All the People in Lebanon

Dedicated to the 60,000 Palestinian men,
women, and children who lived in Lebanon from
1948–1983.

I didn't know and nobody told me and what
could I do or say, anyway?

They said you shot the London Ambassador
and when that wasn't true
they said so

what
They said you shelled their northern villages
and when U.N. forces reported that was not true
because your side of the cease-fire was holding
since more than a year before
they said so
what
They said they wanted simply to carve
a 25 mile buffer zone and then
they ravaged your
water supplies your electricity your
hospitals your schools your highways and byways all
the way north to Beirut because they said this
was their quest for peace
They blew up your homes and demolished the grocery
stores and blocked the Red Cross and took away doctors
to jail and they cluster-bombed girls and boys
whose bodies
swelled purple and black into twice the original size
and tore the buttocks from a four month old baby
and then
they said this was brilliant
military accomplishment and this was done
they said in the name of self-defense they said
that is the noblest concept
of mankind isn't that obvious?
They said something about never again and then
they made close to one million human beings homeless
in less than three weeks and they killed or maimed
40,000 of your men and your women and your children

But I didn't know and nobody told me and what
could I do or say, anyway?

They said they were victims. They said you were
Arabs.
They called   your apartments and gardens   guerrilla
strongholds.

They called   the screaming devastation
that they created   the rubble.
Then they told you to leave, didn't they?

Didn't you read the leaflets that they dropped
from their hotshot fighter jets?
They told you to go.
One hundred and thirty-five thousand
Palestinians in Beirut and why
didn't you take the hint?
Go!
There was the Mediterranean: You
could walk into the water and stay
there.
What was the problem?

I didn't know and nobody told me and what
could I do or say, anyway?

Yes, I did know it was the money I earned as a poet that
paid
for the bombs and the planes and the tanks
that they used to massacre your family

But I am not an evil person
The people of my country aren't so bad

You can expect but so much
from those of us who have to pay taxes and watch
American TV

You see my point;

I'm sorry.
I really am sorry.

Tornado Watch

Thunder.
More thunder.
Lightning.
Thunder.
More thunder.
More thunder.
The rain reaches me through the window
nine feet away.
I read your letter again.
Lightning.
More thunder.
More. More. More thunder.
I turn out the lights.
The curtains swing to the left.
Rain becomes the coloring of the air.
Hailstones attack the roof of my room.
Like marbles.
More. More. More thunder.
I am afraid to close the window.
The blue spruce cracks.
And crashes among the marbles.
Its trunk slashed to the flesh
jaggedly.
I feel like a woman
who says to herself:

"That kid is leaning too far
out of the car.
My God.
The kid has fallen out.
On his head."

Then wonders where
should she make her report.

Another Poem about the Man

the man who brought you the garbage can
                    the graveyard
                    the grossout
                    the grimgram
                    the grubby grabbing
                    bloody blabbing nightly news
                    now brings you
                    Grenada

helicopters grating nutmeg trees
rifles shiny on the shellshocked sand
the beautiful laundry of the bombs falling into fresh air
artillery and tanks up against a halfnaked girl
and her boyfriend

another great success
brought to you
by trash delivering more trash to smash
and despoil the papaya
the breadfruit and bloodroot
shattered and bloodspattered
from freedom
rammed down the throat
of Grenada now Grenada she
no sing no more

Grenada now Grenada she
no sing no more she lose
she sky
to yankee invaders
Grenada now Grenada she
no sing no more

Story for Tuesday

Into the gnat infested twilight of the woods
we walked across pine needles stuck
in the soon to be moonlit mud
discussing the cities of the world
as far away as Rome

Hovering like the suspicion of a freshwater
pond in the forest or what water implies
to a wilderness grown by one tree at a time
was the music interrupted by the piano tuner
earlier that day

Almost home again we saw the piano tuner
in his pickup truck. With his wife and child
beside him he keyed the ignition.
The engine burst into flames.
Flames flew to his face.
He went to a telephone for help.
While waiting around he played
Chopin's Revolutionary Étude
on the well-tuned piano
rather well.

Outside
his wife and child
watching the truck burn.

War Verse

Something there is that sure must love a plane
No matter how many you kill with what kind of
bombs or how much blood you manage to spill
you never will hear the cries of pain

Something there is that sure must love a plane
The pilots are never crazy or mean
and bombing a hospital's quick and it's clean
and how could you call such precision insane?

Something there is that sure must love a plane!

Poem Written to the Heavy Rain through the Trees, or An Update on the Moonlight Sonata

Where are you?
Torso precise at the corner of the wall.
Eye casting me into a mystery.
Hand of the hungry and wrong.

They drink.
They dance.
They shoot.

We drink.
We dance.
We don't.

Where are you?
Quietly.
Quick.
Keen.
Close.

I sleep parallel to the river.
I move without shadow.
I stand below the cataclysms of the moon.

By myself.

I Am No More and I Am No Less

As the Lebanese disqualify the Lebanese
As the Lebanese soldier scalps the head
    of the Lebanese civilian
As the Lebanese man rebukes the Lebanese
    woman
As the Lebanese girl pretends she is not
    Lebanese
I wonder when they will organize the rest
    of us
to evict the children from the hospital ward
to bulldoze the babies crawling among the rocks
to declare even the last refuge from our
    self-hatred

illegal.

1980: Note to the League of Women Voters

Dear Ladies:

As a child my parents taught me not
to deal with bullies, fools, or bums.
Strangers were forbidden. Kooks excluded.
Perverts ostracized. In addition every grown man
was my enemy unless (in some constructive way)
he proved himself a member of my family.

Now I am a woman of modest abilities: I
cannot well discriminate between disgusting
and obscene between incompetent
and criminal between apocalyptic
and malodorous between blind
and deaf between
ruthless and blundering between inertia

and insanity between one lie and another
lie

For these reasons I am forced to decline
your invitation to the vote: I am moreover forced
to decline your remarkable attributions
of responsibility as when you say
it's up to me:

What's up to me?

On Life After Life

For the Poet Nancy Morejón

If you take three or four tulips from a cold
day
lavender tulips for example
and place them solid as a hot
room
where people do not touch
even the walls
they will forgive the shriveling
of their petals finally
but they will not forget the heat
of the hand
that carried them blooming
into the palm of your dream

Adrienne's Poem: On the Dialectics of the Diatonic Scale

Supposing everytime I hit this key
somebody
crumples to the ground or stops

breathing for a minute or begins to strangle
in the crib

Supposing everytime I play this chord
ribs
smash
brain-cells shrink
and a woman loses all of her hair

Supposing everytime I follow a melody
the overtones irradiate five Filipino
workers
burning their bodies
to bone

A-Flat. *A. A*-Sharp.
C. F. G. C.
Suppose my music is a hyper-
homicidal harp
and I'm just playing

Grace

To end my pestering my friend
said okay I'll come over and show you how you dred
your hair. She came by and told me I
should take a shower and apply a little bit
of plain shampoo then rinse.
I did and when I asked her, "Well, now what!"
She said, "That's it!"
And I been dredding ever since.

Poor Form

That whole way to Delphi
The children wrecked loaves of bread
smeared cheese banged each other
on the nose
and I must admit
I tried to obliterate such dread
disturbance of the dead the bother
of the beeline to the rose
the yowling of the healthy

Hoping to hear the gods
Having to wait on goats
we drove
not very fast
against the freeze that height promotes
the odds
against the living
that don't last

In bed
your hair beside my face
I do not sing
instead
I brace against the ending

The Test of Atlanta 1979–

What kind of a person would kill Black children?
What kind of a person could persuade eighteen
different Black children to get into a car or
a truck or a van?
What kind of a person could kill or kidnap
these particular
Black children:

Edward Hope Smith, 14 years old, dead
Alfred James Evans, 14 years old, dead
Yosef Bell, 9 years old, dead
Milton Harvey, 14 years old, dead
Angel Lanier, 12 years old, dead
Eric Middlebrooks, 14 years old, dead
Christopher Richardson, 11 years old, dead
Aaron Wyche, 11 years old, dead
LaTanya Wilson, 7 years old, dead
Anthony B. Carter, 9 years old, dead
Earl Lee Terrell, 10 years old, dead
Clifford Jones, 13 years old, dead
Aaron Jackson, Jr., 9 years old, dead
Patrick Rogers, 16 years old, dead
Charles Stevens, 12 years old, dead
Jeffrey Lamar Mathis, 10 years old, missing
Darron Glass, 10 years old, missing
Lubie "Chuck" Geter, 14 years old, dead

What kind of a person could kill a Black child
and then kill another Black child and then
kill another Black child and then kill another
Black child and then kill another
Black child and then kill another Black
child
and stay above suspicion?
What about the police?
What about somebody Black?
What sixteen year old would say no to a cop?
What seven year old would say no thanks to me?
What is an overreaction to murder?
What kind of a person could kill a Black
child and then kill a Black child and then
kill a Black child?

What kind of a person are you?
What kind of a person am I?

What makes you so sure?

What kind of a person could save a Black child?

What kind of a people will lay down its
life for the lives of our children?

What kind of a people are we?

Notes towards Home

My born on 99th Street uncle when he went to Canada
used to wash and polish the car long before coffee
every morning outside his room in the motel
"Because," he said, "that way they thought I lived
around there; you ever hear of a perfectly clean car
traveling all the way from Brooklyn to Quebec?"

My mother left the barefoot roads of St. Mary's
in Jamaica for the States where she wore
stockings even in a heat wave and repeatedly
advised me never to wear tacky underwear
"That way," she said, "if you have an accident
when they take you to a hospital they'll know you
come from a home."

After singing God Bless America Kate Smith
bellowed the willies out of Bless This House O
Lord We Pray/Make It Safe By Night and Day
but my cousin meant Lord keep June
and her Boris Karloff imitations out of the hall
and my mother meant Lord keep my husband out
of my way and I remember I used to mean Lord
just pretty please get me out of here!

But everybody needs a home
so at least you have someplace to leave
which is where most other folks will say
you must be coming from

Relativity

It's 5 after 4 A.M. and nothing but my own
motion stirs throughout the waiting air
the rain completely purged earlier and all
day long. I could call
you now but that would join you to this
restless lying down and getting up to list
still another act I must commit
tomorrow if I ever sleep if I ever stop
sleeping long enough to act upon the space
between this comatose commotion
and the next time I can look into your
face. I hope you're laughing at the cans
of soup the house to clean the kitchen curtains
I will wash and iron
like so many other promises I make
myself: to sweep the stairs down
to the front door
and to answer every letter down to no
thanks.
     My own motion
does not satisfy tonight and later
in the daylight I'll be speeding through the streets
a secret messenger a wakeup agent walking
backwards maybe walking sideways
but for damn sure headed possibly southeast
as well as every other whichway
in your absolute
direction

Roots for a.b.t.

There is something wonderful about the limits of a tree
But not most wonderful:

There is the flag
There is the licenseplate
Where are the trees?

Silently astir under the nervous covering of one
finger
of your hands
the veins invisible to that skin that will
not conceal the joining of the parts
the sequence
the comprehensive present tense
allowing for all alchemies
of your determination

They grow there
inside the possible and everlasting
grasp
of your own breath
your own
changeable air

Home: January 29, 1984

I can tell
because the ashtray was cleaned out
because the downstairs coconut is still full of milk
because actually nothing was left
except two shells hinged together pretty tough
at the joint
I can tell
because the in-house music now includes

the lying down look of gold and your shoulders
because there is no more noise in my head
because one room two hallways two flights of stairs
and the rest of northamerica remain
to be seen in this movie about why
I am trying to write this poem

                    not a letter
                    not a proclamation
                    not a history

I am trying to write this poem
because I can tell
because it's way after midnight and so what
I can tell
eyes open or shut
I can tell
George Washington did not sleep
here
I can tell
it was you
I can tell
it really was
you

The Cedar Trees of Lebanon

Bursting soft but kept by the structure of a spine
the green parts of the tree cloud under the clouds.
Under the axe the branches bleed red
dust. The tree bleeds red. The blood
of the cedar is red blood red body
enfolded by unmistakable brown skin.

At the end of this century massacre
remains invisible unless the victim's
skin reads white.

Night air and the smoke from the chimney
puffs into a humid atmosphere obsessed
by particles from burned up cedar trees
a smell so defiantly sweet
the stars freeze to resist that violent and swollen
odor of a life transformed by fire.

At the end of this century massacre
becomes a cluster of phosphorous
events described by a woman carrying
a mattress on her head without
a destination.

At the end of this century a girl
stands her ground next to a tree
the Cedrus Libani
that the thunder does not shake
that the lightning cannot strike down

Nightline: September 20, 1982

"I know it's an unfortunate way to say it, but
do you think you can put this massacre
on the back burner now?"

The Beirut Jokebook

1. June 8, 1982: This is not an invasion.

2. July 9, 1982: This is a ceasefire.

3. July 15, 1982: This is a ceasefire.

4. July 30, 1982: This ceasefire is strained.

5. August 4, 1982: This is not an invasion.

6. As a gesture of humanity we ask you to please pile all of
   your clothes and food and pots and pans and furniture
   and children on a bicycle and leave your homes. Our
   planes will be along, shortly.

7. You could go to the Sudan.

8. As another humanitarian gesture we have turned off the
   water and the electricity in order to speed peaceful
   negotiations.

9. What has 500,000 people and flies?

Here

The words sliding from the large glass table
into the still river
tiger lilies diluted by the windows of a gray sky
On the 36th floor of a Manhattan apartment building I try
to understand French
for the sake of Adrian Diop who thought
he would teach me by speaking so fast
I lost my own name among the messages from Senegal
for the sake of Etel Adnan who thought I would know
because she slipped her words under the feet of
Lebanese children
for the sake of the workmen who smash the cathedral
that does not rise into bread
for the sake of a city where no river stays
still
the same river.

Moving towards Home

"Where is Abu Fadi," she wailed.
"Who will bring me my loved one?"
The New York Times, 9/20/82

I do not wish to speak about the bulldozer and the
red dirt
not quite covering all of the arms and legs
Nor do I wish to speak about the nightlong screams
that reached
the observation posts where soldiers lounged about
Nor do I wish to speak about the woman who shoved
her baby
into the stranger's hands before she was led away
Nor do I wish to speak about the father whose sons
were shot
through the head while they slit his own throat before
the eyes
of his wife
Nor do I wish to speak about the army that lit continuous
flares into the darkness so that the others could see
the backs of their victims lined against the wall
Nor do I wish to speak about the piled up bodies and
the stench
that will not float
Nor do I wish to speak about the nurse again and
again raped
before they murdered her on the hospital floor
Nor do I wish to speak about the rattling bullets that
did not
halt on that keening trajectory
Nor do I wish to speak about the pounding on the
doors and
the breaking of windows and the hauling of families into
the world of the dead
I do not wish to speak about the bulldozer and the
red dirt

not quite covering all of the arms and legs
because I do not wish to speak about unspeakable events
that must follow from those who dare
"to purify" a people
those who dare
"to exterminate" a people
those who dare
to describe human beings as "beasts with two legs"
those who dare
"to mop up"
"to tighten the noose"
"to step up the military pressure"
"to ring around" civilian streets with tanks
those who dare
to close the universities
to abolish the press
to kill the elected representatives
of the people who refuse to be purified
those are the ones from whom we must redeem
the words of our beginning

because I need to speak about home
I need to speak about living room
where the land is not bullied and beaten to
a tombstone
I need to speak about living room
where the talk will take place in my language
I need to speak about living room
where my children will grow without horror
I need to speak about living room where the men
of my family between the ages of six and sixty-five
are not
marched into a roundup that leads to the grave
I need to talk about living room
where I can sit without grief without wailing aloud
for my loved ones
where I must not ask where is Abu Fadi
because he will be there beside me

I need to talk about living room
because I need to talk about home

I was born a Black woman
and now
I am become a Palestinian
against the relentless laughter of evil
there is less and less living room
and where are my loved ones?

It is time to make our way home.

≈ 1989

from *Naming Our Destiny*

For Tanzua
and
with my love and gratitude to
Mark Ainley, Sara Miles, and Adrienne Rich

✑ NORTH STAR

North Star:

Stellar guide to freedom for African men and women making their escape from slavery

Signpost in the sky for sailors on the open sea

The Abolitionist newspaper founded by Frederick Douglass in 1847

Famine

Fifty or maybe just five flies eat at the chin
of that child: Thin except for the bloat
at the belly and the bulging eyes that watch or
more accurately
that stop
in the direction he expects his mother
to come from
if she returns
if she can
walk back
carrying water that anyway
may kill
whoever gets to drink it: It's
heavy:
Water for a day weighs more than the boy
by now
weighs more than anything else
on her mind
the woman who leaves him
possibly to die
while she hunts in the sand
mile after mile looking
for water
that will not boil roots even
or bones

because not even carcasses
of trees or animals
rot
anymore
anywhere

around

2

On line
the elderly wait for the armory or
the church doors
to open
magnanimous with surplus saltine crackers
margarine and velveeta cheese
if you eat enough of the stuff
nobody wants to pay
money for
you fill up the freckling flesh
of what's left

3

On line
the boys who deal
the girls who trick
somersault
suck
sneak
slide
steal
break for the sake of a meal
they feel
nothing at all

4

But we the holy roller
passers-by
we wallow among calories that glut
the braincells/overload
the willing gut
and stupefy
inert

Mustering meretricious rosaries
of hell-bent penitence
we disavow our power
saying:

"This is not the house of my father
There is no longer the lingering scent of the roses
grown on a mortgage
There is no more to the story of the fish that got
away

This is not the land of my mother

There is no mountain becoming the breast of the earth
There is no feeding us
according to need"

But suppose that we live on the land
of our people
Suppose we live in the houses
of our rightful lives
but we do not believe it
we do not insist on quick
redistribution
of these gifts/then
who are we
and how shall we defend
ourselves as members of what
family?

Intifada

In detention
in concentration camps
we trade stories
we take turns sharing the straw mat

or a pencil
we watch what crawls in and out
of the sand

As-Salāmm 'Alaykum

The guards do not allow the blue
woolen blanket
my family traveled far
to bring
to this crepuscular and gelid cell
where my still breathing infant son
and I
defy the purgatory implications
of a state-created hell

Wa 'Alaikum As-Salām

The village trembles from the heavy
tanks that try
to terrify the children:
Everyday
my little brother runs behind the rubble
practicing the tactics of the stones
against the rock.
In January soldiers broke his fingers
one by one. Time has healed
his hands but not the fury that controls
what used to be
his heart.

Insha A'llāh

Close the villages
Close the clinics
Close the school
Close the house
Close the windows of the house

Kill the vegetables languishing under the sun
Kill the milk of the cows left to the swelling of pain
Cut the electricity
Cut the telephones
Confine the people to the people

Do Not Despair of the Mercy of Allah

Fig trees will grow and oranges
erupt from the desert
holdings on which plastic
bullets (70% zinc, 20% glass, and 10%
plastic) will prove blood
soluble and fertilize the earth
where sheep will graze
and women no longer grieve and beat
their breasts
They will beat clean
fine-woven rugs outside a house
smelling of cinnamon
and nutmeg

Ahamdullilah

So says *Iman*
the teacher of peace
the shepherd on the mountain of the lamb
the teacher of peace
who will subdue the howling of the lion
so that we may kneel
as we must
five times beginning just after dawn
and ending just before dusk
in the *Ibādah*
of prayer

Allāhu Akbar
Allāhu Akbar
Allāhu Akbar

GLOSSARY

As-Salāmm 'Alaykum: peace be unto you. *Wa 'Alaikum As-Salām:* and peace be unto you.
Insha A'llāh: as/if Allah wills it. "Do Not Despair of the Mercy of Allah": verse from
the Qur'ān. *Ahamdullilah:* praise be to Allah. *Iman:* faith. *Ibādah:* worship in a ritual sense.
Allāhu Akbar: Allah is the Greatest.

Ghazal at Full Moon

I try to describe how this aching begins or how it began
with an obsolete coin and the obsolete head of an obsolete Indian.

Holding a nickel I beheld a buffalo I beheld the silver face
of a man who might be your father: A dead man: An Indian.

I thought, "Indians pray. Indians dance. But, mostly, Indians do not live.
In the U.S.A.," we said, "the only good Indian is a dead Indian."

Dumb like Christopher Columbus I could not factor out the obvious
denominator: Guatemala/Wisconsin/Jamaica/Colorado: Indian.

Nicaragua and Brazil, Arizona, Illinois, North Dakota, and New
    Mexico:
The Indigenous: The shining and the shadow of the eye is Indian.

One billion-fifty-six, five-hundred-and-thirty-seven-thousand people
breathing in India, Pakistan, Bangladesh: All of them Indian.

Ocho Rios Oklahoma Las Vegas Pearl Lagoon Chicago
Bombay Panjim Liverpool Lahore Comalapa Glasgow: Indian.

From a London pub among the lager louts to Machu Picchu
I am following an irresistible a tenuous and livid profile: Indian.

I find a surging latticework inside the merciless detritus of diaspora.
We go from death to death who see any difference here from Indian.

The voice desiring your tongue transmits from the light of the clouds
     as it can.
Indian Indian Indian   Indian Indian Indian Indian.

Poem from Taped Testimony in the Tradition of Bernhard Goetz

1

This was not I repeat this was not a racial incident.

2

I was sitting down and it happened to me
before that I was sitting down or I was standing
up and I was by myself because of course
a lot of the time I am by myself because
I am not married or famous or super-im-
portant enough to have shadows or body-
guards so I was alone as it happens when
I was sitting down or let me retract that
I wasn't with anybody else regardless
who else was there
and I know I am not blind I could see
other people around me but the point
is that I wasn't with them I wasn't
with anybody else and like I said
it happened before two three
times it had happened that I was
sitting down or I was standing up
when one of them or one time it was
more than one I think it was two
of them anyway they just jumped
me I mean they jumped on me like

I was chump change and I know
I am not blind I could see they were
laughing at me they thought it was
funny to make me feel humiliated or I don't
know ugly or weak or really too small
to fight back so they were just laughing
at me in a way I mean you didn't
necessarily see some kind of a smile
or hear them laughing but I could feel
it like I could feel I could always
feel this shiver thing this fear take
me over when I would have to come into a room
full of them and I would be by myself
and they would just look at you know what
I mean you can't know what I mean
you're not Black

3

How would you know
how that feels when mostly you move through
outnumbered and you are the one doesn't
fit in doesn't look right doesn't read
right because you're not white
but you live
in this place in this city where
again and again
there you are inside but outside or off
and you're different and I would never know when
it would happen again that the talking
would stop or the talking would start
or somebody would say something
stupid or nasty to me like nigga
or honey or bitch or not say
anything at all like the drugstore on Sunday
and I was standing in line but the girl
behind the counter couldn't get it
together to say, "Yes. Can I help

you?" or anything at all she was counting
on silence to make me
disappear or beg or I don't know
what and okay I'm visiting New Hampshire
but also
I live here I mean in this country
I live here and you should have seen
the look of her eyes they were shining
I know I am not blind and she wanted
to make believe me this irreducible this me
into a no-count what you gone do about
it/zip

4

So one of them a policeman a long
time ago but I remember it he kicked
in the teeth of Jeffrey Underwood who
lived on my block and who had been the best
looking boy in the neighborhood and he was tall
and skinny even and kind of shy and he/
Jeffrey went up on the roof with fire
crackers I mean it was the roof of the house
of a family that knew him and they knew
Jeffrey's parents too and
my cousin told me the next morning how
this policeman asked Jeffrey to come
down so Jeffrey left the roof and came
down to the street where we lived and
then the policeman beat Jeffrey
unconscious and he/the
policeman who was one of them he kicked
Jeffrey's teeth out and I never wanted to see
Jeffrey anymore but I kept seeing
these policemen and I remember how
my cousin who was older than I was I remember how
she whispered to me, "That's what they
do to you"

5

and the stinging of my face when some of
them my mother told me they were
Irish and when some of them shot at me
with zip guns and howled out "li'l nigga"
I was eight years old by myself walking
with my book bag to a public school
and I remember my mother
asking me to kneel down beside her to pray
for the Irish

6

So much later and of course this is not something
I keep on the front burner but then again
it's nothing you want to forget because
enough is enough and it has happened before
and it happens so often but when you turn around
for help or the punishment of these people
where can you go I mean I was raped six
years ago by one of them who was good he told me
with a rifle and he raped me and his
brother was the judge in town and so forth all
of them have brothers all over town there
are so many of them everywhere you go so
either you become the routine
setup
or you have to figure out
some self-defense

7

I was sitting down and it had happened
before that I was sitting down and I was
by myself because not one of them was
with me not one of them was cognizant
(to use a better word) of me where I
was sitting down and they filled up
the room around me and one of them

sat down to my left and another one
of them sat down beside my right fist
on the table (next to the silverware) and
I was sitting there quiet and mild-
mannered which is how I am you can
ask my neighbors you can read about
it in the papers everyday the papers
tell you I am quiet and mild-mannered which is
how I sat there at this table in a room
full of them and then the one to the right
of my right fist she started up about this South
African novel she was reading and she said to the one
to my left by which I mean she ignored me in the middle
and it felt like I was
not there but I was I was sitting
in my chair at the table where
she the one to my right said to the one
to my left she said, "And the writer
expects the reader to be sympathetic
to that character!" And then the
one to my left said to the one to my
right she said, "Exactly! And it's
so cheap. It's so disgusting. She (the
writer) makes her (the character)
marry not one but two Black revolutionaries!" And something
        snapped
inside me I could see across the table
more of them just sitting there eyes
shining
and I know I am not blind
I could see them laughing at me and I went
cold because in a situation like that
you have to be cold a cold
killer or they will ridicule you
right there at the dining table and
I wanted to murder
I wanted them to hurt and bleed I wanted
them to leave me alone

and so I became cold I became a cold
killer and I took out my gun and
I shot the one to my right and then
I shot the one to my left and then I looked
across the table and I thought, "They
look all right," and so I shot them too
and it was self-defense I wanted
them to stop playing with me
I wanted them to know it's not cheap
or disgusting to love a Black
revolutionary and
as a matter of fact
I wanted them to know you'd
better love a Black revolutionary before she
gets the idea

that you don't

Aftermath

Morning sun heats up the young beech tree
leaves and almost lights them into fireflies

I wish I could dig up the earth to plant apples
pears or peaches on a lazy dandelion lawn

I am tired from this digging up of human bodies
no one loved enough to save from death

To Free Nelson Mandela

Every night Winnie Mandela
Every night the waters of the world
turn to the softly burning
light of the moon

Every night Winnie Mandela
Every night

Have they killed the twelve-year-old girl?
Have they hung the poet?
Have they shot down the students?
Have they splashed the clinic the house
and the faces of the children
with blood?

Every night Winnie Mandela
Every night the waters of the world
turn to the softly burning
light of the moon

They have murdered Victoria Mxenge
They have murdered her
victorious now
that the earth recoils from that crime
of her murder now
that the very dirt shudders from the falling blood
the thud of bodies fallen
into the sickening
into the thickening
crimes of apartheid

Every night
Every night Winnie Mandela

Every night Winnie Mandela
Every night the waters of the world
turn to the softly burning
light of the moon

At last the bullets boomerang
At last the artifice of exile explodes
At last no one obeys the bossman of atrocities

At last the carpenters the midwives
the miners the weavers the anonymous
housekeepers the anonymous
street sweepers
the diggers of the ditch
the sentries the scouts the ministers
the mob the pallbearers the practical
nurse
the diggers of the ditch
the banned
the tortured
the detained
the everlastingly insulted
the twelve-year-old girl and her brothers at last
the diggers of the ditch
despise the meal without grace
   the water without wine
   the trial without rights
   the work without rest
at last the diggers of the ditch
begin the living funeral
for death

Every night Winnie Mandela
Every night

Every night Winnie Mandela
Every night the waters of the world
turn to the softly burning
light of the moon

Every night Winnie Mandela
Every night

Dance: Nicaragua

NI SE RINDE   NI SE VENDE
NI SE RINDE

Nicaragua
Todas las armas al pueblo
Todo el pueblo al sueño
Nicaragua Nicaragua
Todo el pueblo al sueño

Nicaragua Nicaragua
Bluefields/Estelí/Managua

Picking coffee in the morning
Playing basketball at night
Pencil manifestos under new electric light

Nicaragua
going back to Nicaragua
to the land of Sandinistas
to the land of New World vistas

GOING BACK
GOING BACK TO
Nicaragua Nicaragua
Bluefields/Estelí/Managua
going back to little Nica
not Honduras/Costa Rica
going back to little Nica

Fill my plate with rice and beans
Talk with parrots from the hushed up hills
of green
Swim beside the blown up bridges
Fish inside the bomb-sick harbors
Farm across the contra ridges

Dance with revolutionary ardor
Swim/Fish/Farm/Dance
Nicaragua   Nicaragua

NI SE RINDE   NI SE VENDE
NI SE RINDE

nicaragua

vivir libre
vivir libre
vivir libre
o morir

Verse for Ronald Slapjack Who Publicly Declared, "I, Too, Am a Contra!"

You said it.
You got that right.
Finally you told it to the people:
"I, too, am a contra."
All except the "too" stuff:
How you mean that "too"?
Too compared to what/who stalks
around the planet like you do?
You the crown conniver
You the jivetime star
You the megajoint
You the program you the point
to every hotline launchpad eagle
program spying high
and spying low
for any signs of independent life (uh-oh)
Oops!
Swoop down! Pounce
and seize it,

Undercut them vital signs:
"Independent life," indeed.

"I, too, am a contra."

You got that right.
You the founding father
for the morally retarded
    the armed with butter-for-brains and truly mean
    the burn and brag
    the mercenaries
    the leftover lackeys from last year's greed freak
    the do-anything-go-anywhere for the thrill
        of a little killing or
        if flexible
        a big kill

You the founding father
But still
that ain' no news
we seen the pot-rot way back
when
we seen you

        contra-dictory
        we seen you
        contra-dicted
        we seen you
        contra-factual
        we seen you
        contra-verified
        we seen you
        contra-Constitution
        we seen you
        contra-Bill-of-Rights
        we seen you
        contra-sanctuary
        we seen you

contra-smart
we seen you
contra-all-intelligence
we seen you
contra-hospital-ship
we seen you
contra-heart
we seen you
contra-any-sign-of-independent-life

Fact is
Mister Slapjack Quack-Quack
in a happy
peaceful
law-abiding scheme of things
you jus' contra-indicated!

Poem Instead of a Columbus Day Parade

Yes Baby:

"Unrest in the Philippines":

Is it 7,000 islands
Am I 7,000 fragments from a country
Christopher Columbus
wrecked the reputation of the compass
by?

Did somebody ask an Indian
to pay for parking anywhere at all?

Yes Baby:

"Unrest in the Philippines":

My daily politics
an open hydrant pouring water
into late November rain

An Always Lei of Ginger Blossoms for the First Lady of Hawai'i: Queen Lili'uokalani

Dedicated to Philip and Diana Chang

Never mind
Even the Be-Still tree will never stop
the spirit rivers of the Ko'olau Mountains
nor the twisting smash surf drown
the great gong
pounded by the living
for the right to live

On your island dolphins
slope below belief
then rise in somersault or triple flip affection
for the laughter of the weary
ones who need

more than African tulips
more than bareback riding of a whale
more than banyan roots
more than Diamond Head above their shoulders
more than mango guava sugarcane or pineapple and papaya
more than monkey pod elegance of shelter
more than the miracle revised to feed the blue and silver and
        yellow and spotted and large and small fish who receive
        bread from the fingers of a hand
more than forgive and forget about "the secret annexation
        society"

                mainlander businessmen who held you
                prisoner

inside the 'Iolani Palace
kept you
solitary in confinement
nine months
minus even pencils or a piece of paper
nine months
before the businessmen relented
and allowed you your guitar

more than the southern star skies
and the delivering wild ocean swells
that rule the separating space
between Tahiti and the statue
of Your Highness
schooling Honolulu into secret conduct
suitable for thimbleberries
suitable for orchids
suitable for the singing ghost of your guitar

On your island dolphins
slope beyond belief
then rise

On your island (*never mind*)
the weary ones throng
faithful to the great song
once again to pound
the great gong
sounds again and then
again

Something like a Sonnet for Phillis Miracle Wheatley

Girl from the realm of birds florid and fleet
flying full feather in far or near weather
Who fell to a dollar lust coffled like meat

Captured by avarice and hate spit together
Trembling asthmatic alone on the slave block
built by a savagery traveling by carriage
viewed like a species of flaw in the livestock
A child without safety of mother or marriage

Chosen by whimsy but born to surprise
They taught you to read but you learned how to write
Begging the universe into your eyes:
They dressed you in light but you dreamed with the night.
From Africa singing of justice and grace,
Your early verse sweetens the fame of our Race.

Poem for Benjamin Franklin

who said,
"I do not believe we shall ever have a firm peace
with the Indians,
till we have well-drubbed them."

My Daddy, Mr. Franklin, my truculent
no-paunch
crack a coconut with one whack
of a handy homeowner's hammer-axe/my
Daddy, Mr. Franklin, my fastidious
first runaway from a true calypso/my
Daddy, Mr. Franklin, my Daddy give this
little girl
your glorified life story she
must read
or else
when she didn't know much better than to trust
some pontiff-politician talk about save pennies/
take a stitch in time

anyway

you the one gone out there in the lightning
with a kite?

Let me electrify the ghost
of your redoubtable achievements!

The Indians been well drubbed
The Palestinians been well drubbed

firm peace prevails
in 2 out of every 3 American bedrooms
and
on the nighttime city sidewalks
Firm peace prevails

and
underneath the hanging tree
and
moaning down at Wounded Knee
and north of Ocotal
and east of Ilopango
and
censored in the sandpits of an occupied West Bank
and
all around Johannesburg where boiling water in a tin can
has become a crime

Firm peace prevails
Mr. Franklin
Firm peace prevails

We been well drubbed
but
like my Daddy could have told you/my
Daddy whistling in the ghetto
of your legacy/my
Daddy could have told you after he done beat me
how I laid real low but didn't hardly overlook to pay him

back
(big men must sleep sometime)
My Daddy/Mr. Franklin/my Daddy could have told you
firm peace ain' peace it's truce
and truce don't last
but temporarily

The Torn Sky: Lesson #1

chlorofluorocarbons
chlorofluorocarbons
chlorofluorocarbons

start at Antarctica

chlorofluorocarbons
chlorofluorocarbons
chlorofluorocarbons

like a Spanish speaking Afrikaner
(or
an Afrikaner speaking Spanish)

start at Antarctica

(now you're getting it)

chlorofluorocarbons
chlorofluorocarbons
chlorofluorocarbons

start at Antarctica

(to tear up the sky)

Take Them Out!

Take them out!

Rain forests of the world
only provide x amount of oxygen
for everybody including some
you don't like anyhow

Rain forests of the world
only provide x amount of refuge
for x amount of living creatures
most of which you never seen
even in the movies

Take them out!

From Alaska to Brazil you want
to keep that kind of uncontrolled
diversity in stock?

Poem for Jan

Dedicated to Jan Heller Levi

Crushed marigold or
a child's hand
crushed
the colors blurring into sunset
or royalty spelled by liquid pastel
implications of delight

Crushed marigold or
a child's hand
crushed

In what context you may ask me
For what reason
                    that small flower
                    that small hand
                    as commonplace as lechery
                    third degree burns
                    or quietly contriving torture
                    of a little bit of hope

To do that thing

regardless of aesthetics
regardless of some use

Crushed marigold or
a child's hand
crushed

I cannot imagine an excuse

Solidarity

For Angela Y. Davis

Even then
in the attenuated light
of the Church of le Sacré Coeur
(early evening and folk songs
on the mausoleum steps)
and armed
only with 2 instamatic cameras
(not a terrorist among us)
even there
in that Parisian downpour
four
Black women (2 of Asian 2
of African descent)

could not catch a taxi
and
I wondered what umbrella
would be big enough to stop
the shivering
of our collective impotence
up
against such negligent
assault

And I wondered
who would build that shelter
who will build and lift it
high and wide
above
such loneliness

In Paris

Dedicated to Pratibha Parmar and Shaheen Haque

I do not dare to reject the quarter moon
that perforates a clear night
sky

Adamantine above dark trees
the sliver of its lucid invitation
emulates
the willing calm of lovers
fallen
almost asleep

Between stone walls the tourist
boats float
silently electrified
under le Pont Royal

What would Louis the Fourteenth
make
of my two friends and me
our eyes as commonly tender
as the mud
our vision tempered by diaspora?

And who cares?

We stand beside the river
speaking quietly somewhere
comfortable
below the stars

At this moment
the water itself
begins to melt

Nothing
Not tears
Not even the rain
As soft as the Seine

Poem on the Second Consecutive Day of Rain

It just don't stop/flood
levels falling/if the meadow was a Tub
of Butterflies Blue Violets
and Harebells (not to mention)
Morning Glories
Foxglove
Purple Loosestrife
Indian Paint Bursh
Oxeye Daisies and
Stiff Asters
at the grassy birds' nests bottom

then I'd swim the surface of this birdsong
sanctuary
on my belly looking down
and float
complacent as the quietly pointed white pine needles
in such water saturated air

But this meadow got no bottom/
base line/absolute: This meadow sucks it up:
A rich man running after money/more
rain more more
more rain

It just don't stop!

Out in the Country of My Country (*Peterborough, New Hampshire*)

Filling my eyes with flowers of no name
that I can call aloud: This northernmost retreat
of white pine or aching birch
of meadow mouth opening the body of a perfect land
that throws away birdsong on the rushes
of hard rain

Testing my heart with precipice and crest
accumulating timber trails or fern
beside the mica sparkling road that peaks
at mountain heights of granite situated
next to purple lilac feeling out the light
of short cold days

Choosing my mind between mosquitoes and the moon
that dominates a darkness larger than the stars
close by: I (what do you suppose)
I battle with the spirits of a winterkill

that spoils the summer berries: Blunts the nipple points
of love

Chasing my face among displacements of a stream
I behold the Indian: I become the slave
again I am hunting/I am hunted in these snowy woods
again I am eagle/I am scrambling on the summit rocks
I slip I scream I soar I seek the dancing of the spirits
from the grave

A Richland County Lyric for Elizabeth Asleep

His wet nose pushing at the screen
the big dog indicates he's had enough
inside
the table oilcloth flaps beneath a cabin lamp

I let him go and follow
slowly
held by full moon on the flying ants
the flying hawk at large and silent in its odd
nocturnal drift towards mysterious emergency –

How soft it seems! The misted termination
of that hillside: (Solid black beside the easing
only human light
a mile away)

A forest breast/a midnight
nursing of the cirrus
clouds that lead the hawk beyond its vision
and beyond my own into the trusting evolution
of apparently pale flowers that ignite
the darkening prairie surf
like stars

The Madison Experience

Dedicated to Nellie McKay

I

Lake Michigan
(like so much hearsay:
Who says, "lake" and who
can hold this surging body
thrust against these cities?
Who can prove the limits of original wild water
how?
But then
Lake Michigan is not the point)

2

I am in Miami/no
Waikiki/no
It's Oxford on the definitely northern Lake
Mendota floats along with Women's
Studies/Big Ten Football
and canoes/the sailboats
tease the students and their teachers
from a coming summer's ease with beer and yoghurt
and next Friday night
at 6 o'clock
a rally for Soweto

3

Crayola was right:
Color this farmland green and blue
and yellow pastels
Make the barn red
Look at the silo and notice the cows
in the middle
of the University

4

How many Black people live in Madison?
How many buffaloes sleep in the park?
How many Indians came to the bar-be-cue?
When is the last time it rained?

5

Bicycles deliver urban lyrics
uphill:
hard labor habits from a hearty breakfast
for a stiff day's work on the difficult
but rolling
earth

6

Yesterday I went out
Looking for traffic

7

As far as I know
Sundays come and Sundays go
but there won't be no
Gay Pride March (unless somebody plans to show
by accident)

8

Shelling beans
snow peas/onions/hosed
down beets/potatoes/ornamental cabbages
Planned Parenthood or fathers
for Equal Rights/whole wheat sticky
buns/potted tiger lilies/"Cheese
Curds Guaranteed to Squeak" and "What
Can One Man Do
to Stop Rape?" at The Farmers' Market
Saturdays

around the domed white Capitol building
scrubbed clean like most
of the children fingering the flowers
and the homemade fudge

   9

7:30 A.M.
and my neighbor Bonnie
brings me a pile of still hot chocolate
chip cookies because
"They taste better like that" but
her daughter burned her forearm on the oven
and underneath my barefeet the bristling July
grass
as delicate as last October

   10

Inside the always unlit hardware store
where no more than one customer per half
an hour opens or shuts the door
Mrs. Schensky mans a cash
register probably full of Romanian jewels
that remind her of the orchids
planted all around her kitchen sink
or else those – "Well
they look like morning glories but
they grow on bushes
thousands of them – Oh, hibiscus! Do you know
hibiscus?"
I am there to buy a rubber floor mat that spells
WELCOME but that translates
into PLEASE: NO MUD

"I don't want anything to hurt you," she
declares. And so I wait
obedient
as Mrs. Schensky first removes the stapled price

tag from the floor mat
she will finally allow me
to accept
into my own two tenderly
astounded hands

11

Drought around the eyes
Drought around the mouth
and words falling out like logs
from the irresistible
big trees

12

Five days stretch thick skin
across the skull
of quick romance

Above the backyard mulberry tree leaves a full moon
        Not quite as high as the Himalaya Mountains
not quite as high as the rent in New York City
summons me beyond my mind into the meat and mud
of things that sing

13

The Chancellor The Mayor The County Executive
Somebody and Jesus
all played volleyball
together
and I don't remember anybody
losing it.

14

Who is a small burrowing mammal
head-over-heels in bona fide hog heaven

plumb full of sunlight/veal brats
and an opening heartland of surprise?

A Sonnet from the Stony Brook

Studying the shadows of my face in this white place
where tree stumps recollect a hurricane
I admire the possibilities of flight and space
without one move towards the ending of my pain.
I conspire with blackbirds light enough to fly
but grounded by the trivia of appetite
I desist decease delimit: I deny
the darling dervish from a half-forgotten night
when mouth became a word too sweet
to say aloud and body changed to right
or wrong ways to prolong new irresponsibilities of heat
new tunings of a temperature with weight and height.

For all I can remember all I know
only shadows flourish; shadows grow

A Sonnet for a.b.t.

But one of these Wednesdays everything could work
the phone and the answering machine: Your voice
despite the 65 miles that would irk
or exhaust a fainthearted lover: Your choice
of this distance this timing between us bends
things around: Illusory landmarks of longing and speed.
A full moon the flight of summer sends
to light a branch the leaves no longer need.
A top ten lyric fallen to eleven
But meaningful (*meaningful*) because the music still
invites a kind of close tight heaven
of a slowdown dance to let me kill the chill.

You know what I mean
My Love: Seen or unseen

Poem on Bell's Theorem, or Haying the Field by Quantum Mechanics

The tractor stuck between the strewn or
uncollected and the baled-up grass
mounded circles because somebody worried
about spontaneous combustion if you cubed
that igneous that throttled mass
drenched to the centermost stalk
and the farmer gone home to drink
(his son slipped from his lap since noon)
through this unpromising but slight
disaster
this intermittent and torrential rain
bringing to a halt a poor man's bare
rituals of preparation for the hushed-
up months
when green becomes an obscene
color for a discount
portable TV
                    Now
it seems that water holds the land
in faulted frieze
but no stopped trucks or turned-off key
originated here along this flooding dirt path
where I see what I may see

More likely melted glacier molecules
capricious in flirtations with an underground
magnetic tease
Or Chinese peasants killing cattle that upset
new market monetary rules
Or beaten farmers' wives who commandeer

a neighbor's car/jump-start the pickup for a get-
away from on-and-off the bottle boys
more likely these
far probabilities
making connections faster than light
compelled the man's machine to lose its energy
abandon aim
and caused the sunburned driver
just to walk himself
out of my local my mistaken sight

Poem Number Two on Bell's Theorem, or The New Physicality of Long Distance Love

There is no chance that we will fall apart
There is no chance
There are no parts.

Last Poem on Bell's Theorem, or Overriding the Local Common Sense of Causes to Effect

No:
I did not buy this sweatshirt with
    NORTH STAR
imprinted on the front
because:
       I found it on sale.
       It fit.
       I am a Minnesota hockey fan.
Look at me
and guess again.

Romance in Irony

            I would risk ticks
and Rocky Mountain Spotted Fever
stop smoking
give up the car and the VCR
destabilize my bank account
floss before as well as after meals
and unilaterally disarm my telephone connection

                                        to

other (possible) lovers
if
we could walk into the mountains then
come home again
together

But instead
I lie in bed
fingering photographs from Colorado
that conceal more than they illuminate
the hunter of the elksong or the deer

I resent the radiator heat
that nightly rises almost musical
in a wet hot air
crescendo
or I exaggerate some not bad looking trees
that 2 or maybe 3 feet there (away from me)
and out the window
grow
oblivious above a miscellaneous
debris
(I yearn for non-negotiable abutment
to the beauty of the world)

And with the courage that the lonely or the
                        foolish keep

I set the clock
turn out the light
and do not dream and do not sleep

Trying to Capture Rapture

The point is not to pacify the soul
Or sleep through torments measuring the night
And I concede I hold no trust or goal
That, trembling, yet retains the body's light.
And I admit I hardly understand
The motions of a hand that wants a hand
Or deadlines for a love that perseveres.
But I cannot survive the blurring of the years:
Untouched, unknown, estranged and, now, alone.

And having said, "I cannot," here I do
Again declare: I will not beg for you.
And love will say, "Nobody asks you to!"
But I have died for rapture other days.
Oh, I have tried for rapture other ways!

Winter Honey

Sugar come
and sugar go
Sugar dumb
but sugar know
ain' nothin' run me for my money
nothin' sweet like winter honey

Sugar high
and sugarlow
Sugar pie
and sugar dough

Then sugar throw
a sugar fit
And sugar find
a sugar tit
But never mind
what sugar find
ain' nothin' run me for my money
nothin' sweet like winter honey

Sugar come
and please don' go
Sugar dumb
but oh-my: Oh!
Ain' nothin' run me for my money
nothin' sweet like winter honey

At Some Moment the Confidence Snaps

At some moment the confidence snaps
that tomorrow or next year or in the middle of spring
you will be
around
to run errands/drink coffee/want love/write
history
does not know about the inside snap
but this is not
historical
this is me
by myself on a quiet Friday night
not at all sure
about the future tense
of my single life
limited
by time already taking away
my arrogance
or easy postponement
of anything whatsoever

How much do I hope
that the memories of my minute
among so many strangers
will mainly taste
sweet
to the mouth of judgment

Double Standard Lifestyle Studies: #1

For example I would slit
my eyes
if I supposed your close and ravenous
inquiries might reach into a corpus
not my own

Or I would assume you would assume
Me/solitary on a gorgeous night
of tropical compulsions from the flesh
or astral incantations to the ecosystems
of my lust

But I take this call from California/
an aerogram arrives
and I watch for signals from Tibet
while you perhaps return
from Washington, D.C.

                          Baby
I guess I have trouble getting the geography
on screen

Could be monogamous monopolies
will have to wait
until some footloose wizard can identify
exact locations
on this high risk undertaking
for conventional cartographers

Or should I build implacable
my homebase
right around that millimeter where
imagination will not tempt me from the mesmerizing marvel
of your honest or deceitful
lips?

Poem for Joy

Dedicated to the Creek Tribe of North America

Dreaming
    Colorado where the whole earth rises
    marvelous high hard rock higher than the heart can
    calmly tolerate: The hawk
    swoons from its fierce precipitation
    granite in its rising opposition to the bird
    or rabbit
    Sapling leaf or stallion loose among the chasmic
    crevices dividing continental
    stretch into the small scale appetizers
    then the lifted meal
    itself

And dazed
    by snowlight settled like a glossary
    of diamonds on the difficult
    ice-bitten mountain trails that lead
    to fish rich waters

I reach
    the birthplace for the stories of your hurt
    your soft collapse
    the feelings of the flat wound of the not forgotten graves
    where neither rain nor dawn
    can resurrect the stolen pageantry the blister
    details of the taken acreage

that scars two million memories of forest
blueberry bush and sudden
mushrooms sharing dirt
with footprints tender as the hesitations
of your hand
     who know obliteration
     who arise from the abyss
     the aboriginal
     as definite as heated through as dry
     around the eyes
     as Arizona
     the aboriginal
     as apparently inclement as invincible
     as porous
     as the desert
     the aboriginal
     from whom the mountains slide
     away
     afraid to block the day's deliverance
     into stars and cool air lonely
     for the infinite invention of avenging fires

And now the wolf
And now the loyalty of wolves
And now the bear
And now the vast amusement of the bears
And now the aboriginal
And now the daughter of the tomb.

And now an only child of the dead becomes the mother
of another life,
And how shall the living sing of that
impossibility?
    She will.

Poem at the Midnight of My Life

I never thought that I would live forever:
Now I light a cigarette
surprised by pleasures lasting past
predictions from the hemorrhaging of fears
and I reflect on faces soft above my own
in love

The implications of all heated ecstasy that I have known
despite the soldier fist on broken bone
despite the small eyes shrinking flesh to stone
surround me in this tender solitude
like teenage choirs of gullibility
and guts

(How many bottles of beer will it take
to make a baby?)

I understand how nothing ever happens on a one-
plus-one equals anything predictable/
how time rolls
drunk around the curvilinear conventions
of a virgin
and eventual as passion's lapse
just peters out
indefinite

(92 bottles of beer on the wall
92 bottles of beer)

           how sorry brings you
to the graveside
on an afternoon of trees entirely alive

(if one of the bottles should happen to fall...)

the chosen focus tortured true
between a homeless woman lying frozen
on the avenue
and a flying horse or legs to carry you or race
into the hungers of a problematic
new embrace

(...91 bottles of beer on the wall)

I understand the comfortable temptation of the dead:
I turn my back against the grave
and kiss again the risk of what I have
instead

The Female and the Silence of a Man

cf. W.B. Yeats's "Leda and the Swan"

And now she knows: The big fist shattering her face.
Above, the sky conceals the sadness of the moon.
And windows light, doors close, against all trace
of her: She falls into the violence of a woman's ruin.

How should she rise against the plunging of his lust?
She vomits out her teeth. He tears the slender legs apart.
The hairy torso of his rage destroys the soft last bastion of
    her trust.
He lacerates her breasts. He claws and squeezes out her heart.

She sinks into a meadow pond of lilies and a swan.
She floats above an afternoon of music from the trees.
She vanishes like blood that people walk upon.
She reappears: A mad *bitch* dog that reason cannot seize;
A fever withering the river and the crops:
A lovely girl protected by her cruel/incandescent energies.

Poem for Buddy

Dedicated to André Morgan

In that same beginning winter
when the rains strained all credulity
swallowed highways
rolled mountains of mud down
mountains
buried boundaries
left 20,000 families homeless

In that same beginning winter
of the rivers rising up
some of the people rose
organic
secretly
out loud
and irresistible

In that same beginning winter
of the gods asleep
rain
rain
rain
flood
mudslide and
the powerful at large and
lies
lies
lies
the river burst torrential
to attack to overcome
the limitations of all compromise

In that same beginning winter
when Duvalier and Marcos
fell into the torrents

streaming full and efflorescent out
between the blank walls and the sea
streaming aboriginal
as female

when the ku klux klan
the Duck Club and other crackpot
rah-rah
butchered Charles and Annie Goldmark
in Seattle
hung Timothy Lee
from a California weed tree
and captured two top nominations
in the State of Illinois
when Reagan reigned
from the Gulf of Sidra to the asinine appeal
of right-to-life
explosives and warmongering
cutbacks on the already alive

when the great lakes trembled
when volcanoes shook
when the desert flowers failed
when the farmers lost the land
when the Challenger blew up
when the Chairman of the Board skipped lunch

when the rain the lies lies lies
and the rain
and the rain
when the rivers burst torrential
to attack to overcome
the limitations of all compromise

from Pretoria to Port-au-Prince
from Manila to Managua
from the hanging tree for Timothy Lee
to Washington, D.C.

when the rivers burst torrential
it was then that
in Manhattan
one Black homosexual
in a gym
by himself
he turned to the taunting cocksure
multitude of forty-five
miscellaneous straight men preoccupied by musculature
and scores of conquest
tight men tight against gay
rights gay everything around them gay
hey/whatever happened to
dictatorship
anyway
next thing you know and your dog will be gay
and your wife and the cop on the corner gay gay
teachers in the classroom gay
victims of aids gay soldiers
in uniform gay fathers
of children gay
athletes on the U.S. Olympic teams
of whatever gay
members of the city council gay
lovers who love themselves gay
mothers gay
brothers-in-law gay
nuns gay priests gay
gay T.W.A. pilots gay
lumberjacks
gay rockstars gay
gay revolutionaries they
were saying, "Enough
enough!"
when he
in the gym
by himself
this Black homosexual this man

took on the question: *if not here then where if not now –*
And he spoke to them saying:
"Okay! Look at me!" And in front of them he stood
thinking
they should march into a stadium
and gathering there by the hundreds
tear out their eyes
that they might no longer see him or
me/this despicable growing minority
here
outside but gathered as strong as we stand.
They should tear out their eyes
so the world will look only
the way they believe to be
beautiful!
Because
we are everywhere
gay
and today you just can't be sure
anymore
who's who
or
what's what
now
can you?

But they did not move they
did not say anything and they broke
into the locker of this Black homosexual this
human being and they broke they smashed his glasses
that let him deal
real
among the gay and the grim
and he left that gym
by himself

In that same beginning winter
when the first rivers burst torrential

to attack to overcome
the limitations of all compromise

he slipped into the rising up
we who will irreversibly see
and name our own destiny
with our own
open eyes

Smash the Church

I am eating
I am eating ⅔ of a half pound of cashew nuts
dry roasted
filling the cavity full
with cashew nuts
because I still don't understand
why I wanted to win so much
I hit my nine-year-old
best friend
because she didn't feel like playing
ball
softball
on the day of the final play-offs
for the championship of Central Valley
New York
okay
I was nine years old
but so what
and I knew we couldn't win without her
and she Jodi
played third base I think
and didn't hit me back she
hit that ball
pretty damn good
and we won

nothing to take home
nothing to wear
nothing to eat

I am eating ⅔ of a half pound of cashew nuts
dry roasted
filling the cavity full
with cashew nuts
because I still don't get it
why I had to hit her
why we had to win
that game
I wish that I could burn my hand
I can't because I am
a coward
just like any intermittent psychopath
salivating hellbent towards whatever
she wants
she tells herself
I want that so I need
fresh raspberries in December
⅔ of a half pound of cashew nuts
I am eating them
because I want to
        I need to
eat them
up
devour the itch the tickle
the pinch the probing pierce elements of my
appetite
because I still don't understand it
because I still don't understand it
I am eating
I am eating ⅔ of a half pound of cashew nuts
        I can't figure out why
I thought another friend of mine was weird
or funny
see

because she offered me
some bread
not fancy
not nut
not spice
but bread
one loaf of plain bread
hot from a bakery we
passed by
why did I turn shy
against the basic thing
that bread
that we might choose as something
rare
something precious we could share
like soldiers?

Food will fortify your body:
Where's the war?

I am eating
I am eating ⅔ of a half pound of cashew nuts
not bread
I am writing this tonight although I could be eating
with a friend instead
because I still don't understand my
appetite
what's wrong with bread
what's nuts about these nuts
what's right about this poem in my head
        does monopoly capital fit
into it
I'm sorry that I hit
my best friend
And the basic story of this basic loaf of bread
will not end
here

Take: Eat,
This is My Body
I wish that I could burn my hand.
The body of Christ.
The bread of heaven.

Jodi
pushed away
the movie magazine that she'd been reading
and she said
straight and simple
as   daily bread,
"Okay.
Let's play."

The game is still a test of grace.

Raspberries in December
Thin wafer and thick wine
The blood shed
so that the hungry could recognize and savor
basic bread.

We wish that we could win
against the furies of original
unalterable sin.

The trouble with church
is
somebody has to let you in and
nobody knows how
to let you out.
However
cashew nuts do not
conclusively
attest to crime
and ceremonies of self-hatred

do not truly make you
beautiful.

Dear Jodi
from as long ago as bubble gum
I come
apology in hand

I know it's good
at last
I say it's possible
at least
to let the bad stuff go

Don't Estimate!

I need to know
exactly
how many stars separate Brooklyn from the Rockies
How many light-years filled with what
passionate ash will float
into a visible position
blazing liberties of tenderness
to captivate the Denver sky

I do not detect the fragile
morning stars
that smile with my confusion
I cannot see the molten
or ethereal trace recollections
of this into-my-body experience
expanding circular canopies
of planets ruled by lust
as welcome
as suddenly regular
as daybreak

But I am found by fantasies
that even here
on the third floor walk-up of a city hideaway
may force me
down into indifferent urban
circumstances that include (I hope!)
a near-by travel agent ready/
waiting
on my urgent lover's
trust

Financial Planning

A poem commissioned by *Forbes* magazine

Fifty cents more an hour would get me
     a house in the country
     hilarious friends calling
     an Airedale that wakes me up only for brunch
     a lover lusting insatiate
     liberation from my own daily routines
10,000 more a year would get me
     in debt for the house in the country
     part of the car that will slide up the driveway
     tennis lessons in the neighborhood
     installment plan travel out of that
     neighborhood entirely
     an A-1 recommended kennel for my dog
50,000 beyond that would get me
a whole lotta trouble
I'm sure
for example
I would have to revise this poem
and I don't know
how

Poem for Mark

England, I thought, will look like Africa
or India with elephants and pale men
pushing things about
rifle and gloves
handlebar mustache and tea
pith helmets
riding crop
The Holy Bible
and a rolled up map of plunder
possibilities

But schoolboys with schoolbags
little enough for sweets
wore Wellingtons into the manicured
mud
and Cockney manners
("I say
we've been waiting 45 minutes
for this bus, we 'ave! It's
a regular disgrace,
it 'tis!"
"Yes, love: I'm sorry! But
step up/move along,
now! I'm doing the best I can!
You can
write a letter if you please!")
quite outclassed the Queen's

And time felt like a flag
right side up and flying
high while mousse-spike haircuts
denim jackets strolled around
and Afro-Caribbean/Afro-Celtic men
and women comfortable in full
length Rasta dreads

invited me to dinner
or presented me with poetry

And we
sat opposite but close
debating Nicaragua
or the civil liberties of countries
under siege
and you said
"Rubbish!" to the notion of a national
identity
and if I answered,
"In my country –"
You would interrupt me, saying,
"You're not serious!"
but then I thought I was
about "my country"
meaning where I'd come from
recently
and after only transatlantic static for a single
phone call
up against my loathing to disrupt and travel
to the silly land of Philip and Diana
never having hoped for anyone (a bebop-
antelope) like you
so quietly impertinent and teasing
it was 4 A.M. the first time
when we stopped the conversation
And long before my face lay nestling on the hotel
pillows/well
I knew
whoever the hell "my people"
are
I knew that one of them
is you

DeLiza Come to London Town

A birthday poem for Mark

DeLiza walk across the Waterloo
at night
She short but happy that she maybe have
one inch or two
on Bonaparte
who (anyway) look peculiar up against the backdrop
of Big Ben

She cogitate
on glory and the sword/she
smoke a cigarette among a hundred homeless
white men
them the Queen forget to decorate
with bed or blanket
softening the bottomline along the lamp-lit
dirty river

DeLiza race away from Waterloo
at night
She run she clutch she hotel key real tight:
DeLiza shaken from the speculation
on The Empire and The Crown:

> Them that will not kiss the family
> like as not to kill
> the strangers that they meet

DeLiza and the TV News

DeLiza watch one hostage then
she watch two hostage
then she think it must be
she descend

from something like that
only some may call it slavery and
a middle passage

DeLiza say you call it
what you want to
she think
the original hostage
holocaust kill some 22 million
African hostage
so they die

And somebody real popular
have high-jack that history
to this very day

Sometimes DeLiza

Sometimes DeLiza
she forget about location
and she wondering what to do
to make she Black self
just a little more
conspicuous

(She thinking
maybe she wear pink
or smoke a pipe)

But when she realize
she altogether in New Hampshire
not
The Planet

Then
DeLiza laugh out loud

War and Memory

Dedicated to Jane Creighton

I

Daddy at the stove or sink. Large
knife nearby or artfully
suspended by his clean hand handsome
even in its menace
slamming the silverware drawer
open and shut/the spoons
suddenly loud as the yelling
at my mother
no (she would say) no
Granville no
about: would he
be late/had she
hidden away the Chinese laundry shirts
again/did she think
it right that he (a man in his own house)
should serve himself a cup of tea a plate
of food/perhaps she thought that he
should cook the cabbage and the pot roast
for himself
as well?
It sure did seem she wanted him to lose
his job because she could not find
the keys
he could not find
and no (she would attempt to disagree)
no Granville no
but was he
trying to destroy her with his mouth
"My mouth?!" my daddy hunkered down
incredulous and burly now
with anger, "What you mean, 'My mouth'?! You, woman!
    Who
you talk to in that way?

I am master of this castle!" Here
he'd gesture with a kitchen fork
around the sagging clutter
laugh and choke the rage tears
watering his eyes: "You no to speak to me
like that: You hear?
You damn Black woman!"
And my mother
backing up or hunching smaller
than frail bones should easily allow
began to munch on saltine
crackers
let the flat crumbs scatter on her full lips
and the oilcloth
on the table

"You answer me!" he'd scream, at last:
"I speak to you. You answer me!"
And she might struggle then
to swallow
or to mumble finally out loud:
"And who are you supposed to be? The Queen
of England? Or the King?"
And he
berserk with fury lifted
chair or frying pan
and I'd attack
in her defense: "No
Daddy! No!" rushing for his knees
and begging, "Please
don't, Daddy, please!"
He'd come down hard: My head
break into daylight pain
or rip me spinning crookedly across the floor.
I'd match him fast
for madness
lineage in wild display
age six

my pigtails long enough to hang me
from the ceiling
I would race about for weaponry
another chair a knife
a flowered glass
the radio
"You stop it, Daddy! Stop it!"
brandishing my arsenal
my mother
silently
beside the point.
He'd seize me or he'd duck the glass
"You devil child!
You damn Black devil child!"
"And what are you supposed to be?"
My mother might inquire
from the doorway:
"White? Are you supposed to be a white man
Granville?"
"Not white, but right!" And I would have to bite and kick
or race away
sometimes out the house and racing
still for blocks
my daddy chasing
after me

                2

Daddy at the table reading
all about the Fiji Islanders or childhood
in Brazil
his favorite National Geographic research
into life beyond our
neighborhood
my mother looking into
the refrigerator
"Momma!" I cried, after staring at the front page
photo of The Daily News.

"What's this a picture of?"
It was Black and White,
But nothing else. No people
and no houses anywhere. My mother
came and took a look above my shoulder.
"It's about the Jews": she said.
"The Jews?"
"It's not! It's more about those Nazis!" Daddy
interjected.
"No, Granville, no!
It's about the Jews. In the war going on,"
my mother amplified, "the German soldiers
take away the Jewish families and they make
them march through snow until they die!"
"What kind of an ignorant
woman are you?" Daddy shouted out, "It's
not the snow. It's Nazi camps: the concentration
camps!"
"The camps?" I asked them, eagerly: "The Nazis?"
I was quite confused, "But in this picture,
Daddy, I can't see nobody."
"*Any*body," he corrected me: "You can't see
anybody!" "Yes, but what," I persevered, "what is this a
picture of?"
"That's the trail of blood left by the Jewish girls
and women on the snow because the Germans
make them march so long."
"Does the snow make feet bleed, Momma?
Where does the bleeding come from?"

My mother told me I should put away
the papers and not continue to upset myself
about these things I could not understand
and I remember
wondering if my family was a war
going on
and if
there would soon be blood

someplace in the house
and where
the blood of my family would come from

3

The Spanish Civil War:
I think I read about that one.

4

Joan DeFreitas /2 doors up
she latched onto a soldier
fat cat bulging at the belt
and he didn't look like Hollywood
said he should
so I couldn't picture him defending
me or anyone
but then I couldn't picture war or North
Korea
at that time

5

There was TV
There were buses down to Washington, D.C.
You could go and meet your friends
from everywhere.
It was very exciting.
The tear gas burned like crazy.
The President kept lying to us.
Crowd counts at the rallies.
Body counts on the news.
Ketchup on the steps of universities.
Blood on the bandages around the head of the Vietnamese
women shot between the eyes.
Big guys.

Aerial spray missions.
Little people
Shot at close range
"Hell no! We won't go!"
"Hell no! We won't go!"
Make love
Kill anything that moves.
Kent State.
American artillery unlimited at Jackson State
Who raised these devil children?
Who invented these Americans with pony
tails and Afros and tee shirts and statistical
arguments against the mining of the harbors
of a country far away?

And I remember turning from the footage of the tat-tat-tat-
tat-tat-tat
helicopters
and I wondered how democracy would travel from the graves
at Kent State
to the hidden trenches
of Hanoi

6

Plump during The War on Poverty
I remember making pretty good
money (6 bucks an hour)
as a city planner and my former
husband married my best
friend and I was never positive
about the next month's rent but
once I left my son sitting
on his lunchbox in the early rain
waiting for a day-care pickup and I went
to redesign low-income housing for the Lower
East Side of Manhattan and three hours after that
I got a phone call from my neighbors
that the pickup never came

that Christopher was waiting
on the sidewalk
in his yellow slicker
on his lunchbox
in the rain.

7

I used to sometimes call the government
to tell them how many parents
ate real butter or stole sugar
from The Victory Rations
we received

I sometimes called the Operator
asking for Police
to beat my father up for beating me
so bad
but no one listened to
a tattletale
like me:

I think I felt relieved
because the government didn't send a rescue
face or voice to my imagination
and I hated
the police
but what else could you do?

Peace never meant a thing to me.

I wanted everyone to mold
the plastic bag for margarine
save stamps
plant carrots
and
(imitating Joe "Brown Bomber" Louis)
fight hard

fight fair
And from the freedom days
that blazed outside my mind
I fell in love
I fell in love with Black men White
men Black
women White women
and I
dared myself to say The Palestinians
and I
worried about unilateral words like Lesbian or Nationalist
and I
tried to speak Spanish when I traveled to Managua
and I
dreamed about The Fourteenth Amendment
and I
defied the hatred of the hateful everywhere
as best I could
I mean
I took long nightly walks to emulate the Chinese Revolutionaries
and I
always wore one sweater less than absolutely necessary to keep
    warm

and I wrote everything I knew how to write against apartheid
and I
thought I was a warrior growing up
and I
buried my father with all of the ceremony all of the music I
    could piece together
and I
lust for justice
and I
make that quest arthritic/pigeon-toed/however
and I
invent the mother of the courage I require not to quit

from *Haruko/Love Poems*

dedicated to love

New Year

For Haruko

Here comes the dragon!
Here comes the dog!
Here comes the monkey!
Here comes the apple tree!
Here come the apples!
Here come the acolytes!
Here comes the church!
Here come the shoes!
Here comes the drum!
Here comes the rain!
Here come the blues!
Here comes the shark!
Here comes the head!
Here comes the tail!
Here come dumplings in a little tin pail!
Here comes the snow!
Here come the cows!
Here come the clowns!
Here comes the hill!
Here comes the pearl!
Here come the waves!
Here comes the bread!
Here comes the call!

Here comes the dragon!
Here comes the dog!
Here come the apples!
Here come the acolytes!
Here comes the church!
Here come the shoes!

For Haruko

Little moves on sight
blinded by histories
as trivial or expansive
as the rain
seducing light
into a blurred excitement

Then
she opens
all of one eye
as accurate as longing
as two hands beholden to the hunger of green leaves

and
rinsing them back
into regular breath
she who sees
she frees each of these
beggarly events
cleansing them
of dust and other death

Poem for Haruko

I never thought I'd keep a record of my pain
or happiness
like candles lighting the entire soft lace
of the air
around the full length of your hair/a shower
organized by God
in brown and auburn
undulations luminous like particles
of flame

But now I do
retrieve an afternoon of apricots
and water interspersed with cigarettes
and sand and rocks
we walked across:
                How easily you held
my hand
beside the low tide
of the world

Now I do
relive an evening of retreat
a bridge I left behind
where all the solid heat
of lust and tender trembling
lay as cruel and as kind
as passion spins its infinite
tergiversations in between the bitter
and the sweet

Alone and longing for you
now I do

12:01 A.M.

                For Haruko

        I

Rushing like white
waters rapid toward precipitous
and killer rocks
the blood of time alone
escapes control and leaking
useless
dries and quantifies
the liquid loss of impulse

purified by any of your fingertips
that touch my face

2

The rain does not become a clock
does not become the rain

3

Thinking about chocolate
I woke up
and tried to move
but where you kept me
nipples and the milk
of mystery bestirred the mouth
of my imagination

4

Forget about fever
Forget about healthy or unhealthy
this or that
At times
the flesh below the thin skin
of your naked leg
seems to my pilgrim lips
a living column smooth but swollen
with the juice of my new
destiny

5

Then how should I
subsist
without the benediction of our bodies
intertwined
or why?

6

Somebody else might think I mean
the epiderm the tissues
and the cells
that matter into tangible configurations
only

7

I am my soul adrift
the whole night sky denies me light
without you

"Why I became a pacifist"

Why I became a pacifist
and then
How I became a warrior again:

Because nothing I could do or say
turned out okay
I figured I should just sit
still and chill
except to maybe mumble
"Baby, Baby:
Stop!"
AND
Because turning that other cheek
        holding my tongue
        refusing to retaliate when the deal
        got ugly
And because not throwing whoever calls me *bitch*
        out the goddamn window
And because swallowing my pride
        saying I'm sorry when whoever don't like
        one single thing

about me and don't never take a break from
counting up the 65,899 ways I talk wrong
I act wrong
And because sitting on my fist
neglecting to enumerate every incoherent
rigid/raggedy-ass/disrespectful/killer cold
and self-infatuated crime against love
committed by some loudmouth don't know
nothing about it takes 2 to fuck and
it takes 2 to fuck things up
And because making apologies that nobody give a shit
about

and because failing to sing my song

finally
finally

got on my absolute last nerve

I pick up my sword
I lift up my shield
And I stay ready for war
Because now I live ready for a whole lot more

than that

"*"CLEAN!"*"

"CLEAN!"
you spelled out: "Make it"/"Break it
clean!"
But you meant <u>mean</u>
as in

mean
hard
gone

like how you done me

      mean
      hard
      gone
      hard

      done

Update

For Haruko

More than two months since a carousel of misery
accursed and violent ensnared my mind and
spinning me vertiginous in solitude and
alternating trustful lust with lyrical delirium
or pain irregular as drought or rain
crushed out the flowering of surprise and still today drains
all the colors of the world into the pointless
pulverizing dry bed of a dried up hand

So I arrive a neophyte to unconditional
and passionate but passive vigil undercut
by flares of anger or despair that at the last
subside to core forbidden appetite for cigarettes or food
especially Chinese to take out/not too spicy
hot but what I need means hot and shrimp fried
rice becomes three boxed up coals of fire
I hold as close as possible against this wistful skin
this frozen covering for all my love

Still I am learning unconditional and true
Still I am burning unconditional for you

Poem about Process and Progress

For Haruko

Hey Baby you betta
hurry it up!
Because
since you went totally
off
I seen a full moon
I seen a half moon
I seen a quarter moon
I seen no moon whatsoever!

I seen a equinox
I seen a solstice
I seen Mars and Venus on a line
I seen a mess a fickle stars
and lately
I seen this new kind a luva
on an' off the telephone
who like to talk to me
all the time

real nice

Resolution #1,003

I will love who loves me
I will love as much as I am loved
I will hate who hates me
I will feel nothing for everyone oblivious to me

I will stay indifferent to indifference
I will live hostile to hostility
I will make myself a passionate and eager lover
    in response to passionate and eager love

I will be nobody's fool

A Poem for Haruko 10/29

because
it's about my anger
smoldering
because your stillness
kills simplicity
and chills
this willing ardor
swept back
into realms of doubt
and ordinary feats
of regular and unimpassioned
sensible retreat
wherein an ending to my love
for you
will stretch its scaly
full length into light
that shrivels
innocence
and warps the silent mouth
of adoration
into bitten
blighted
bloom
Oh! If you would only walk
into this room
again and touch me anywhere
I swear

I would not long for heaven or
for earth
more than I'd wish to stay there
touched
and touching you

"Admittedly"

Admittedly
I do not forget
the beauty of one braid
black silk that fell
as loose as it fell long
and everlasting as the twilight
anywhere

"Boats afloat"

Boats afloat
Kayaks capsizing
A skyhawk falling asleep
Wind chimes murmuring into the atmosphere
and high above this peaceful
house
a 90 year old willow tree
sucks on the sunlight
with a thousand toothless leaves
and what do I care
if I never will hear your fast
words slurring
near to my eager ears
again

Taiko Dōjō

Messages from Haruko

No! No!
No. No. No. No.
No! No!
No. No. No. No.
No-No-No-No/No-No-No-No/No-No-No-No
No-No-No-No
No! No!
No. No. No. No.
No! No!
No. No. No. No.
No-No-No-No/No-No-No-No
No-No-No-No
No! No!
No-No-No-No
No! No!

NO!

Poem about Heartbreak That Go On and On

bad love last like a big
ugly lizard crawl around the house
forever
never die
and never change itself

into a butterfly

Speculations on the Present Through the Prism of the Past

For Haruko

At 29
I climbed on a motorcycle
for my first date
with this guy in front of me
my arms around his waist
as tight as my excitement
my chin nestling on a soft spot
in between his shoulder blades

Zoom!
We just took off:
French bread
and a bottle of French wine
my keys
him and me and the bike

We left
after he said, "This –"
(meaning my house/my life)
"is just impossible! It's just too
bare! Too poor!"
And so he carried me and the bike
into the unfamiliar darkness of his opulence his city his
apartment his gigantic bed/he
locked me up/he
kept me well fed/absolutely
clean
and (in general) well satisfied
on the sexual side
but scared to say anything
about the 25 foot leather whip
memento from his military duties
in Algiers

that he uncoiled from time
to time
nostalgic

Through the routine eucalyptus fragrance of his rooms
Through the river-view windows of his paradise
I watched for tail-light jewels on a nearby evening bridge

And I supposed that something
beautiful
might be waiting for me not
too far away
but definitely not
on this side/definitely not
on my side
of the water

Poem for Haruko

All day I did things fast
picking up leaves
scrubbing a saucepan clean
racing through an Asian American anthology
of poems
All because it hurt so much
to think about you hurt
because
I moved so slowly
and in circles
seemingly insensible
to how you held a towel
wide as your slender arms are long
to fold around me
shivering from the bathtub
how you held a children's story
close to my almost closing eyelids

how you held me
free
as I could ever hope
to be

Ichiban

Good bye.

> I do not choose
> to collaborate
> and lose
> the golden blues' delirium
> in this and that
> cynical or reckless
> rat-a-tat tat-tat-tat
> chit-chat
>
> ICHIBAN

Good bye.

> I take back my
> body tractable and loaded up for bliss
> I take back my
> mind become inebriate and apostolic to desire
> I take back my
> heart beating to the intimations of your lips
> I take back my
> spirit riveted in fire
>
> ICHIBAN

Good bye.

Phoenix Mystery #1

The thing about fire
is every kind of moving
light
but the fever that enflames
the blood
ignites the air itself
between two stones
and lifts the world
into a crackling and molecular display
as complicated and seductive
as apocalypse
or else the bated/risen breath
surrendering to the deep
insistence
of uncommon
sexual bliss

The thing about fire
is not unlike all tragedy
that leads you to the house
and takes your hat
your coat
your shoes
and then begins a simmering
destruction of the floor the walls
the ceilings and the door
become a crematorium
a furnace burying the sky
beyond
a mountainous volcanic cloud consumes
the oxygen the photographs
of daily life eternal
as the lover
who survives to search the ashes
for what's hot

a bone chip charred
but irreducible among the burning ruins

Phoenix Mystery #2

For Haruko

The thing about fire
is
ashes in a supermarket
paper bag
but then
you see smoke
rising hot
and serious (and imperious)
again

Postscript for Haruko: On War and Peace

How still these oak and maple trees stand
side by side in slowly melting snow
Not one attacks or seeks incineration
for the other. Not even mysteries of birds
that missed the last sure flight to safety
interject disturbance of this winter
night when patience seems as natural
as the cold air holding all that's there
serene and lifted by a star's light
as specific in its glitter as it's far.

So do we finally outlive the flare and flash
of flame and leaf and feathers violent
as waves that rise because they also fall
away and falling call the waters of the world
one name again.

So do we finally recover side by side
what we have loved enough to keep
in spite of passion or love's sorrow.

"Haruko:"

"Haruko:
Oh! It's like <u>stringbean</u> in French?"

"No:
It's like <u>hurricane</u>
in English!"

Big City Happening

For Haruko

Try exquisite in the New York concept of these tracks
below the subway
platform
far below the sidewalk
concrete
perforated/tricky
mica fireworks
that scatter microscopic
on the almost rising surface
of the street

And I do.
I ride these tracks to meet you:
moving through/an upright register
of shadow and of light
moving through
eclectic ganglia of open cities/nervous
nowhere immaculate nowhere a mystery

to match this urban earthquake traveling
stop by stop
into reunion
with the highway wonder
of your eyes

Poem on the Quantum Mechanics of Breakfast with Haruko

Sutter and Stockton/one block North of Union Square
less than a week ago
seemed simple to me/we
were there

And easy as that San Francisco morning
you ate
memories of Paris
from a plate of sliced papaya
thick
buttered toast
and sent strong current
sidelong glances
towards the handsome white man
(white shirt/no tie)
sitting
possibly oblivious
behind you

One block north of Union Square
but what is union
anyway
or union squared
or North
as I am flying East to London
now
above the secrets of the raw

intractable
blue waters of the blue
Atlantic

and I still stay
willing inches away from your hand
almost too small
to lift the thick
crisp
buttered toast
into the not quite neutral
air
between us

Mendocino Memory

For Haruko

Half moon
cold and low above the poplar tree
and sweet pea petals
pink and white/what
happened
on this personal best night
for casual stars
and silky constellations
streaming brilliant
through the far
forgetful darkness
of the sky

I found the other half
above the pillow
where you lay
asleep
face to one side
with nothing in this world

or the next
to hide

Letter to Haruko from Decorah, Iowa, U.S.A.

In this white space this American
page of immigration from three months
of darkness in Norway/hunger
unrelieved by sun or flowerlight
or playful ambulations through an easy
day
I stand beside a stranger
ice and snow stretched pale for miles
behind me
village streets bare/no
trees/pedestrians/dogs/or shadow
on the hard brick of the local
will to persevere
to stay until the whisperings of spring arrive
to marry
to bake bread
to break a window out of solid log
cabin walls that wheeze with winter
inescapable

A stranger points to handicrafts
traditional
in hand-hewn pine and homemade paints
that sanctify a bed a chair a bowl
with hours of devotion
agitant against a loneliness as unmistakable
as thirst or sex
and I am taken by these florid
refutations of a frozen near horizon
brilliant tokens of a flesh soft loom that held
some woman's sanity together

raveling intelligence
like thread that magical
became a cloth
of loving color

And I am straining to converge
this pain
midwestern/fasting stand of oak trees
quiet as they ramify
in such thin air
with your true
handheld miracles of rain
your expert
California camera capturing
a lush a sudden deluge
from an otherwise
dry sky

But the roots
for a connection that can keep
Japan and San Francisco
and Jamaica and Decorah
Iowa and Norway
all in one place palpable
to any sweet belief
move deep below
apparent differences of turf

I trace them in the lifetime
of an open palm
a hand that works
its homemade heat
against the jealous
hibernating blindness
of the night

"plum blossom plum jam"

plum blossom plum jam
even the tree becomes something
more than a skeleton
longing for the sky

"First full moon of a new and final decade"

First full moon of a new and final decade
so
we're eating pasta
(with pesto plus garlic)
when
the bell rings
and another one of us
shows up
eats the fettuccine
talks about much maybe
it's love much
maybe
it's not exactly love but
anyhow
the pasta's hot/the wine
goes down
real easily and before you know
it
two bottles stand
side by side and we
head
for the beach in San Francisco
and loud on the car box
it's The Gipsy Kings
and Osa's in the back with binoculars
looking at the tail lights of the truck
in the right lane

(or the bridge lights
or the stars)
and we pass the binoculars around
like marijuana
but the visuals seem
better
so we're laughing as we roll
over the Big Bay
and speeding
while each one of us imagines what
romance would look like
through binoculars
(Binocular Romance)
which reminds me
I'm not sure
about the color of your eyes
then
we turn left to find
the Pacific Ocean
and the sand
and the almighty all night
full moon
that begins the end of a whole lot
and I'm thinking
where am I
where are you
and the ocean agitates
the slumber of my curiosity:
Cross currents
slash into the shallow surf
curls of these high tide waters
and the tides dissolve in dizzy
disarray
and how the soft air will accept the breathing
of my timid witness
warm
and restless in the dark
confinement of a moon

as radiant
as imperative
as this lyrical retrieval
of your smile
three thousand miles
away

"I train my eyes to see"

I train my eyes to see
what I am suffering
not to touch

late afternoon and the air
dissolves to luminous and elongated
molecules
a heartfelt mercury as delicate
as compelling
as the melted movements
of your lips

This must be the longitudinal
anatomy of rain

this cosmic commotion twice
bestirred by the exact
infinitesimal
assertions of your body's
dance

These must be the subterranean
beginnings of all light

These shimmer surfaces
that glow arterial below the frosted rooftops
and the thick

surrender of the open
trusted
trees
And like the stars
above the dark far streets
between us
heat
develops into liquid
documents of fire
and there
and here
moving through these beautiful waters
you and I
become the river

Kissing God Goodbye

$$4 \quad y^2$$

and

4   The Student Poet Revolutionaries
Alegría Barclay
Xochi Candelaria
Gary Chandler
Erwin Cho-Woods
Emily Derr
Jill Guerra
Rana Halpern
Dima Hilal
Aaron Jefferis
David Keiser
John Koo
Marisa Loeffen
Belinda Lyons
Maiana Minahal
Alison Peters
Laine Proctor
Marcos Ramírez
Shelly Teves
Marina Wilson
and
Debbie Walker (Datbu)
and
Junichi Semitsu

With my forever love and faith

Poem for a Young Poet

Dedicated to Erwin Cho-Woods
May 27, 1997

Most people search all
of their lives
for someplace to belong to
as you said
but I look instead
into the eyes of anyone
who talks to me

I search for a face
to believe and belong to
a loosening mask
with a voice
ears
and a consciousness
breathing through
a nose
I can see

Day to day
it's the only way
I like to travel
noticing the colors of a cheek
the curvature of brow
and the public declarations
of two lips

Okay!
I did not say male
or female
I did not say Serbian
or Tutsi
I said
what tilts my head

into the opposite of fear
or dread
is anyone
who talks to me

A face
to claim or question
my next step away
or else towards

fifteen anemones
dilated well beyond apologies
for such an open centerpiece
that soft
forever begs for bees

one morning
and the birdsong and the dew-
struck honeysuckle blending
invitations to dislodge
my fingers tangling with my sunlit
lover's hair

A face
to spur or interdict
my mesmerized approach
or else
my agonized reproach

to strangulations of the soul
that bring a mother
to disown
her children
leaving them alone to feed
on bone and dust

A face
despite a corpse

invasion of the cradle
where I rock my love
alive

A face
despite numb fashions
of an internet connection between nobody
and no one

A face
against the narcoleptic/antiseptic
chalk streaks
in the sky
that lie
and posit credit cards
and starched de facto exposés
as copacetic evidence
that you and I
need no defense
against latrine
and bully bullet-proof decisions
launched by limousines
dividing up the big screen
into gold points
cold above the valley
of the shadow of unpardonable
tiny
tiny
tiny
this breathing and that breath
and then
that and that
that death

I search a face
a loosening mask
with voice
ears

and a consciousness
breathing through
a nose
that I can see

I search a face
for obstacles to genocide
I search beyond the dead
and
driven by imperfect visions
of the living
yes and no
I come and go
back to the eyes
of anyone
who talks to me

November Poem for Alegría: 1996

I have seen concrete
disintegrate
under the weight of water

I have seen stone and steel
yield
to students
civil
disobedient
and fasting
and lasting
open to the rain

And goodbye to the men
and goodbye to the women
angry at the wind
frightened by the bright light
horrified by strangers

Goodbye!
Goodbye!

I have heard
the tender speaking
of many tongues

I have heard
the breaking voice beg

Here ends civility
Now we know the strategy of stars
continuous
exempt from tinkering
and beyond numerical reduction

Now we know the strategy of trees
that flourish
roots protected or exposed
above the famished
or the flooded
earth
and lifting
always
lifting up the air
itself

No more polishing of pain!

Here ends surrender:

I have seen the face
of every promise from the sun

I have seen the bestial
kneel
beside the bodies of young poets

standing
in your tears

What Great Grief Has Made the Empress Mute

N.Y. Times headline

Dedicated to the Empress Michiko and to Janice Mirikitani

Because it was raining outside the palace
Because there was no rain in her vicinity

Because people kept asking her questions
Because nobody ever asked her anything

Because marriage robbed her of her mother
Because she lost her daughters to the same tradition

Because her son laughed when she opened her mouth
Because he never delighted in anything she said

Because romance carried the rose inside a fist
Because she hungered for the fragrance of the rose

Because the jewels of her life did not belong to her
Because the glow of gold and silk disguised her soul

Because nothing she could say could change the melted music of
     her space
Because the privilege of her misery was something she could not
     disgrace

Because no one could imagine reasons for her grief
Because her grief required no imagination

Because it was raining outside the palace
Because there was no rain in her vicinity

Argument with the Buddha

Dedicated to Shelly Teves
2/15/96, Berkeley

We agree
about the suffering
disease
decrepitude
and incremental
death

or
nobody hold the child
nobody bless the scar
nobody change the meaning
of the land
        the regular
insensibility of trying to farm
the rocks
        trying to beg a meal
from shadow offerings
of your body
        trying to reduce the craziness
of motion without trace

We disagree
about desire

I own a whole address book
full of names and numbers
I no longer care about
and the moral of that story
        contradicts (in sum)
The wisdom of whoever forgets
to want somebody else
alive and troublesome
despite the slide

towards sleep
I need new names!

And I have never done one single thing
for 49 days straight
much less to sit myself beneath some tree
And no one entertains
me
with ten thousand dancing
girls/
a feast of fruit and fresh
killed
curry lamb
or jewels strewn across my table
top

So I renounce
renunciation!

This hand that writes
and waits
and writes and waits
again
These ears that listen
for the rain
or wind that catapults
the tree
into a standing hazard

ignorant of roots

I choose and cherish
all that will perish
The living deal
The balance of my bliss
with pain

excites my soul

perhaps to no enlightenment
but

rather than transcend
what makes me ache

I hope to fend
off enemies
and bend with
lovers
endlessly

I choose
anything
anyone
I may lose

I renounce
renunciation

I breathe
head to head
with suffering

and after that

nothing
for sure

merry-go-round poetry

For one second there
you laid your face against
the brass
support on which the earth
turned high and low

a carousel of horse and rider
in electrical affinity
and I saw
that pole become like melted gold
impressionable and precious
from that momentary contact
with the reckless
question
of your cheek
and I knew the music of your rising
through the air
would not subside
or disappear

Lebanon
Lebanon

Dedicated to the people of Lebanon and to Laura

I

Faces I have never seen before
language I have never heard
before
        between me
        and the enemy
the difference blurred
by blood
dried
only yesterday

(I would have loved to walk beside the sand
the turquoise water
tickling at the fingers of my idle
hand)

this amputation of my tongue
this clotted artery that starts
a fatal stuttering

this massacre
I photograph
the withered aftermath
the oozing consequence
the swollen stump
the burned out cranial configuration
of a 6 year old
recovering
from abrupt incineration
of her dress her hair
her plastic daisy bracelet singed
into a 3rd degree
tattoo
       do I exaggerate?
or not
recovering

and shrunken to a charcoal
junked life shifted
into shadows
upon shadows of the shadows
fire borne
the lasting flash
outlasts
the leaking
scar
become
a relic
of its breathing
minimum

Or how shall I collect
the rubble of the landscape/
flesh smell
on the floor

or cave containers
of the throat

that livid
howls
a huge hole
in the house wall
fallen loose
the left
leg blown away
below
the howling
livid
knee
or how will I begin
to guarantee a denudation
to the bone of knowing
from
the meat of bodies
of the howling
livid
one eye
shot to pieces
two eyes
shot to pieces
of the meat
of the shattering
of the rain
of the bodies
howling
livid

how

2

I would have loved
I would
I would
I would have
            water of one glass

passing
hand to hand
the ceremony of the stacked-up
photos of the no more
no more mother no
more mother's
mother's
son
no father no
more no
more
from one to twenty four
no more no
village family
still
alive

I would have loved
I would
I would
I would have
          touched the buttons of his shirt
          traced my longing light
          along his shoulders

how
does he survive

this hospital
this public bed
these daily saviors
without name
          his bearded face
          as beautiful
          as hushed
          his everlasting tilted
          stare
          as liquid

as deliberate
as deep

as what will he
never say

as what will he
never see

again

without that blasted
limb
exploded from its socket

blasted
taken without anesthesia
or amnesia

I would have loved
I would
I would
I would have loved
        what he will never see
        again

   3
As usual
I have to ask
where's Jesus
when you need him

The miracle of water into wine's
just fine
but what about
a miracle of blood

delivering a river
we can drink

4

behold the woolly lamb
beside the children
shivering
in shock

behold the refugees
aroused by soap
and blankets
(maybe
blankets)

behold a people
lost inside the landscape
that belongs to them
behold a landscape
taken by the fiend
of force

5

How do you evacuate
a country?

offshore
the gunboats have begun
the shelling
of the highway
and the houses

above
the orange groves
the F-16s drop
death

and from a balding hilltop
only eyeball meters
distant from a field
of rusted car parts
dissolute among wild
flowers
trusting all that color from the sun
artillery
destroys the heated laughter
of another
lost
civilian afternoon

Lebanon
Lebanon

the mountain of the people of the mountain

Lebanon
Lebanon

the cedar trees forever foraging the air
for earth for space
for non-negotiable longevity

Lebanon
Lebanon

the sea refusing to recede
the open sky that will not blink
the wailing of the soul that does not sleep
the worry beads that spell
    apocalypse specific to this man
    this woman

Lebanon
Lebanon

the 12 year old who sings aloud
to calm the other children
terrified by murder

Here do I discover
the humility
the miracle of suffering
without surrender
the miracle of suffering
without defeat

Short Takes

1

Somebody works up a sweat
in the vineyard
I drive by

2

I am not your East Coast weather
cyclical
and always coming
back
in your direction

3

Those grapes!
Growing in such straight rows!
Who will savor
the smell and the flavor
(the madness)
of all that wine!

4

Leaves loosening lost
your or my eyes turned away
this spiral spins slow

Sometimes Clarity Comes in the Dark

I turn my body to the side
where formerly you lay
asleep
or whispering
or hot
where you are not
now
or ever
close
to me

Poem After Receiving Voicemail from You After (*I Don't Even Know Anymore*) How Long!

Your voice and the weighted
stammering between us
evident
and the train of my routine
adjustment to nothing anywhere
as unforgettable
as your bare feet on the flagstone
pathway
next to bunched up honeysuckle
blooming aromatic in the A.M.
of a daily life
we shared but never dared
to lock and key

into
our problematic/
intersection –
That train derailed/my
regular defenses failed
to lower the volume
of the million and one
or zero
meanings
of your call

Tanka Trio

1

Fallen on the street
Black woman wrestling with air
Bloody hair and teeth
No small change in her pockets
Big change always pass her by

2

El campesino
stoops all day above the dirt
strawberries flourish
strange wages for sweat and strain
Darkness cover him with rain

3

What I need right now
after the rising water
What I need right now
after the pounding collapse
body surf a new wave fast

Ghaflah

In Islam, *Ghaflah* refers to the sin of forgetfulness

Grief scrapes at my skin
she never
"Be a big girl!"
wanted to touch
much
except to disinfect
or bandage

I acknowledge nothing

I forget the mother of my hurt
her innocence of pride
her suicide

That first woman

lowered eyes
folded hands
withered limbs
among the plastic flowers
rhinestone bracelets
eau de toilette
trinkets from slow
compromise

Where did she go?

After swallowing fifteen/twenty/thirty-five pills
she tried to rise
and rising
froze
forever trying to arise
from compromise

And I do not remember finding her
like that
half seated half
almost standing up
just dead
by her own hand
just dead

I do not remember finding her
like that

I forget the burned toast/
spinach
cold eggs
taste-free tuna fish
and thin spread peanut butter
sandwiches
she left for me

I erase
the stew the soup
she cooked and carried
everywhere
to neighbors

I forget three or four other things
I cannot recall
how many pairs of pretty shoes
how many dressup overcoats
I saved my nickels
dimes and quarters
all year long
to buy
at Christmas time
to give to her
my mother
she

the one who would wear nothing
beautiful

Or how I strut
beside her walking anywhere
prepared for any lunatic
assault
upon her shuffling
journey
to a bus stop

I acknowledge nothing

I forget she taught me
how to pray
I forget her prayers
And mine

I do not remember
kneeling down
to ask for wisdom
high-top sneakers
or linoleum chips
to animate
my zip gun

I have never remembered
the blistering fury
the abyss
into which
I capsized
after her last
compromise

I wish I had found her
that first woman
my mother

trying to rise
up

I wish I had given her
my arm

both arms

I have never forgiven her
for going away

But I don't remember anything

Grief scrapes at my skin
she never
"Be a big girl!"
wanted to touch
much

Haiku for the Would-Be Killers of a Teacher

Dedicated to Janet Hill

You cut down that tree
Tore off the new leaves and left
Roots to bless that dirt

Bridget Song #1

Late in the day and near
a growing edge of redwood
trees
and following a solitary
trail
I saw you/fern

ravine nirvana
passing by

but then you changed
direction
and came back
to walk with me

and I will never be
the same

Before you knew my name
I knew
nobody treads the earth
as close
as light
as you

And I am turned around
because
the ceremony of your movement
slides along
the shadow of a shining
sound

Study #1

Let me be
very
very
very
very
very
specific

Let me not forget about
or

Let me not forget about
anything like
anything like
an eyelash
lost above your lips

When the President says no to legislation
to make cocaine more criminal like crack
or crack less criminal like cocaine
so that white men as well as black
get nailed for jail

When the President says no
When the President says no
When the President says no to Fidel Castro
When the President talks about Human Rights
and moral guiding lights and then
The President says yes
to a total mess of multi-multi-
millionfold
marketplace
potentate
Toms and Dicks and Harrys and then
And then when the President
says no to Fidel Castro

Let me be
very
very
very
very
very
specific

The criminal inertia
The criminal morality of inertia
The criminal morality of inertia nothing
nothing

nothing
not even the junked baby tied to the chair
not even the smashed face woman
  dragged through the house by
    what's left of her hair

nothing
nothing
interdicts
the criminal inertia
of suit and tie/
or my
complacency

Nothing
Nothing
Not even the beautiful man
parking my car or
sweeping the airport terminal floor
only because so far no
robot can
absolutely replace a beautiful man
while unemployment and huge profits rise
amid official spokesmanly lies
about the no jobs future
we're definitely due for

Nothing
Nothing interdicts
the criminal inertia
of suit and tie
or my
complacency

Or let me not forget
Or let me not forget about 2 miles
below my house
a train moves

moaning through the night
(I said:) 2 miles below my house
a train moves
moaning through the night

Let me be
very
very
very
very
very
specific
Now that the U.S. Congress agrees
That nobody American
has a right to anything besides
acute emotional
      physical
      and economic
      anxieties

Let me be
very
very
very
very
very
specific

Let me not forget about
or
Let me not forget about
anything like
anything like
an eyelash
lost above your lips

(please baby please)

The Eclipse of 1996

Everybody out of the house!
Everybody up on the roof!
Run to the top of the street!
Pull back the branches of the trees!
Abandon all cars!
Do you hear me?
Bring the children!
Carry your babies into the night!
THE LIGHT'S ABOUT TO GO OUT!
We've finally managed to shut down the shining of the moon!

And you wouldn't want
to miss that

wouldya?

Message from Belfast

For Justice and for Gerry Adams

At 4 A.M.
I imagine you somewhere safe
and sunny
and I pray that you stay there
far away from here
where I watch for the daring
of dawn and men
again on these dangerous
streets
way below the window
of my lovely most-blown-up-hotel-
in-Europe
room
where I pace with cigarettes

and a useless telephone
trying to last through the night

From half a mile away
I see
that stacked slum
high-rise
concrete monstrosity
where Catholic families
crumble from a cruel
chronic surveillance
exercised
by British teenage soldiers
spilling loose on the sidewalk
assault rifles cocked
while they stalk backwards
into plastic toys and tricycles
and children
blown apart
the papers say
by accident

And in-between my untouched bed
and the kitchen chaos
of such incendiary
occupation
I see
railroad tracks but no trains
I see
one highway overpass
carrying no traffic
I smell blood
but I see
none of the bodies
buried close to each other
father/brother
son

This afternoon
the car grew dark before my eyes
and I looked up and up and up
into the towering
effrontery of a British tank
parked
killer casual
across the corner of a street
of homes so humble
this one intrusion
smashed the sanctuary purpose
of the neighborhood
I began to eat my notes
I began to make comparisons to police
in Harlem or the Nicaragua contras
I began to stop bothering about comparisons
I began to count each close and opening of my eyes
each proof of breath not death
        among my friends
        not one of us
        shot down
        dragged out and beaten
        or "detained"
        indefinitely
        without charge
        or tortured
        without recourse
        for however long some military sadist
        might find imperial
        abuse
        amusing

I thought, "This might be it –
(around and behind
ubiquitous combat boots
a foreign Army flagrant
with
its lockstep slur in front of church

or posing on a housing project
wall with SLR and SA-80 semi-
automatic rifles
eager
to go off –
This heavy thread through heavy terror
for a secret cup
of tea
and hands across an oilcloth covered
tabletop)
This might be it"

And listening to the stories
and the songs
of all my comrades
bickering/hilarious and loud
and anticipating (any
minute) the explosion
that would blast
our whole thing
into a statistical
addition
to "The Troubles"

I thought
This has always been
the deal: The danger
The derogation of my image of my gods
The enemy invasion
The tank on the cobblestone
The tip of the bayonet puncturing your skin
The bullet longing for your very best flesh

Well
it rained for 20 minutes
and a rainbow
gorged its colors from the gun gray weather
of this Irish no-man's zone

This city is so small
You could never murder anybody
by mistake
And there is not a playground to be found
for all the babies
– Only War –

I am afraid to fall
asleep
but I am proud
to stand before the morning
breaks
awake with no one near
and with my conscience clear
for once
I am completely where
I ought to be

In the city
of Belfast
I have lost and found myself
at home

Letter to Mrs. Virginia Thomas, Wife of Whatzhisname Lamentably Appointed to the Supreme Court, U.S.A.

And here I thought I hated him!
I mean I thought that he was loathsome to the nth
degree
I saw him as some kinda clown
a first class
colored fool
an Uncle Tom
a Peeping Tom
a creepy eager pornographic Tom

a hypocrite
a liar and a fake
a make-
believe Black man
a mediocre mediocrity of apple polish
brown nose cut-throat
and an insult to his elders
a menace to his peers
a hazard to the under seventeen
a joke
a serious mistake
a cynical disjuncture between race
and history
a cruel interlocutor between the needy
and relief
a bullet to the family
a bully to the female
a pietistic turncoat
and a trivializing renegade
a jerk
a cornball hustler and a trifling no 'count crocodile
a sacrilegious opportunist
and a hitman for the pitiless

But
I'm completely off the track/mistaken/out of line and
off the wall
(it seems)
which brings me to this letter I must write to you:
I write to thank you for your revelation!
I declare
I don't know how
the truth escaped my understanding
I can't explain the blindness that concealed
the facts
from me

But suddenly
I looked at you and Clarence
happy as 2 pods in a poke (or 2 pigs in a pea or
whatever)
on the cover of *People* magazine
and things just clicked
They really did!
I mean like *click:*
I realized you're right
and I been dense and dumb and bigtime
into criminal denial
see
because
I probably was
(as you say) probably I was
in love with Clarence!
Probably I lusted after him/your husband:
Yes I guess
I probably did!
And here I thought I hated him!
But then
you never know:
Sometimes it's awful hard to tell
now isn't it:

You never know!

First Poem after Serious Surgery

The breath continues but the breathing
hurts
Is this the way death wins its way
against all longing
and redemptive thrust from grief?
Head falls
Hands crawl

and pain becomes the only keeper
of my time

I am not held
I do not hold
And touch degenerates into new
agony

I feel
the healing of cut muscle/
broken nerves
as I return to hot and cold
sensations
of a body tortured by the flight
of feeling/normal
registrations of repulsion
or delight

On this meridian of failure or recovery
I move
or stop respectful
of each day
but silent now
and slow

The Bombing of Baghdad

I

began and did not terminate for 42 days
and 42 nights relentless minute after minute
more than 110,000 times
we bombed Iraq we bombed Baghdad
we bombed Basra/we bombed military
installations we bombed the National Museum
we bombed schools we bombed air raid
shelters we bombed water we bombed

electricity we bombed hospitals we
bombed streets we bombed highways
we bombed everything that moved/we
bombed everything that did not move we
bombed Baghdad
a city of 5.5 million human beings
we bombed radio towers we bombed
telephone poles we bombed mosques
we bombed runways we bombed tanks
we bombed trucks we bombed cars we bombed bridges
we bombed the darkness we bombed
the sunlight we bombed them and we
bombed them and we cluster bombed the citizens
of Iraq and we sulfur bombed the citizens of Iraq
and we napalm bombed the citizens of Iraq and we
complemented these bombings/these "sorties" with
Tomahawk cruise missiles which we shot
repeatedly by the thousands upon thousands
into Iraq
(you understand an Iraqi Scud missile
is *quote* militarily insignificant *unquote* and we
do not mess around with insignificant)
so we used cruise missiles repeatedly
we fired them into Iraq
And I am not pleased
I am not very pleased
None of this fits into my notion of "things going very well"

2

The bombing of Baghdad
did not obliterate the distance or the time
between my body and the breath
of my beloved

3
This was Custer's Next-To-Last Stand
I hear Crazy Horse singing as he dies

I dedicate myself to learn that song
I hear that music in the moaning of the Arab world

4

Custer got accustomed to just doing his job
Pushing westward into glory
Making promises
Searching for the savages/their fragile
temporary settlements
for raising children/dancing down the rain/and praying
for the mercy of a herd of buffalo
Custer/he pursued these savages
He attacked at dawn
He murdered the men/murdered the boys
He captured the women and converted
them (I'm sure)
to his religion
Oh, how gently did he bid his darling fiancée
farewell!
How sweet the gaze her eyes bestowed upon her warrior!
Loaded with guns and gunpowder he embraced
the guts and gore of manifest white destiny
He pushed westward
to annihilate the savages
("Attack at dawn!")
and seize their territories
    seize their women
    seize their natural wealth

5

And I am cheering for the arrows
and the braves

6

And all who believed some must die
they were already dead

And all who believe only they possess
human being and therefore human rights
they no longer stood among the possibly humane
And all who believed that retaliation/revenge/defense
derive from God-given prerogatives of white men
And all who believed that waging war is anything
        besides terrorist activity in the first
        place and in the last
And all who believed that F-15s/F-16s/ "Apache"
        helicopters/
B-52 bombers/smart bombs/dumb
        bombs/napalm/artillery/
battleships/nuclear warheads amount to anything other
than terrorist tools of a terrorist undertaking
And all who believed that holocaust means something
        that only happens to white people
And all who believed that Desert Storm
        signified anything besides the delivery of an American
        holocaust against the peoples of the Middle East
All who believed these things
they were already dead
They no longer stood among the possibly humane

And this is for Crazy Horse singing as he dies
because I live inside his grave
And this is for the victims of the bombing of Baghdad
because the enemy traveled from my house
        to blast your homeland
        into pieces of children
        and pieces of sand

And in the aftermath of carnage
perpetrated in my name
how should I dare to offer you my hand
how shall I negotiate the implications
        of my shame?

My heart cannot confront
this death without relief
My soul will not control
this leaking of my grief

And this is for Crazy Horse singing as he dies
And here is my song of the living
who must sing against the dying
sing to join the living
with the dead

October Snowpea Poem

So as the sun declines below Detroit
(the lake a cool
assurance of alternatives to hard
dark high-rise
miscellaneous)
the colors of the end of light
relax along the horizontal edge of this
blue place
with burnt sienna
rose and oranges
that soften into regular
domestic tragedies
of night
without a lover's willing
face
to stop the desperation of the chase
for daytime stars
that glint and blur and mix and lift
like mica sprinkling
on a concrete hieroglyph of altered space
where
by himself
a young black man

sits
still

for no good reason

so do I turn to memorize
the soft excitement of the homestretch of your lips
and close to the hypnosis
of your almost closing eyes
I spin to the surprise
of no pain/no pain
whatsoever

Campsite #21

For Y^2

Next to so many stars
next to a meadow of wild oats rising to dry
next to a barrel full of flame and remnants of flame
next to the water bubbling full of rice
next to the knives
next to the feast of the wooden skewers
next to the roasted mushrooms/onion/shrimp and chunks
        of ripe red pepper
next to the wine and the cooler and the candle and
        the flashlights
next to the gigantic redwood tree
next to the mountains receding but never
        shadowy or lost
next to the very spot where Venus
        blinked delirious as I felt close
                enough to feel the Milky Way
        collapse into the aerial Big
        Dipper poised above our bodies
        close enough to feel

            our bodies close
                together

    2½ miles up
    from the beginning of the forest
    2½ miles up
    from the ending of a regular road
    pretty damn high
    after
    tying knots

    of white nylon to aluminum
    stakes
    or bending bamboo poles
    into the pockets
    of our borrowed tent
    or shooing our ground
    away from possible killer
    ants
    but next to squirrels and a curious
    raccoon
    soon you were blowing on the fire
    and sparks burst from the dark
    few inches left
    between us
    like the incandescent tremor
    of a moon
    that will not spoil an expectation
    with its full disclosure

    Next to you
    the 2 blue sleeping bags
    zipped tight
    together
    and I felt the lifted
    lifting
    positive security of a well-made
    kite

and I felt the irresistible
the naked nature of the right
enclosure

               your handiwork
               your arms
around me

while the lone hawk of the evening
he forgot about the hungers
of the sun

and glided by

Bosnia Bosnia

Too bad
there is no oil
between her legs

that 4-year-old Muslim girl and
her 5-year-old sister
and the 16-year-old babysitter
and the 20-year-old mother of that 4-year-old/that
Muslim child gang raped
from dawn to dark to time become damnation

Too bad
there is no oil
between her legs

Too bad there is no oil
between Srebrenica and Sarajevo
and in between the standing of a life
and genocide

Too bad
there is no oil

Too bad
there is no oil
between her legs

the woman in Somalia
who weighs 45 pounds and
who has buried village elders and
who has buried village children
who weighed even less
than she weighs after so many days
of hunger gaping open
to the flies

Too bad
there is no oil
in South Central L.A.
and in between the beaten men and beatup women
and in between the African and Asian throwaways
and in between the Spanish and the English speaking
homeless
and in between the dealers and the drugged
and in between the people and criminal police
too bad
there is no oil

Too bad
there is no oil
between her legs
that 4-year-old Muslim girl

Too bad
there is no oil
between her legs

Focus in Real Time

Poem for Margaret who passed the California bar!

A bowl of rice
          as food
          as politics
          or metaphor
          as something valuable and good
          or something common to consume/exploit/ignore

Who grew these grains
Who owned the land
Who harvested the crop
Who converted these soft particles to money
Who kept the cash
Who shipped the consequences of the cash
Who else was going to eat the rice
Who else was going to convert the rice to cash

Who would design the flowers for the outside of the bowl
Who would hold the bowl between her hands
Who would give the bowl away
Who could share the rice
Who could fill that bowl with rice how many times a day
          how many times a week
Who would adore the hands that held the bowl that held the rice
Who would adore the look the smell the steam of boiled rice
          in a bowl

Who will analyze the cash the rice becomes
Who will sit beside the bowl or fight for rice
Who will write about the hands that hold the bowl
Who will want to own the land
          A bowl of rice

Poem in Memory of Alan Schindler, 22 Years Old

Except for the tattoo
how could I recognize
my son
what with the way that monster
crushed
his skull
what with the way that monster
broke
then pulverized his jaw
what with the way that monster
kicked apart
the rib cage of my only son/
except for the tattoo
how could I recognize
my boy
my manchild grown into a sailor
for the Navy

I have buried him
my son
who lived and died loving
other men
I have buried him now
beneath the earth that allows for no
distinctions among men
except for the tattoo
that personal flag
of an honest body
as courageous
as ordinary
as continuing to breathe
when the world demands your death
as courageous
as ordinary
as an everyday parade

across mined territory
as courageous
as ordinary
as all of that
except
Thank God!
except for the tattoo

Poem Because the 1996 U.S. Poet Laureate Told the San Francisco Chronicle *There Are "Obvious" Poets — All of Them White — and Then There Are "Representative" Poets — None of Them White*

Dedicated to Laura Serna

So the man said
Let there be obvious people
and representative others.
Let there be obvious poets
and representative
others
Let the obvious people be white
Let the others
represent what happens
when
you fail to qualify
as obvious

And the representative other
not obvious people or poets
worried a lot about just what should you do
if you fall into
such a difficult
such a representative
slot

Except for one representative
sista poet
who said, "Mista
Poet Laureate!
Please clarify:
Was Timothy McVeigh
was he
obvious?

And what about media experts
certain that the murdering terrorist
must look like somebody, 'Middle
Eastern'?
Would you say that expertise was
representative?

And how about the cops trying to stop
then
trying to kill
Rodney King?

And Sheriff's deputies
Racing to vilify
and humiliate
Twenty-one Mexican men and women wannabe
working for minimum
wages
in America/how
about those
deputies who chose
on camera
to vent the venom
of their obvious
territorial assertions over land
that (truth to tell)
belongs to Mexico?

How about all histories
of all the deputies
hellbent to freeze inverted boundaries
according to some Anglo-Saxon
Christian
English Speaking
Crock of Conquest-As-The-Best
Of-Destinies?
And Patrick Buchanan!

Is he obvious?
Is he legal?

That no way
alien
neo-nazi wannabe
neo-nazi 'über alles'
promising death to 'José'
and to *Niggas Jews* and *Queers*
That obvious
clear
leader
for obvious
clear
people
would you say
he's the bees' knees'
representative?"

Yes?
No?

Not all of us must come and go
by pick-up truck
And you can't yank each one
of us
right off the driver's seat

to beat up
on our heads and bloody backs!

And after twisted kicks
and billy sticks
to knock us down to
knock us down
to ground
our fathers and our mothers
sanctified/sweat
laboring to escape
the leather whip
you label who
illegal
or unqualified?

And dangerous to standards
and a way of life
that venerates brutality
and turns around to smirk
with overt
obvious
and homicidal
pride
you label who
illegal?

And burrowing under everything you think
you know
some of us move slow
like inch worms
softening the earth
to bury you

And how I hope the obvious
necessity for me to write
this poem
Translates into Spanish

Mandarin
Cantonese
Punjabi
Japanese
Xhosa
Arabic

and every African
and every Asian
language

Of every people representative
of people
kept unequal
on the planet

Mista
Poet Laureate
I close this disquisition
on the obvious
with the words of representative
Poet Hero
Langston Hughes:

"The night is beautiful,
So the faces of my people.

The stars are beautiful,
So the eyes of my people.

Beautiful, also, is the sun.
Beautiful, also, are the souls of my people."

poem to continue a conversation

for Erwin Cho-Woods

changing through the day
or night
      words never stay the same
sounds bounding to a brain
without my mouth

      old syllables
aim
away from the night
      the revelations
of a glance
      or gaze
confound
      statistical inequities
like zero
      this kind of a life
      or that
blueberries
buffalo
      nothing anywhere
      extinct

if you if I
if we
just
face it

Christmas Poem

Dedicated to the one and only Adrienne B. Torf

1

Clouds flying across the sky
and the moon
and the moon
and I hold
still

2

All that milky light full
enough to push and pull
the open sea
and lull that tipsy trickster
to her knees

3

And around
the infinite surf
and the sound
of its infinite pounding
little else
besides two yellow breasted sugar birds
domestic
among jasmine murmurs

4

And how
the lone blue heron
stands
wherever
wherever it lands

Poem at the End of the Third Year

Free from an earlier debility
an almost ultimate commotion
in the opening mouth of death
I pass by Kezar stadium
where you spent our Sundays
Running
no strain
just speed and gaining stamina
as graceful as the lazy
sunlight boiling up
the air

How we began
a galaxy apart/me
driving on this street
to reach the hospital to take
away one breast
or more
than that

You arriving on this street
to take
and take again
the track
to pre-Olympic competition
training
training
hard and fast as heartbreak

Useless to each other
then and now
except the difference
kept me
keeps me
going

Birthday in Paris

For Peter Sellars
September 27, 1995

Move the buffalo

bird close to its boundless eye

weight and wings one face

Study #2 for b.b.L.

so you're gone
going
away
gone

And I never thought I'd jump
And I never thought you'd deal

And now
And now
And now

You're gone
going
away
gone

        gone
        go
        going away
        gone
ohwellohwellohwell
and the last of the clearing of the skies
and the last of my face inside your eyes

                    away
              going away
        away

Baby, Baby I
what can I say
I
I disappear
                away
              going away gone
from the tease me possibilities
from the going
from the going away gone

possibilities

of your tongue

And I never thought I'd jump
and I never thought you'd deal

but now
but now

                    come back
                    come back back
                    here
                    to my
                    everything I
                    I disappear
                    without/back/here

ohwellohwellohwelloh
flying lowdown slip
flow
skip
baby
baby

so you're gone!
what can I where can I
what
without you

why would I what could I
what
without you/you're
what I what
would I
do
without
do
without
you
so you're gone
going away gone
and I don't care
I don't
                I don't care
                you're gone
                I don't care
                you're gone
                I don't care
And now

I need you back
here
I need you back
here
I need you back
here
in my
in my
in my
I need you back
here
in my

everything I
I disappear
without you

back here

going
away
gone

so you're gone
ohwellohwellohwellohwell

I need you back!

Poem #1 for b.b.L.

5 months
eighteen days
three dinners
three countries
two transatlantic
two trans-Mediterranean
flights
one hundred trans-continental
e-mail messages
seven or eight Fed Ex deliveries
four or five letters
2 bowls of granola
146 phone calls
2x playing tennis
one walk
one drive
one salt water
one fresh water
swim

2 hotels
4 or 5 tapes
3 or 4 photographs
one taxi
two books
one movie
and some bimbo
asking me
what's the plan?
one/two/three/four/five months
18 days
3 dinners
spinning into one winner word
like "DUCK!"
that heedless
downy
feathered
thing

that one word
heedless
downy
feathered
three countries
2 transatlantic
okay
okay
so maybe
that's the plan?

Poem #3 for b.b.L.

volcanic particles
between the moon and me
looking for a blue
moon

or a new
moon
or any kind of soon
moon
snuff the particles and stuff
the blues back
where no cold
turkey catch a hold
on me
from fingertips
to nipples
quivering
for some macroscopic
I mean incontrovertible
I mean beyond atomic
      and below the subcutaneous
      and above the epithelial
      and diaphanous (for sure)
      but pedestrian as sweat
      and local like your skin
      taking in
      the/evidence
      baby
      hardcore
      no metaphor
      evidence
      I mean proof
      superluminal
      exploding
      proof
      baby
      evidence of incendiary
      closeup particles
      volcanic
      like a true blue love

Fact Sheets for b.b.L.

No matter how I dawdle
or delay
you do not stay tonight
where only hours ago
you lay
not quite asleep
and close enough
for love
        (to keep)

Poem #4 for b.b.L.

At this beach where the water
rolled emerald as grass
infused by noonday light
and where you could forget
about the sky
because the ocean strayed
left right
forward
forward
hurtling always soft
into a last turn surf
we played
on these striated cliffs
strewn now and then
with rocks
or boulders
hard to touch
but never holding hard
against
your lifted weight
and then this game
of break

this rock
(okay)
then break this bigger
one
(okay)
and then
(okay)
this mountain bit
just try it
and it broke
it crumbled
and it pulverized
to cooling granules
you could shift
about
and sift
for gold
you had to hope nobody else
would notice

Then we raced towards that almost avalanche
that steep/
that risen
sand/we
jumped
and landed
dug-in
hot and staring
at a day
so bright so big
nothing
no one could obliterate
the look
the laughter
of the waves
your lips
precipitate

Poem for Laura

Light as the almond tree petals
cherish each inch
of a solar infusion
that swells into color
and smell

Light as the traveling of land
beyond measure by miles
or the speed of delivery
from need

Light as the infinite wick
of a tiger's eye
kindling its own
appetite

Light as the call against stop
diminishing or dead
to obfuscate
the way to homestead
on the river

Light as the river

Light

Poem #6 for b.b.L.

One room away you sleep or do not wake
to any summons love might make
in competition with all hummingbirds/
those wings of utmost stutter
at the starting source
for rapture

infinitesimal
I take away the noise the words
that might disturb
or curb
your flight
and think how you will
curling
pearl into the night
with all my world
at stake

Poem #7 for b.b.L.

Baby
when you reach out
for me
I forget everything
except
I do try to remember
to breathe

Intifada Incantation: Poem #8 for b.b.L.

I SAID I LOVED YOU AND I WANTED
GENOCIDE TO STOP
I SAID I LOVED YOU AND I WANTED AFFIRMATIVE
ACTION AND REACTION
I SAID I LOVED YOU AND I WANTED MUSIC
OUT THE WINDOWS
I SAID I LOVED YOU AND I WANTED
NOBODY THIRST AND NOBODY
NOBODY COLD
I SAID I LOVED YOU AND I WANTED I WANTED
JUSTICE UNDER MY NOSE

I SAID I LOVED YOU AND I WANTED
BOUNDARIES TO DISAPPEAR

I WANTED
NOBODY ROLL BACK THE TREES!
I WANTED
NOBODY TAKE AWAY DAYBREAK!
I WANTED
NOBODY FREEZE ALL THE PEOPLE ON THEIR
KNEES!

I WANTED YOU
I WANTED YOUR KISS ON THE SKIN OF MY SOUL
AND NOW YOU SAY YOU LOVE ME AND I STAND
DESPITE THE TRILLION TREACHERIES OF SAND
YOU SAY YOU LOVE ME AND I HOLD THE LONGING
OF THE WINTER IN MY HAND
YOU SAY YOU LOVE ME AND I COMMIT
TO FRICTION AND THE UNDERTAKING
OF THE PEARL

YOU SAY YOU LOVE ME
YOU SAY YOU LOVE ME

AND I HAVE BEGUN
I BEGIN TO BELIEVE MAYBE
MAYBE YOU DO

I AM TASTING MYSELF
IN THE MOUTH OF THE SUN

Tanka Metaphors or Not for b.b.L.

Dedicated to Dr. Jennifer Ross
and to Dr. Marilyn Milkman, 11/3/96

Rose-tinged waters break
Lilacs blossoming soft stars
uterine reprieve
waters burst through body's thirst
love past ache alive at last

Haiku for b.b.L.

Lover help me love
New waves wash away my fears
Rain carry me home

Poem #9 for b.b.L.

I could as soon forget
about the wrapped-in newsprint
roses
As you could forget
(apparently all)
about me

Kissing God Goodbye

Poem in the face of Operation Rescue
Dedicated to Jennie Portnoff

You mean to tell me on the 12th day or the 13th
that the Lord
which is to say some wiseass

got more muscle than he
reasonably
can control or figure out/some
accidental hard disk
thunderbolt/some
big mouth
woman-hating/super
heterosexist heterosexual
kind of a guy guy
he decided who could live and who would die?

And after he did what?
created alleyways of death
and acid rain
and infant mortality rates
and sons of the gun
and something called the kitchenette
and trailer trucks to kill and carry
beautiful trees out of their natural
habitat/Oh! Not that guy?

Was it that other guy
who invented a snake
an apple and a really
retarded scenario so that
down to this very day
it is not a lot of fun
to give birth to a son of a gun?
And wasn't no woman in the picture
of the Lord?
He done the whole thing by himself?
The oceans and the skies
and the fish that swim and the bird
that flies?

You sure he didn't have some serious problems
of perspective
for example

coming up with mountains/valleys/rivers/rainbows
and no companionship/no coach/no
midwife/boyfriend/girlfriend/
no help whatsoever for a swollen
overactive
brain
unable to spell
sex

You mean to tell me that the planet
is the brainchild
of a single
      male
      head of household?

And everything he said and done
the floods/famines/plagues
and pestilence
the invention of the slave and the invention of the gun
the worship of war (especially whichever war
he won)
And after everything he thought about and made 2 million
megapronouncements about
(Like)
"Give not your strength to women"
and
"You shall not lie with a male as with a woman"
and
"An outsider shall not eat of a holy thing"
and
"If a woman conceives and bears a male child
then she shall be unclean
seven days... But if she bears
a female child, then she shall be unclean
2 weeks... "
and
"The leper who has the disease
shall wear torn clothes and let the hair

of his head hang loose
and he shall cover his upper lip
and cry, 'Unclean,
unclean!'"
and
"Behold, I have 2 daughters
who have not known a man,
let me bring them out to you, and do
to them as you please"
and
"I will greatly multiply your pain
in childbearing:
in pain shall you bring forth children"
and
"Take your son, your only son Isaac,
whom you love,
and go to the land of Moriah, and offer
him there as a burnt offering"
and in the middle of this lunatic lottery
there was Ruth saying to Naomi:
"Entreat me not
to leave you or to return
from following you; for where you go
I will go
and where you lodge I will lodge, your people
shall be my people
And your God my God;
where you die I will die,
and there I will be buried. May the Lord do so to me
and more also
if even death parts me from you."
and
David wailing aloud at the death of Jonathan who loved
        him
"more than his own soul" and David
inconsolable in lamentation
saying
"...very pleasant have you been to me;

your love to me was wonderful,
passing the love of women"
and
"If I give away all I have, and if I deliver
my body to be burned,
but have not love,
I gain nothing..."
and this chaos/this chaos
exploded tyrannical in scattershot scripture
(Like)
"...those who belong in Christ
Jesus have crucified the flesh
with its passions and desire"
and
"Cast out the slave and her son"
and
"If in spite of this you will not hearken
to me, then...
You shall eat the flesh of your sons,
you shall eat the flesh
of your daughters. And I will
destroy your high places... I will
lay your cities waste... I will
devastate your land... And
as for those of you that are left,
I will send faintness
into their hearts in the lands of their enemies
the sound of a driven leaf
shall put them to flight..."
etcetera etcetera
That guy?
That guy?
the ruler of all earth
and heaven too
The maker of all laws
and all taboo
The absolute supremacist
of power

the origin of the destiny
of molecules and Mars
The father and the son
the king and the prince
The prophet and the prophecy
The singer and the song
The man from whom
in whom
of whom
by whom
comes everything
without the womb
without that unclean
feminine
connection/
that guy?

The emperor of poverty
The czar of suffering
The wizard of disease
The joker of morality
The pioneer of slavery
The priest of sexuality
The host of violence
The Almighty fount of fear and trembling
That's the guy?
You mean to tell me on the 12th day or the 13th
that the Lord
which is to say some wiseass
got more muscle than he
reasonably
can control or figure out/some
accidental hard disk
thunderbolt/some
big mouth
woman-hating/super
heterosexist heterosexual

kind of a guy guy
he decided who could live and who would die?

And so
the names become
the names of the dead and the living
who love
Peter
John
Tede
Phil
Larry
Bob
Alan
Richard
Tom
Wayne
David
Jonathan
Bruce
Mike
Steve
And so
our names become
the names of the dead
and the living who love
Suzanne
Amy
Elizabeth
Margaret
Trude
Linda
Sara
Alexis
Frances
Nancy
Ruth
Naomi

Julie
Kate
Patricia
And out of that scriptural scattershot
our names become
the names of the dead

our names become
the names of the iniquitous
the names of the accursed
the names of the tribes of the abomination
because
my name is not Abraham
my name is not Moses/Leviticus/Solomon/Cain or Abel
my name is not Matthew/Luke/Saul or Paul
My name is not Adam
My name is female
my name is freedom
my name is the one who lives outside the tent of the father
my name is the one who is dark
my name is the one who fights for the end of the kingdom
my name is the one at home
my name is the one who bleeds
my name is the one with the womb
my name is female
my name is freedom
my name is the one the bible despised
my name is the one astrology cannot predict
my name is the name the law cannot invalidate
my name is the one who loves

and that guy
and that guy
you never even seen upclose

He cannot eat at my table
He cannot sleep in my bed
He cannot push me aside

He cannot make me commit or contemplate
 suicide

He cannot say my name
without shame
He cannot say my name
My name
My name is the name of the one who loves

And he
has no dominion over me
his hate has no dominion over me
I am she who will be free

And that guy
better not try to tell anybody about who
should live
and who should die
or why

His name is not holy
He is not my Lord
He is not my people
His name is not sacred
His name is not my name
His name is not the name of those who love the living

His name is not the name of those who love the living
and the dead

His name is not our name
we
who survive the death
of men and women
whose beloved
breath
becomes (at last)
our own

Last Poems

1997 birthday poem for b.b.L.

Knowing or not
knowing
as you go

days rise
nothing dies

A tiger's eye
and snow

Poem on the Death of Princess Diana

At least she was riding
beside
somebody going somewhere
fast
about love

For Alice Walker (*a summertime tanka*)

Redwood grove and war
You and me talking Congo
gender grief and ash

I say, "God! It's all so huge"
You say, "These sweet trees: This tree"

Poem Against the Temptations of Ambivalence

Quit?
Save?
Sign off?
ARE YOU SURE?

ARE YOU SURE?

Poem towards the End of a Winter Evening

For Philip and Diana Chang

Chill light blue sail slow
Slice moon curve surf low
Wind fall wave small fast
Cloud strip star bright snow

T'ang Poem #2

Homage

Rain grow gold dim stay
Plum branch flame break gray
Ditch rinse dirt steam rise
Wind keep wing make way

1998 Mid-Day Philadelphia Haiku

For Chuck and Jane James

Black men sleep homeless
Freeze far away from Iraq
Still sleeping still men

T'ang Poem #3

Written on Transcontinental Flight #147
February 16, 1998

Tongue glow silk graze skin
Rough touch trick stone thin
House last hold night fast
Rouse tree brush bird spin

First Anniversary T'ang Poem

for bbL 2/28/98

Hush bowl heave deep see
Spume sleep shell rock free
Tide slide sand drift stop
Fish sweet fruit trail tree

Poem of Commitment

Dedicated to 3-year-old Antonio Guerra

Because cowards attack
by committee
and others kill with bullets
while some numb by numbers
bleeding the body and the language
of a child

And because as far as I can tell
less than a thousand flowers blooming
means a putrid termination of night jasmine
randomly transporting strangers
into close caress
proximity and sometimes even

more than that
sometimes jasmine startles
the entire sleeping world awake
with lust
for what can't be accounted for
and sometimes even
more than that
a thousand flowers wilted
on a locked-down classroom
windowsill
and sometimes even more than that
the bleached the monotone
interposition of all regulations
for the changing face of fire

Who would behold the colorings of a cloud
and legislate its shadows
legislate its shine?

Or confront a cataract of rain
and seek to interdict its speed
and suffocate its sound?

Or disappear the trees
behind a nomenclature
no one knows by heart?

Or count the syllables that invoke
the mother of my tongue?

Or say the game goes the way
of the wind

And the wind blows the way
of the ones who make
and break
the rules?

And because as far as I can tell
less than a thousand children
as particular
as dark as pine needle earth at dusk
as pink as the pastel crenulations of a sea-struck shell
as brown as the spread wings of a starling
as Cantonese
Nigerian and Irish
as a thousand words
that violate the law
that violate a kiss beyond
syntactical control
because
because
because as far as I can tell
less than a thousand children playing
in the garden of a thousand flowers
means the broken neck
of birds

I commit my body and my language
to the sheltering of any Antonio/Tyrone/Valerie/Yunjong
just about to choose his
or her own
name
for the family and the strangers
still not listening
to the great good news
of his or her
own voice

The End of Kindness:
Poem for Dr. Elizabeth Ann Karlin

Boys choosing birthday balloons
A couple selecting condoms for Sunday afternoon
A woman waiting for the traffic so she can't
Turn left or right
Liam taking his first step to his mother's
Predictable delight
Walter washing his truck –

There was no luck
With the peace lily plan
For the Doctor dying of brain tumor
The Doctor trying
To die

In Wisconsin
They had to send away
For the little plant the peace lily
I sent
Because I meant
It to sit
Beside the morphine drip
To reinforce her will to let life slip
Free from the clutch and claw
Of that disease that saw
Intelligence and speech become
Impossible

She who was always kind
Could not in death agree
To cruelty
To sorrow longer than the mind
Can comprehend

She is choosing now to end
Her own death with her own breath

I grow numb
With grief and think perhaps I follow
Dumb
With love

And then a kitchen knife by accident cuts up
My thumb.
And I feel it feel that pain
That ironic welcome gain:
I am still here still clear
About what hurts
What really hurts
And what
Does not

Holding to all pain
I remain
Faithful to the one
Who let pain go

Poem for Annie Topham, Partner of Dr. Elizabeth Ann Karlin

As you know
I loved her too
And that was not so long ago
I will not forget the laughter
Or the mock fights
That came after
Tears
Mosquito bites
And bike rides through
The wildly blooming arboretum near the lake

I loved her too
The woman who loved you
The woman you sleep next to
On a makeshift cot
The makeshift lot
Of the beloved one who listens
To the rattling last
Encounter with the future and the past
As useless sunlight glistens
On the useless world beyond that
Final gloom of light

Oh! Bright grief beyond relief!

I loved her too
As now it is my privilege
To love you now I love you now
Forever
For love's sake

I guess it was my destiny to live so long

Death chase me down
death's way
uproot a breast
infest the lymph nodes
crack a femur
rip morale
to shreds

Death chase me down
death's way
tilt me off-kilter
crutch me slow
nobody show me
how

you make a cup of coffee
with no hands

Death chase me down
death's way
awkward in sunlight
single in a double bed at night
and hurtling out of mind
and out of sight

Don't chase me down
down
down
death chasing me
death's way

And I'm not done
I'm not about to blues my dues or beg

I am about to teach myself
to fly slip slide flip run
fast as I need to
on one leg

Bridget Running

12/24/98-1/4/99

back from fury cataracts
revengeful frothings strict
vindictive
trivial as short- or long-term terminal
warfare
infiltrates the atmosphere
the throat
the pointless gasping
everywhere

from all casual carnage
and the ragged details
of a broken
hand
the cracked-up landscape
freezing flowers
wasted
on the frozen
eye

Bridget running

from disputes that do not tally
smashed teeth in the mouths
of children
and the quiet killing
of all lullabies
and laughter
after that

Bridget running

into cosmic conjugations
clipped by laser amputations
of the spirit
fluttering to flight
despite
the sometimes stuttering spirit
spills
into the world
as clear
as light and letting
go
as first-day snow

Bridget running

Pleasures of Love

For b.b.L.

So much birdsong slow boat surf and sky
and waves that light and light
that braves the trembling orbit of my eye
negotiate a treaty between cowardice
and lustful trust
that floats along the privilege of your nipples
on my thigh

Shakespeare's 116th Sonnet in Black English Translation

Don't let me mess up partner happiness
because the trouble
start
An' I ain' got the heart
to deal!
That won't be real
(about love)
if I
(push come to shove)
just punk

Not hardly! Hey:
Love do not cooperate
with cop-out
provocations: No!

Storm come. Storm go
away
but love stay
steady
(if you ready or

you not!)
True love stay
steady
True love stay
hot!

Poem to Take Back the Night

What about moonlight
What about watching for the moon above
the tops of trees and standing
still enough to hear the raucous crickets
chittering invisible among the soon lit stones
trick pinpoints of positions even poise
sustained in solitary loss

What about moonlight
What about moonlight

What about watching for the moon
through the windows low enough to let the screams
and curses of the street the gunshots
and the drunken driver screeching tires
and the boom box big beat and the tinkle
bell ice cream truck
inside

What about moonlight
What about moonlight

What about watching for the moon
behind the locked doors and bolted shut bedrooms
and the blind side of venetian blinds and
cowering under the kitchen table and struggling
from the car and wrestling head
down when the surprise when the
stranger when the surprise when the

coach when the surprise when the
priest when the surprise when the
doctor when the surprise when the
family when the surprise when the
lover when the surprise when the
friend when the surprise

lacerates your throat
constricted into no
no more sound

who will whisper
what about moonlight
what about moonlight

What about watching for the moon
so far from where you tremble
where you bleed where you sob
out loud for help or mercy for
a thunderbolt of shame and
retribution where you plead
with God and devils with
the creatures in-between
to push the power key
and set you free
from filth and blasphemy
from everything you never wanted to feel
or see

to set you free

so you could brush your teeth
and comb your hair and maybe
throw on a jacket
or maybe not

you running
curious and so excited and

running and running into the
night
asking only asking

What about the moonlight
What about the moonlight

Kosovo Fugue in Seven Parts

1. APRIL 7, 1999

Nothing is more cruel
than the soldiers
who command
the widow
to be grateful
that she's still alive

2. APRIL 9, 1999

only the ones without water
only the ones without bread
only the ones without guns

There is international TV
There is no news

The enemies proliferate
The homeless multiply
And I
I watch   I wait

I am already far
and away
too late

too late

3. APRIL 9, 1999 (FOR ETHELBERT)

In Brooklyn when the flowering
forsythia escaped the concrete patterns
of tight winter days
I didn't think about long
distances
or F-117s in contrast
to a lover or an army
on the ground
up close
and personal as washing out a shirt
by hand
the soapsuds and the fingers and the cloth
an ordinary ritual
to interdict the devils of 2,000-lb. bombs
dropped from 25,000 feet above
the children
scrambling from the schoolyard
suddenly aflame
until you called from Washington
D.C.
to say
"Oh, let me be
that shirt!"

4. APRIL 10, 1999

The enemies proliferate
by air
by land
they bomb the cities
they burn the earth
they force the families into miles and miles of violent exile

30 or 40 or 81,000 refugees
just before this
check-point

or who knows where
they disappear

the woman cannot find her brother
the man cannot recall the point of all
      the papers somebody took
         away from him
the rains fail to purify the river
the darkness does not slow the trembling
      message of the tanks
Hundreds of houses on fire and still
      the enemies do not seek and find
         the enemies

5. APRIL 11, 1999 (FOR M.R.)

Through nights of bleeding
feet and babies lost to one
mis-step on ice or
stony mountain trail

my peaceful friend relinquishes
his pencil
and begins to inch his way
towards a gun
as I release the rifle
nestling in my head
and then attempt
to hold him
close

6. APRIL 12, 1999

Sex, food, and war
cyberspace addicts
insist the buttons and the on-line
icons indicating universal on and off and stop
and go
deliver just about everything you know

and more
everything (just about)
as good as actual
anesthesia actual
caress

And like the (e-mail) lover
claiming
"Love! Love!"
who will not alter all the virtual
terms of the engagement
that obliterate the (anyway invisible)
beloved
so do computer-driven warriors
claim "Rescue!" "Mercy!" "Moral
Imperative!" but
meanwhile blast and kill
the living
who need real time face
to face
and mouth to mouth

recovery

7. APRIL 29, 1999

> Dedicated to the Third World Liberation Front
> Students at U.C. Berkeley

You can't help but worship
with this raggedy last
vigil
against ethnic cleansing
under a full moon
close to the campanile
where all the bells hold still

And not the President
And not the Chancellor
And not the C.E.O.
And not the Army Chief of Staff
And not His Holiness Himself
can influence the candles
lit
intermittent and among the young
believers
breaking bread at midnight
as their oath
to stay together
aching for another light
to bless the weather and the outcome
of this whispering
this unruly
witness

From Kosovo to Berkeley

no more starve or freeze
no more torch or shoot or seize
no more purging of the people!

(so they talk and sign their names in chalk)

They give up food and bed and roof
as proof
they will not sleep
before the morning wakes the world
on just
such sweet demand

and hungering
and few
they stand
the darkness down

T'ang Poem

For Trinh Minh-ha

Word roll wall fill light
swell lock slide thrill sight
blue floor red turn tease
drape air wrap space bright

New Year Poem

Dedicated to Sara Glickstein
(which means "luck stone" in German)

Say, Vashahva!
That's Warszawa
or
(to you and me)
just WARSAW

But to Sara/
Sarenka/ Saruch
that's where Nazis murdered
her relatives unable
fast enough
to alter into refugees
who fled
East to Soviet prisons thrusting
them
into Siberia
where mosquitoes and
starvation killed
one uncle
and then almost
stole herself
a baby girl
away

Now sixty-one
she tells me, "Stalin, we survived. And we escaped
from Hitler. But today my landlord's
trying to evict us!"

So small
Sarenka stands inside a bookstore
with a lightly woven shawl
around her narrow shoulders

as she blinks
excited
wistful
just to recommend
another something beautiful
a thought
an English sentence
she will whisper to her friends
delighted
not to lose
another lovely word
beyond the Russian
and the Polish
lost already
lost
"And how are you?" she
always asks.

It may be
I am thinking of tomorrow's
chemotherapy
or the hatred of white
people
for my people

the erasure of my face
the structured eclipse

of every wish
to count

to amount to more than ⅗
of some/anyone's
imagination

but I listen to her inquiry
I note the nascent trembling
of her aerial composure

and I answer her,
"I'm fine."

As the sun sets all the water lets the sky slip away

Epitaph for Amigo,
August 5, 1989–January 27, 2001

Who never looked back
except (in fact) to see
me
and moved on
today
I know
however I may go from here
I move towards you
and so
I leave no
one
behind

2/27/01

heat sound pound plum spill
ground rise fruit fall fill
air splash branch rain wash
chance start heart kill chill

Scenario Revision #1

Or
suppose that gorgeous
wings spread
speckled
hawk
begins to glide
above my body lying
down
like dead meat
maybe start to rot
a little bit
not moving
see just flat
just limp
but hot
not moving
see
him circle closer
closing closer
for the kill
until
he makes that dive
to savage
me
and inches
from the blood flood lusty
beak

I roll away
I speak
I laugh out loud

Not yet
big bird of prey
not yet

Buzz Off: Romantic Poem #1

After pecking and pecking and pecking after
Crumbs
The bird
(sometimes soon enough)

remembers how to fly

away

Interim Mystery Poem for Haruko

This is a new development/this
distance this
fighting for your happiness
behind your back
tenacious
as a snake engorged by what
it thought
would taste so good/
the bite that bulged
into a bursting tension
of its skin
seemed worth the almost suffocation
of that stupendous
swallow

Oh! I guess
I am incorrigible
or that this love
resists
the tepid
meretricious tease
of termination
altogether
or
that there must be
a snake
in every paradise

Lo que tengo que decir

in words without melody
or hum
words crass as cracked neck
backyard chickens
scattering from no escape
scattering from too soon slaughter
twisting into dust and blood
deliveries
weird
unheard
bewilderment
becoming pleasant
family meals
nobody eats together
anymore
What I have to say
is something
dumb

like that

Ode #2 Written during Chemotherapy at UCSF, or Ode to I'd Really Rather Be Sailing

Or failing to dive fast enough so fish
Marvel at the rapidity of my descent into the sea
So deep even sperm whales move on sound
So dark even what's electrical will not ignite into a luminous event

Oh, I'd rather be flying
Or lying beside somebody lift
My lips to lips
Averse to words
Lips articulate as colorings of an eye
About to blink me just beyond just lust

I'd rather be no answer
Or no cancer always stuck inside gray company
Of frail and bald and sagging melodrama
Intravenous drips and problematic pokings in my veins
And daily pills that kill acuity of consciousness
And stats that say, "That's it! That's that!"

Oh, no lie!
I'd really rather be somebody's
Sweet potato pie!

Poem at the End of the Third Week

Rooster Husband and Monkey Wife
Dragon Husband and Dog Wife
Snake Husband and Rat Wife
Dear Love
It says here
that sheep and rats
"do not relate well to each
other"

and that you and I
"have nothing much
in common"

But we will never fit
inside a horoscope
invented long before
the 2 of us could read or
write

And we do not belong
inside a system that will tolerate
the drowning of a baby
if she's female

And we will never qualify
according to a book composed
without the impact
of your legs mixed
easily
with mine

And as far as I can tell
what we possess together
pushes history out
the door
and begins
the making of a romance
that was never known
or told
before

A Couple of Questions

Dedicated to Derrick Gilbert

How many Indians?
How many Indians left?
How many Africans?
How many Africans now?
How many Indians?
How many Indians left?
How many Mexicans?
How many Mexicans here?
How many Chinese?
How many Jews?
How many Jews anywhere?
How many?
How many Catholics?
How many Queers?
How many Indians?
How many Indians left?
How many Muslims?
How many Muslim women and girls?
How many Indians?
How many Palestinians?
How many?

I can't handle the numbers
Who runs the lottery on what percent of who
ends up dead on the street
and
what are the odds that a drive-by
shooting will take out a 2-year-old
and her 15-year-old mother?
or
what is the cost of an LAPD surveillance
helicopter or an anti-personnel armored vehicle
for use in situations of civil unrest?

And how many people
listening to these questions do
not have a clue
How many?
How many Indians?
How many Indians left?

How many minutes
How many hours before we agree that loving ourselves
does not require our hatred of somebody else?

I have someplace to go
and candles to light
and I live 3,500 miles and 3 time zones away
from the only lover in the world
who can keep me
awake when I'm actually fast
asleep

And all of this hatred sorely aggravates my soul
all of this hatred aggravates my soul
and hate will not obliterate
3 time zones
plus 3,500 miles
of Unadulterated Baby I'm Here By My Lonesome Self Reality
and so I'm trying to handle this math
I know
it's a fact
you can't take a political meeting
to bed
it's a fact
and there are these other
several happy things I want to find out about
instead
like
when will you love me enough
to move
just a little bit closer

or
my imagination of the snow that knows the furnace
of the secret of your face
but
regular life feels difficult
feels fleeting and not
what
anybody (serious) could describe or
categorize
as SAFE
and so how about a political
meeting
a really big marathon
meeting
of everybody
tired of The President The Governor The Army The Marines
The cops
and white supremacy and racial purity
and religious and gender crusades?

How about a meeting
of (about) how many (would you say)
today?

How many Indians?
How many Indians left?

"Drizzle spills soft air"

Drizzle spills soft air
jasmine smothering a storm
darkness surrounds me

(*Thoughts of*) *A Teenage African Girl Standing on the Auction Block*

The
That
No
That
That no
The
Mother
Mother
That
The
No tree
Water
Dirty
Dirty
No air
No
Hurt me
Hurt me
No
No
No

"Bay waters rolling"

Bay waters rolling
birds glide above broken rocks
I am not alone

"Trumpet vine sneaks in"

Trumpet vine sneaks in
dressing up the window screen
tendrils wreck the wall

For Mohammed al-Direh

1

India's monsoon destroys another boy
no story
on his struggling termination in that risen
water
just a photograph
just
before he drowns

2

At least we know they called you
(12 years old)
"a scamp"
a runner among the ruins
a bubbling from the rubble
a humbled
crumbling bull's-eye
for Israeli soldiers
firing and firing and firing
at your head your chest your head
falls into its own blood
bleeding on its own dirt
evidence of territory
yours

at last

My Victim Poem

The soldiers are stirring hot stones in the soup,
to force feed the hungry ones out on the street
My children need carrots and muffins and meat,
but I am not part of a tough enough group.

Woe is me, woe is me, woe is me.

My ancestors died from the whip and the lash
My mother was treated like pitiful trash
My father spoke softly, afraid of his voice,
and I say, I'm sorry, I don't have a choice.

Woe is me, woe is me, woe is me.

I know I'm a woman, my fate is the same
as the millions of females who live without name
The world takes me lightly, or makes me its mule,
and I feel I am meant to be somebody's fool.

Woe is me, woe is me, woe is me.

Insanity rules out the song of my soul
The people in power lift death as the goal
My brothers and sisters beg wretched with fear,
but all I can do is contend with despair.

Woe is me, woe is me, woe is me.

My friends see me raging and shaken by truth
I meditate daily, and eat only fruit
Inner peace and transcend have become my pursuit,
and struggle seems ugly and tired, uncouth.

Woe is me, woe is me, woe is me.

I am the victim, I am the dead.
I am the meaning of grace without pride.
I am the meaning of race suicide.
I am the victim, I am the dead.

Woe is me. I could start fighting instead.
But no, I am the victim. I am already dead.
Woe is me. Woe is me. Indeed.

Snowpea

SHE IS THE ONE
WHO
STANDING IN THE SUN
DOES NOT CAST A SHADOW

T'ang Poem for Amadou Diallo

Branch break rain bring blood
Lake light fold close mud
Storm wreck chime rhyme air
Shoot stop heart lose flood

December Snowpea Poem

I use a stiff bristle brush
to loosen then dislodge
mashed bits of dog shit
stashed
between hard rubber
cleats
of Hi-tech hiking boots
I wore

this morning
not on some mountainside trek
with you
but out back in the backyard
bagging
your dog's defecation
or to be exact
your and my dog's doo
the dog you blew away
same like you threw
not just your tee shirts
and your jeans
but finally our love
into a slew of many colored
plastic garbage bags/ like that
you bagged your stuff
and flew
away
in big time pain and rain
and yes I willingly digress I guess
because I never knew
you really never
had a clue I'd end up
in a backyard
wearing Hi-tech boots
to pick up baby canine particles of shit

I later extricate
by bristle and by streams
of ordinary water in the bathroom sink
that lovely fake/ that marble basin
where you rinsed your sleepy face
awake
2 weeks ago

      shoes
      shit
      face

time
place
all flow together

And I suppose I know
what folks mean now
about how things come clear
and clean

Love Song about Choosing Your Booze

On a rainy Ireland night
way west towards the sea
and quite inside the wee Leewiston Bar
and also close to 3 guys shooting pool
and (must be) awful close to God
(considering we found 2 seats
while everybody else
was standing
perched
with Guinness Stout
or Power's or Paddy's whiskey
well in hand)
I listened to this eloquent
and stammering
Belfast poet
read to me his new
translation
of *Le bateau ivre*
"Drunk Boat!" he emphasized
the 2 stressed syllables:
"Drunk Boat!"
And then began to sing real
slow
he sang to me deep and he sang to me low:
"A-ma-zing grace

how sweet the sound
That saved a wretch
like me
I once was lost
but now I'm found
was blind
but now I see..."

And I slipped back to Mississippi
And to Brooklyn
And to Belfast
But I returned
intoxicated
to the shock of that song/my
song no longer
or
not only mine

And I decided
I didn't really much care
if it was Power's or Paddy's
filling up my glass

so long as it was Irish
I'd be fine:
just fine!

Racial Profile #1

     sort of small but
     black but
     older but
     sort of strong but
     short but
pissed off but
     slow but

sort of laughing a lot but
    black

    and not that slow!

Racial Profile #2

You bring out the Jamaica in me
The killer hotsauce hot head knock
Dead slap face yell bellow yellow
Curry goat and ackee egomania
Mango maniac attack smack codfish
Salt to shrink a hippopotamus
In me

You bring out the best behavior Sunday
Rice and peas in coconut oil and ganja
Fantasy and Arawak free or gone
To Rasta fury and a cane-field
Flaming slave revolt
In me

Me no repent
Me no relent

You bring out the Jamaica in me
The violent cradle for my temper
Tantrum reggae and banana basic no way
Blues in me

You bring out the typhoon flinging hurricane swinging
Doors and roof tops got to go
In me

Me no repent
Me no relent

You/Calypso
Palm tree dirt path to the big wink
Crocodile the now
You see me now you
Won't believe
How close how hot
How kiss the queen how
Crop the king Jamaica
I can really be

You betta to make room for the mongoose poet
Spill no relent and no repent juice
Over you over
And over you over
And over
And over
you

Racial Profile #3

A boat in the water
Not so big
Sails full
Or buckling
Or drenched
Or furled up tight and tied
To a torn-up masthead

A boat in the water
Not so big
A boat

Still in the water

Poem for Black English

Dedicated to Dr. Geneva Smitherman

You don' never write me off
Because you ignorant
Don' know nobody got my
name
my low lights
softstone hometown
street
my rollin high Apollo style
my sweet
two babies wait
for food I ain' figured
out about
yet but you bet
I will
I'll get
them somethin serious goin on
just let
me sit here
half a minute
on the sidewalk
next to Willie's
Burgers
watch that ole man
suited up besides
the blues
can' touch that faithful

finery

can' mess up walk-to-Jesus shoes
he clean
he shine and shave and lose
a weeklong shuffle
steppin

close to music
from the signifyin red
dress of some woman
do not care

the world stay blind
to all the glory all the heavy
invitation of a red dress radiate
a whole day
that she wear no stretch no
stress
she overturn the law
of gravity
she dare you
don' believe it

yeah
she dare you!

Owed to Eminem

I'm the Slim Lady the real Slim Lady
the real Slim Lady just a little ole lady
uh-huh
uh-huh
I'm Slim Lady the real Slim Lady
all them other age ladies
just tryin to page me
but I'm Slim Lady the real Slim Lady
and I will
stand up
I will stand up

I assume that you fume while the
        dollar bills bloom
and you magnify scum while the

critics stay mum
and you anguish and languish runnin
    straight to the bank
and you scheme and you team with
    false balls so you rank
at the top and you pop like the jury the
    victim
the judge
but the ghetto don't trip to the light
    stuff you flip
on the chain saw you skip
with
the rope and the knives and that bunk
    about tying who up like a punk in the
back of the trunk
or that dope about mothers and wives
    give you worse than a funeral hearse
fulla
hickies and hives
you fudge
where you come from or whether you
    mean it
the shit you can't make without
    sycophants see'n it
but nobody's dumb
enough to believe that you grieve
    because folks
can't conceive that you more than a
    moron
or why would you whore on
the hole in your soul?

At this stage of my rage
I'm a sage so I know how you blow
to the left then the right and you maim
every Columbine game about "No!
    Cuz he's white!"

But I am that I am
and I don't give a damn
and you mess with my jam
and I'll kill you
I will!

And if you insist listenin close for a dis
then you missin more than the gist in
      this
because
I gotcha pose by the nose

I hear how you laugh and cut corners
      in half
And I see you wigglin a line that's not
      flat
while you screwin around with more
      than all that

But I am that I am
and I don't give a damn
and you mess with my jam
and I'll kill you
I will!

Don't tell me you pissed or who's
      slashin whose wrists
or pretend about risks
to a blond millionaire
with a bodyguard crew that prey
behind shades and that pay
to get laid – What?
What's that about fair?

I'm not through with you!

I'm the bitch in the bedroom the
      faggot

you chump I'm the nigga for real so get
     ready to deal
I'm tired of wiggas that whine as they
     squeal
about bitches and faggots and little
     girls too!
I'm a Arab I'm a Muslim I'm a
     Orthodox Jew!

I'm the bitch come to take you
I'm the faggot to fake you
outta the closet
outta the closet
fulla the slime you deposit
for fun

rhyme and run
you the number one
phony-ass gun

Oh! I am that I am
and I don't give a damn
and you mess with my jam
and I'll kill you
I will!

(Hey, Shady
you know what I'm sayin
I'm just playin!
You know I love you!)

Sincerely,

Slim Lady

Democracy Poem #1

Tell them that I stood
in line
and I waited
and I waited
like everybody
else

But I never got
called
And I keep that scrap
of paper
in my pocket

just in case

Owed to Eminem #2

For Wen Ho Lee

Go back!
It's a pitiful Fact that that 1882 Chinese Exclusion Act
gives a whole lotta people a real inspiration
about what they can do about how much they hate you
inside this lily-white nation

You almost a nigga a arab a terrorist too
because you Chinese you never will please
the Aryan order
Crawl back to the border
You never belong
You always look wrong
Got a criminal slant to a criminal spine
and besides alla that you got eyes dark as mine

They got shadows decipherin a espionage pad
to freeze atom bombs at Los Alamos Lab
but really it's simple as poppin a pimple
Jump on a scientist (one you can twist)
and supposin he looks like he
looks like he's
apparently
apparently
Chinese
Then yell about how all the brightstuff's gone straight to hell
while the F.B.I.'s
trying to squeeze and to tease and to shackle and seize
all the gooks
all the spies all the lies and whoever denies
it's (apparently)
he's
(apparently) Chinese

You come from Taiwan or maybe Saigon
which – it don't matter
let bygones be bygones
and fall off the ladder
you got nobody to call
NO MORE!
You been kicked out the door
You been slammed to the floor
You been labeled a snivelin ingrate/a whiz-kid/ a treacherous
    whore

A threat to my god-damned national security
A fantastic affront to my paranoid maturity

And just because you dint do nothin
don' mean you got rights to fly life on the wing
Forget that!
You never ever gonna be free
Not with some name like Mr. Chinese
Wen Chinese Ho

Chinese Wen Ho Lee!
You a prisoner of profile
a case of the face of a race the big boys revile
and that's why they pile on
the treasonous charges they style on

Because
you musta busted up some laws!

And no matter how you plead innocent or pretty pretty please
You just look like you (apparently)
apparently Chinese

So after all the Federal hot shot deployment
of slander and free-base accusation
you got no employment
you got no nothin no rent-payin reputation

An' you never ever gonna be free
walkin around lookin way too much
exactly like me
See I get arrested just drivin my car
(which is just about par for the regular gar-
bage we seem to inherit
entirely without merit)
An' you don' need to keep screenin the Feds for the meanin
of pre-trial detention
and don' even mention
36 weeks of miserable consignment
to a punishing/unprecedented solitary confinement

You the prize
you the neo-nazi invention
of the right size
the right (I mean wrong)
complexion
Forever Alien! You a national
infection!

They cleanin and cleanin
you out!

You out!

Oh you never ever gonna be free!
An' that's that
Unless we, you an' me
change that story,
Dr. Wen Ho Lee!

Poem for The New York Times *Dedicated to Dr. Elizabeth Ann Karlin*

I think
I have decided
I wish it to be understood
that the Pope
should not and shall not
have
an abortion

I think
I have decided
I wish it to be understood
that the Pope
should and shall restrict
his bodily concerns
to what happens underneath
all those clothes
he loves to put on
and never take off

I think
I have decided
I wish it to be understood

that the Pope
should not and shall not remain
oblivious to the fact
that billions of folks out here/Catholics
and Buddhists and Muslims and Jews and
Protestants and Atheists
do not really appreciate
his
pronouncements
on everything
except the infinite mystery
of his own
personal life

I think
I have decided
I wish it to be understood
that the Pope
should not and shall not
trouble
his celibate brain
with questions
about anyone's sex life
because
if you don't know
and if
you don't do
it
that in itself
should be
a big clue
to
the absurdity
of your having any
opinion
whatsoever

I think
I have decided
I wish it to be understood
that the Pope
should not and shall not
have an abortion

Ode to the Gun Lobby

Because you got more guns
And more people support for more
People and more guns more people
Insisting on more guns more
People more guns more
Everything
Than I gotta right

To smoke my cigarette

It's Hard to Keep a Clean Shirt Clean

Poem for Sriram Shamasunder
And All of Poetry for the People

It's a sunlit morning
with jasmine blooming
easily
and a drove of robin redbreasts
diving into the ivy covering
what used to be
a backyard fence
or doves shoving aside
the birch tree leaves
when
a young man walks among

the flowers
to my doorway
where he knocks
then stands still
brilliant in a clean white shirt

He lifts a soft fist
to that door
and knocks again

He's come to say this
was or that
was
not
and what's
anyone of us to do
about what's done
what's past
but prickling salt to sting
our eyes

What's anyone of us to do
about what's done

And 7-month-old Bingo
puppy leaps
and hits
that clean white shirt
with muddy paw
prints here
and here and there

And what's anyone of us to do
about what's done
I say I'll wash the shirt
no problem
two times through
the delicate blue cycle

of an old machine
the shirt spins in the soapy
suds and spins in rinse
and spins
and spins out dry

not clean

still marked by accidents
by energy of whatever serious or trifling cause
the shirt stays dirty
from that puppy's paws

I take that fine white shirt
from India
the threads as soft as baby
fingers weaving them
together
and I wash that shirt
between
between the knuckles of my own
two hands
I scrub and rub that shirt
to take the dirty
markings
out

At the pocket
and around the shoulder seam
and on both sleeves
the dirt the paw
prints tantalize my soap
my water my sweat
equity
invested in the restoration
of a clean white shirt

And on the eleventh try
I see no more
no anything unfortunate
no dirt

I hold the limp fine
cloth
between the faucet stream
of water as transparent
as a wish the moon stayed out
all day

How small it has become!
That clean white shirt!
How delicate!
How slight!
How like a soft fist knocking on my door!
And now I hang the shirt
to dry
as slowly as it needs
the air
to work its way
with everything

It's clean.
A clean white shirt
nobody wanted to spoil
or soil
that shirt
much cleaner now but also
not the same
as the first before that shirt
got hit got hurt
not perfect
anymore
just beautiful

a clean white shirt

It's hard to keep a clean shirt clean.

To Be Continued:

The partial mastectomy took a long time to execute
And left a huge raggedy scar
Healing from that partial mastectomy took even longer
And devolved into a psychological chasm 2 times the depth
And breadth of the physical scar from the mastectomy that
    was raggedy
And huge
Metastatic reactivation of the breast cancer requiring
    partial mastectomy
That left a huge raggedy scar in the first place now pounds
To pieces
A wound fifty times more implacable and more intractable
Than the psychological chasm produced by the healing process
That was twice as enormously damaging as the surgery
Which left a huge raggedy scar

And so I go
on

Poem for Siddhārtha Gautama of the Shākyas: The Original Buddha

You say, "Close your eye to the butterfly!"
I say, "Don't blink!"

About the Author

JUNE JORDAN was born in Harlem in 1936 and raised in Bedford-Stuyvesant. Poet, essayist, journalist, playwright, novelist, and librettist, she was also a tireless activist and teacher. Jordan taught at City College of the City University of New York, Sarah Lawrence, and the State University of New York–Stony Brook; she was one of the founding poets of Teachers & Writers Collaborative. Professor of African American Studies at the University of California-Berkeley, she founded and directed the Poetry for the People program. Among Jordan's numerous honors and awards were a Rockefeller grant, the Prix de Rome in Environmental Design, a National Endowment for the Arts grant, the Lila Wallace-Reader's Digest Award, the PEN Center USA West Freedom to Write Award, and a special United States Congressional Recognition for "outstanding contributions to literature, the civil rights movement, and in recognition of outstanding and invaluable service to the community." Passionate and prolific, June Jordan lived and wrote on the front lines of American poetry, political vision, and moral witness. She died in Berkeley in 2002.

About the Editors

SARA MILES is a writer and editor; she is the author of *Native Dancer* (poems) and a book of political reporting, *How to Hack a Party Line: The Democrats and Silicon Valley*. She co-edited and contributed to the poetry anthology *Ordinary Women* and a book of essays, *Opposite Sex*. As a reporter based in Central America, she was a contributing writer and editor for *New Thinking: Perspectives on Third World Change*. Sara Miles lives in San Francisco, where she founded and directs St. Gregory's Food Pantry, working with community groups organizing against hunger.

JAN HELLER LEVI is a poet whose first collection of poems, *Once I Gazed at You in Wonder*, won the Walt Whitman Award of the Academy of American Poets; her second collection is *Skyspeak*. Levi is also the editor of *A Muriel Rukeyser Reader*, and she assisted editors Anne Herzog and Janet Kaufman in the new edition of *The Collected Poems of Muriel Rukeyser*. She is working on a biography of Rukeyser. Levi teaches in the M.F.A. Program at Hunter College and divides her time between New York City and St. Gallen, Switzerland.

Index of Titles

Index of First Lines

Copper Canyon Press wishes to acknowledge the support of Lannan Foundation in funding the publication and distribution of exceptional literary works.

LANNAN LITERARY SELECTIONS 2005

June Jordan, *Directed by Desire*

W.S. Merwin, *Migration*

W.S. Merwin, *Present Company*

Pablo Neruda, *The Separate Rose*

Pablo Neruda, *Still Another Day*

Alberto Ríos, *The Theater of Night*

LANNAN LITERARY SELECTIONS 2000–2004

John Balaban, *Spring Essence: The Poetry of Hồ Xuân Hương*

Marvin Bell, *Rampant*

Hayden Carruth, *Doctor Jazz*

Cyrus Cassells, *More Than Peace and Cypresses*

Norman Dubie, *The Mercy Seat: Collected & New Poems, 1967–2001*

Sascha Feinstein, *Misterioso*

James Galvin, *X: Poems*

Jim Harrison, *The Shape of the Journey: New and Collected Poems*

Maxine Kumin, *Always Beginning: Essays on a Life in Poetry*

Ben Lerner, *The Lichtenberg Figures*

Antonio Machado, *Border of a Dream: Selected Poems,* translated by Willis Barnstone

W.S. Merwin, *The First Four Books of Poems*

Cesare Pavese, *Disaffections: Complete Poems 1930–1950,* translated by Geoffrey Brock

Antonio Porchia, *Voices,* translated by W.S. Merwin

Kenneth Rexroth, *The Complete Poems of Kenneth Rexroth,* edited by Sam Hamill and Bradford Morrow

Alberto Ríos, *The Smallest Muscle in the Human Body*

Theodore Roethke, *On Poetry & Craft*

Ann Stanford, *Holding Our Own: The Selected Poems of Ann Stanford,* edited by Maxine Scates and David Trinidad

Ruth Stone, *In the Next Galaxy*

Joseph Stroud, *Country of Light*

Rabindranath Tagore, *The Lover of God,* translated by Tony K. Stewart and Chase Twichell

Reversible Monuments: Contemporary Mexican Poetry, edited by Mónica de la Torre and Michael Wiegers

César Vallejo, *The Black Heralds,* translated by Rebecca Seiferle

Eleanor Rand Wilner, *The Girl with Bees in Her Hair*

C.D. Wright, *Steal Away: Selected and New Poems*

For more on the Lannan Literary Selections, visit:

www.coppercanyonpress.org

The Chinese character for poetry is made up of two parts: "word" and "temple." It also serves as pressmark for Copper Canyon Press. Founded in 1972, Copper Canyon Press remains dedicated to publishing poetry exclusively, from Nobel laureates to new and emerging authors. The Press thrives with the generous patronage of readers, writers, booksellers, librarians, teachers, students, and funders – everyone who shares the conviction that poetry invigorates the language and sharpens our appreciation of the world.

MAJOR FUNDING HAS BEEN PROVIDED BY:

The Paul G. Allen Family Foundation

Lannan Foundation

LEF Foundation

National Endowment for the Arts

Washington State Arts Commission

THE PAUL G. ALLEN FAMILY *foundation*

Lannan

NATIONAL ENDOWMENT FOR THE ARTS

COPPER CANYON PRESS GRATEFULLY ACKNOWLEDGES THE FOLLOWING INDIVIDUALS FOR THEIR GENEROUS ANNUAL FUND SUPPORT:

Mimi Gardner Gates

Carolyn and Robert Hedin

Bruce S. Kahn

Rhoady and Jeanne Marie Lee

Charles and Barbara Wright

FOR INFORMATION AND CATALOGS:

COPPER CANYON PRESS
Post Office Box 271
Port Townsend, Washington 98368
360-385-4925
www.coppercanyonpress.org